The Intensive Phonological Awareness (IPA) Program

The Intensive Phonological Awareness (IPA) Program

by

C. Melanie Schuele, Ph.D., CCC-SLP

and

Naomi D. Murphy, M.S., CCC-SLP

Baltimore • London • Sydney

Paul H. Brookes Publishing Co.
Post Office Box 10624
Baltimore, Maryland 21285-0624

www.brookespublishing.com

Typeset by Integrated Publishing Solutions, Grand Rapids, Michigan.
Manufactured in the United States of America by
Versa Press, Inc., East Peoria, Illinois.

The individuals described in this book are composites or real people whose situations are masked and are based on the authors' experiences. In all instances, names and identifying details have been changed to protect confidentiality.

Library of Congress Cataloging-In-Publication Data
The Library of Congress has cataloged the printed edition as follows:

Schuele, C. Melanie.
The intensive phonological awareness (IPA) program / by C. Melanie Schuele, Ph.D., CCC-SLP and Naomi D. Murphy, M.S., CCC-SLP.
pages cm
Summary: "The IPA Program was developed as a supplemental curriculum to be used with small groups of children in the classroom. The program focuses on four phonological awareness skills, each taught for 3 weeks: rhyming, initial sound, final sound, and complete segmentation. Children participate in 30-minute sessions three times per week for 12 weeks total. After this period, children's phonological awareness skills should have improved enough to be prepared for formal reading instruction."—Provided by publisher.
ISBN 9781598571189WW
1. Reading—Phonetic method—Activity programs. I. Murphy, Naomi D. II. Title.
LB1573.3.S35 2014
372.46'5—dc23 2013047268

British Library Cataloguing in Publication data are available from the British Library.

2018 2017 2016 2015 2014

10 9 8 7 6 5 4 3 2 1

Contents

Contents of the Ancillary Material

About the Ancillary Material

Appendix B of *The Intensive Phonological Awareness (IPA) Program* walks through the steps of creating an IPA Program Materials Kit for implementing the curriculum's sessions. The CD-ROM included with the print book contains session materials (sound cards, game boards, sound files, Child Attendance Record, Daily Implementation Record, Intensive Phonemic Awareness [IPA] Program Implementation Record, and IPA Program Materials Kit Inventory Sheet) for assembling this kit. Purchasers of *The Intensive Phonological Awareness (IPA) Program* may download, print, save, and photocopy the session materials from a computer for their own educational use. Applicable figures in the book are Figures 3.2, 3.4, and 3.5. Refer to the CD-ROM's End User License Agreement for details.

Materials from the CD-ROM (sound cards, game boards, sound files, forms, Child Attendance Record, Daily Implementation Record, Intensive Phonemic Awareness [IPA] Program Implementation Record, and IPA Materials Kit Inventory Sheet, and IPA Program Materials Kit Inventory Sheet) also are available as downloads. Print and e-book purchasers of this book may download, print, and/or photocopy the session materials material for educational use. To access the downloadable versions of the session materials, go to **www.brookespublishing.com/schuele/eforms**

There are two inventory sheets to help you track your IPA Program materials. The first inventory sheet (in Appendix B) is organized by week and lists the materials needed to complete each week's sessions. The second inventory sheet is organized by the IPA Program's four unit areas (Rhyme, Initial Sound, Final Sound, and Segmenting/Blending) and lists the materials according to type (e.g., Rhyme Judgment Cards, Rhyme Generation Cards). The unit inventory appears only on the CD-ROM and in the downloads and includes a Scope and Sequence section listing the unit, week/session number, and session focus for each of the 36 sessions. Purchasers of the IPA Program may choose which way to organize their materials.

About the Authors

C. Melanie Schuele, Ph.D., CCC-SLP, received her doctoral degree from the University of Kansas and is an associate professor at Vanderbilt University in the Department of Hearing and Speech Sciences. Dr. Schuele is a fellow of the American Speech-Language-Hearing Association. She teaches courses in child language acquisition and disorders. Her research and clinical interests include the nature of language and reading acquisition in children with language impairments. Dr. Schuele has many years of pediatric clinical experience in a variety of settings, including public schools, a pediatric hospital, and university clinical and research facilities.

Naomi D. Murphy, M.S., CCC-SLP, is a speech language pathologist working in public school early intervention and in private practice in Walnut Creek, California. She provides speech-language services to children with communication impairments in clinical and public school settings. Ms. Murphy conducted a pilot study with *The Intensive Phonological Awareness (IPA) Program* as her master's thesis. She received her master's degree from the University of Nevada, Reno.

Foreword

Speech-language clinicians and intervention specialists who work with reading disabilities will welcome the publication of *The Intensive Phonological Awareness (IPA) Program*. It fills a decades-long gap within the menu of instructional resources and curricula designed to prevent and ameliorate reading disabilities. While some excellent activity guides and instructional materials have been widely used for teaching phonological awareness in kindergarten and first grade classrooms, only a very few (before this) have been designed specifically for students who demonstrate severe phonological processing difficulties and who need an intensive, structured, systematic program.

Speech sounds (phonemes) are the basic building blocks of words, the smallest units that make one word different from another. Perception of, memory for, and the ability to think about phonemes play a central role in learning to speak, read, and spell. An alphabetic spelling system makes no sense unless the person who is trying to use it can tie each written symbol to the phonemic segments of speech. Yet a substantial number of novice readers are not wired to understand easily or naturally that whole words can be pulled apart into those segments, or to manipulate those segments during oral and written language learning. Approximately 5%–10% of students fail to grasp the fundamental principle that alphabetic writing represents phonemic segments in spoken words. Those are the students most at risk for reading failure and most in need of this intervention.

The IPA Program is unique in several ways. First, it has been piloted and refined by the authors for years, so problem items or activities have been reworked until they can be implemented in typical clinic and school-based settings. The sessions' format and content is accessible to either a speech-language clinician or a reading intervention specialist. Importantly, professionals with varying skills and background knowledge can be successful with students if they follow the program as written. Second, the program incorporates principles of phonological awareness instruction that are strongly supported by research. It follows a clear developmental progression, employs multisensory methods, proceeds in an incremental and cumulative manner, and gradually links students' growing awareness of speech to knowledge of letters and letter-sound associations. Finally, the lessons are informed by the authors' deep understanding of why phoneme awareness is difficult for some children and how, exactly, to forge a path from more transparent to more elusive aspects of language processing.

As the authors discuss in the first chapter, phonological awareness is a broader term than phoneme awareness; it encompasses skills such as rhyme production, syllabification, and perception of stress in multisyllabic words. Phoneme awareness, in contrast, refers specifically to the detection, comparison, segmentation, and blending of individual phonemes within a word. Beginning in the 1970s, research began to focus on the close relationship between phoneme awareness, reading, and spelling. Dozens of studies up until that time, reviewed in the Report of the National Reading Panel (National Institute of Child Health and Human Development, 2000), supported these findings: a) poor readers and spellers typically do poorly on measures of phoneme awareness, especially in the beginning stages of learning to read; b) phoneme segmentation and blending measures are, along with letter naming, the best predictors of reading success or failure in novice readers; and c) training in phoneme awareness improves students' ability to learn the alphabetic principle and to recognize words in print.

Since the National Reading Panel, the *ph* words have been used widely, even finding their way into the Common Core State Standards in kindergarten and first grade. Most published reading programs, at least superficially, include components labeled as phoneme awareness activities. Nevertheless, it is quite common to see instructional programs or activities that use the *ph* words without accurate reference to what they mean or why they are important. More often than not, those programs and activities do not apply the principles of instruction that are best supported by research. As the IPA Program authors state, phonics and phoneme awareness are commonly confused, even in popular textbooks and reading programs. To compound the problem, teachers are seldom trained to understand the nature of speech sound processing, why phonemes are elusive in the first place, or how to lead students through a progression of learning.

In the context of these current realities, the *IPA Program* stands out for its solid grounding in language and literacy research and for its respect for important details. For example, the authors frequently recommend that students feel their mouths as they make the sounds, look in a mirror for visual feedback during articulation, and pay attention to the subtle differences between confusable phonemes. The activities and guidelines for corrective feedback are aligned with Liberman's (1999) profound observation that a phoneme is as much an articulatory gesture, with visual, kinesthetic, and tactile properties, as it is an acoustic or auditory entity. Teachers are often encouraged to ask the question, "How does your mouth feel?" while students are learning a new speech sound or phoneme manipulation. The IPA Program designers appreciate that students are more likely to establish representations of speech sounds in phonological memory if those phonemes are concretized through feeling, looking, and listening combined.

Although it would be ideal if every teacher who uses this program were able to study language structure, particularly the vowel and consonant speech sounds of English, the nature of phonological processing, and the connection between speech and print (Moats, 2010), the program is easily used by teachers who have not been fortunate enough to train at a high level of sophistication. The authors have simplified the session routines so that formal training in speech-language pathology, while very helpful to the user, is not required in order to begin program implementation. At the same time, teachers can learn a great deal about phonology if they use the program faithfully with students at risk for reading failure. Finally, the authors have been realistic about the time necessary to teach the activities of a session and the amount of practice students require to improve their performance on phonological awareness tasks, and in that sense, *The Intensive Phonological Awareness (IPA) Program* is a recipe for success.

In this age of the Common Core State Standards, the foundational skills of reading and writing should be receiving more attention than ever, but in many quarters are receiving less. Literature-based approaches to reading are again gaining ascendance, in spite of the long-standing research consensus around the importance and greater effectiveness of code-focused instruction in the first grade (Adams, 1990; National Institute of Child Health and Human Development, 2000; Snow, Burns, & Griffin, 1998). Until and unless the trend shifts back toward explicit, cumulative, systematic teaching of phoneme awareness, letter knowledge, letter–sound correspondence, and accurate word recognition, along with the language underpinnings for comprehension, it is likely that this program will be needed to salvage the futures of many students who will not otherwise be prepared for early reading instruction. We are fortunate that the authors have given us this valuable tool for preventing and ameliorating reading failure.

Louisa C. Moats, Ed.D.
President, Moats Association Consulting, Inc.
Sun Valley, ID

REFERENCES

Adams, M. (1990). *Beginning to read: Thinking and learning about print.* Cambridge, MA: MIT Press.

Liberman, A. (1999). The reading researcher and the reading teacher need the right theory of speech. *Scientific Studies of Reading, 3*, 95–111.

Moats, L.C. (2010). *Speech to print: Language essentials for teachers* (2nd ed.). Baltimore: Paul H. Brookes Publishing Co.

National Institute of Child Health and Human Development. (2000). *Report of the National Reading Panel, Teaching children to read: an evidence-based assessment of the scientific research literature on reading and its implications for reading instruction.* Washington, DC: NICHD. (1-800-370-2943)

Snow, C. E., Burns, M. S., & Griffin, P. (Eds.). (1998). *Preventing reading difficulties in young children.* Washington, DC: National Academy Press.

For the Reader

The *Intensive Phonological Awareness (IPA) Program* is a systematic, comprehensive, and intensive small group intervention designed for kindergarten and first-grade children who have minimal or no phonological awareness ability. It builds a foundation of phonological awareness critical for developing initial proficiency in decoding and spelling. The ultimate achievement goals targeted in *The IPA Program* is the establishment of children's abilities to segment words into phonemes and to blend phonemes into words. To develop these skills the program initially targets rhyme, followed by initial sounds and final sounds, and lastly, segmenting and blending sounds.

The IPA Program includes thirty-six, 30-minute lessons or sessions, presented over 12 weeks (three sessions per week). The IPA standard treatment protocol is divided into four units:

Rhyme
Initial Sounds
Final Sounds
Segmenting and Blending

Regardless of individual child performance, the sessions are implemented sequentially across 36 days. There is no individualization at the level of the session plan (i.e., repeating a session plan because some children are not catching on) but rather interventionists individualize instruction within each session. The scope and sequence of *The IPA Program* can be found on the accompanying CD.

Across the 12 weeks the intervention moves from simple skills to more complex skills, from phonological awareness skills to phonemic awareness skills. Also within each of the four units, activities are sequenced to move from simple to complex activities so as to gradually build each targeted skill area. Each session plan includes a brief Letter Activity to develop children's alphabet knowledge. *The IPA Program* includes 36 sequentially presented session plans and picture materials to implement the activities (see the CD-ROM and the download). A list of additional materials needed are presented in Appendix B. Each two-page session plan includes activity descriptions, teaching strategies, listing of session stimuli, and implementation suggestions to guide selection and sequencing of stimuli.

Each session begins with a Letter Activity (3–5 min). In the early weeks of the program the focus is on simply knowing sound–letter correspondences (i.e., letter names and letter sounds). As the program progresses, the Letter Activity provides opportunities for children to combine letter-sound knowledge with phonological awareness knowledge.

The bulk of each session (25 min) includes two or three activities to develop the target skill (e.g., rhyme, initial sounds). Nearly all these activities are "pure" phonological awareness activities in that children are asked only to focus on the sounds in words, not a simultaneous focus on speech sounds and the letters used to represent those speech sounds. Within each three-week unit, the complexity and difficulty level of activities increases. For the Rhyme, Initial Sounds, and Final Sounds units, the same activities are used to teach each skill—judgment, odd-one-out, matching, generation, and segmentation (initial, final sounds). New activities are introduced in the Segmenting and Blending unit due to the nature of the targeted skill. Nevertheless, activities progress from simple to complex, first working with CV and VC words, then CVC words, and then words with blends (CVCC, CCVC).

To provide additional learning opportunities, after the first unit some sessions incorporate review of a previously targeted skill. A separate review activity might be included, or a previously taught skill might be targeted alongside the current skill (e.g., segment initial sound of word [current skill] and then give a rhyming word [previous skill]). This repetition and review allows for continued practice for all children, and additional learning opportunities for those children who had not mastered the skill in the three weeks it was targeted.

The *IPA Program* is intended for small group intervention (no more than 6 to 8 children) in educational settings, where the need to provide effective yet efficient small-group intervention is essential. Although small groups are comprised of children with limited phonological awareness, within any one group it is likely that child skill levels will vary. Any professional educator with the appropriate background knowledge in phonological awareness can implement the program. This group of professionals might include speech-language pathologists, reading specialists, and special educators.

Acknowledgments

Learning to decode print is an exciting experience for many children. The accomplishment of fluent decoding opens up wide new worlds and provides a ticket to a most esteemed club, "READERS." Most teachers and speech-language pathologists learned to read easily and effortlessly; they are avid readers as adults. For them reading is a form of entertainment, in addition to a way to gain information. For some children the experience of learning to read is far more challenging and frustrating than exciting and pleasurable. These children have motivated us to think about how to better teach the underpinnings of decoding, phonological awareness.

The idea for *The Intensive Phonological Awareness (IPA) Program* has its roots in Dr. Schuele's master's project, completed at The University of Texas at Austin with Dr. Anne van Kleeck in 1985 (van Kleeck & Schuele, 1987; Schuele & van Kleeck, 1987). The actual development of the *IPA Program* began in 1996 when Ms. Murphy agreed to undertake the development and testing of a phonological awareness intervention protocol for her master's thesis at the University of Nevada, Reno. At the time the research literature provided guidance for treatment, but there were few published treatment protocols.

We are grateful to the children and their families who participated in the initial development of the *IPA Program*. Three children and their families participated in Ms. Murphy's thesis study (Dayton, 1997) at the University of Nevada, Reno, and the following year five children and their families agreed to be part of a second trial run (Schuele, Paul, & Mazzaferri, 1998). We are grateful to Kellie Bozzuto Paul and Karen Mazzaferri, undergraduate students, who implemented the intervention and helped us think about how to teach others to use the *IPA Program*. The parents of these children, who observed most of our sessions, helped us understand the importance of learning to read on time. In 2000 Roxboro Elementary, Cleveland Heights-University Heights Schools (Ohio) and the parents of five struggling readers graciously allowed their children to participate in our third pilot study. Kylie Biggart Volpe and Tina Sharma, master's students at Case Western Reserve University, provided the intervention. We published our first version of *The IPA Program* following these pilot studies.

Further development of the *IPA Program* greatly benefited from our collaboration with Kathy Knighton and Beverly Kingery in the West Virginia Department of Education (WVDE). Over several years we collaborated with many school districts across West Virginia as they implemented a two-tier phonological awareness program with the *Phonemic Awareness in Young Children* (Adams, Foorman, Lundberg, & Beeler, 1998) curriculum and *The IPA Program*. This incredible collaboration with the WVDE and district administrators, teachers, speech-language pathologists, and reading specialists taught us many lessons. Most importantly, this collaboration showed us what teachers can accomplish when they have developmentally appropriate curricula that support their teaching efforts.

Support and patience (as well as much appreciated prodding) from Astrid Zuckerman and Julie Chavez at Brookes Publishing has brought this project to fruition. We greatly appreciate their support in publishing the current version of *The IPA Program*, an intervention program we believe will help clinicians and teachers bridge the research-to-practice gap.

Finally, we would not have finished this project without the support of our husbands and our children.

CMS
NDM

REFERENCES

Adams, M., Foorman, B., Lundberg, I., & Beeler, T. (1998). *Phonemic awareness in young children: A classroom curriculum.* Baltimore: Paul H. Brookes Publishing Co.

Dayton, N. (1997). *Effects of training phonological awareness on three children with specific language impairment.* Unpublished Masters thesis, University of Nevada, Reno.

Schuele, C.M., Paul, K., & Mazzaferri, K. (1998). *Phonological awareness training: Is it worth the time?* Paper presented at the Annual Convention of the American Speech-Language-Hearing Association, San Antonio, TX.

Schuele, C.M., & van Kleeck, A. (1987). Precursors to literacy: Assessment and intervention. *Topics in Language Disorders, 7*(2), 32–44.

van Kleeck, A., & Schuele, C.M. (1987). Precursors to literacy: Normal development. *Topics in Language Disorders, 7*(2), 13–31.

For
Daniel
and
Ben, Emily, and Jack
who remind us daily of the wonders of the journey
of learning to talk and read

DANIEL
When I get home, I am going to go up to my room and read a book. Because I have never done that before.

BEN
Mommy, turn off the CD (audio book). *I don't want to see the bad guy.*

EMILY
I like learning to read. It means you get to know new stories.

JACK
There's the way out. It say's 'EXIT.' (After being praised for being such a good reader) *Of course I can read 'EXIT.' I've seen it a million times.*

I

Overview

1

Development of Phonological Awareness

Our goal in this chapter is to provide a brief overview of development as a means of review for the reader. Several sources are available that provide more extensive summaries of phonological awareness development (Ericson & Juliebo, 1998; Gillon, 2004; International Reading Association, 1998; Schuele & Boudreau, 2008; Torgesen & Mathes, 2000).

WHAT IS PHONOLOGICAL AWARENESS?

Phonological awareness is the ability to analyze the sound structure of language, separate from meaning (Mattingly, 1972). It is one type of metalinguistic skill (van Kleeck, 1994). Some sources suggest that phonological awareness involves the ability to *hear* sounds in words (International Reading Association, 1998). We would suggest that such characterizations are not accurate and cause confusion for educators and parents alike. Children with limited phonological awareness do not have problems hearing (with the exception of children with documented hearing loss), but they do have difficulty *analyzing* the sounds in words. Phonological awareness develops gradually, beginning for many children in the preschool years (Lonigan, 1998).

Children's phonological awareness is evidenced in a range of tasks that require analysis of the sound structure of language; for example, rhyming words, telling the first sound of words, and telling how many sounds are in a word (Yopp, 1988). All the various phonological awareness tasks rely on one underlying skill (Anthony & Lonigan, 2004; Schatschneider, Francis, Foorman, Fletcher, & Mehta, 1999). As children gain more proficiency in phonological awareness, they are successful on increasingly complex phonological awareness tasks (Anthony, Lonigan, Driscoll, Phillips, & Burgess, 2003).

HOW ARE THE TERMS *PHONOLOGICAL AWARENESS* AND *PHONEMIC AWARENESS* RELATED?

Unfortunately, *phonological awareness* and *phonemic awareness* are often used interchangeably. The terms are not synonymous (Scarborough & Brady, 2002). *Phonological awareness* is a broad term that encompasses all activities or tasks that require analysis of sound structure. *Phonemic awareness* is a more narrow term that encompasses only those phonological awareness activities that require children to isolate and produce individual speech sounds or phonemes (e.g., *Say the first sound in* shoe. *Tell me the three sounds*

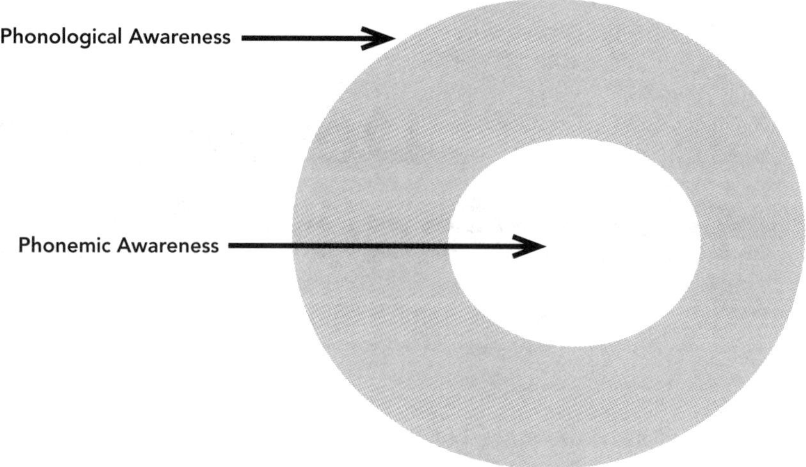

Figure 1.1. Phonemic awareness is a subset of phonological awareness.

in sun). Thus, phonemic awareness should be viewed as a subset of phonological awareness (see Figure 1.1). A few examples may help to clarify the terms. Generating rhyming words (e.g., *Tell me a word that rhymes with* frog) is a phonological awareness task but not a phonemic awareness task. Comparing words based on initial sounds (e.g., *Does* fish *go with* foot *or with* bat?) is also a phonological awareness task, whereas segmenting the initial sounds of words (e.g., *What is the first sound in* fish?) is a phonemic awareness task. All phonemic awareness tasks are phonological awareness tasks, but not all phonological awareness tasks are phonemic awareness tasks.

IS PHONOLOGICAL AWARENESS THE SAME AS PHONICS?

It is critical that educators understand clearly and can differentiate the terms *phonological awareness* and *phonics*. *Phonological awareness* is not just another term for *phonics*. Table 1.1 differentiates these terms by defining the focus, the intervention tasks, and the learning achievements that characterize phonological awareness and phonics. Phonological awareness (and, of course, phonemic awareness) relates to the speech sounds or phonemes in words but has nothing to do with how speech sounds are represented in print. Phonological awareness involves analyzing the sounds of words, but it does not involve understanding or figuring out what letter symbol(s) is used to represent a specific speech sound. Rather,

Table 1.1. Differentiating phonological awareness and phonics

Phonological awareness	Phonics
Focus: Sound structure of words	*Focus:* Print representation of sounds in words
Intervention task: involve identifying, segmenting, and manipulating the sounds in words, without reference to the letters that represent the sounds.	*Intervention task:* involve identifying and categorizing the print symbols (i.e., letters) that are used to represent speech sounds.
Achievement: Ability to segment a spoken word into its component sounds; ability to combine sounds into words	*Achievement:* Ability to represent a spoken word in print with conventional sound–symbol correspondences; ability to create a spoken production of a written word by "sounding out" the written word

I (C.M.S.) had a very difficult time learning to decode in first grade. When I took a phonetics course in my first semester of college, I realized the source of my difficulty learning to read—I was a first grader without an adequate foundation of phonological awareness. In the early 1960s, letters and sounds were taught in first grade, not kindergarten. I easily memorized the letter names and the corresponding sounds but I had no idea what to do with that information. I memorized the spelling of many words. What I read or wrote, I did by memory. Two vivid memories stand out when I think about children who are trying to understand phonics but have limited (or no) phonological awareness. First, I remember the teacher giving directions for a phonics worksheet that included nine pictures, the first two letters for each word, and a space to write the last letter. I listened to the teacher: "Look at the picture. Say the name of the picture. Listen for the last sound in the word and write the letter for the last sound in the word." I thought to myself, looking down at the first picture, *fan: Well, those instructions seem pretty ridiculous. Not sure what she means by sounds in words, and anyways, everyone knows that* fan *ends with the letter* N. And so I wrote an *N* and continued down through the rest of the page, all words I knew how to spell. Second, I remember dutifully sounding out words, producing a sound for each letter in a word such as *cat,* and then putting the sounds together, as instructed, and ending up with something that sounded like "kuhatuh." The teacher's suggestion was always some version of *Say it faster,* but that only resulted in a quicker production of "kuhatuh" but nothing that resembled the target word. When my teacher said "the word is *cat,*" I thought to myself, *Well, if you knew that all along, why are you making me go through these crazy steps?* As I said, college brought new insight into my early reading difficulties when I realized that in first grade, I had no idea that *cat* and *fan* had three sounds and could be divided into those three sounds. Liberman and Shankweiler, 1991, summed my problem up nicely:

> Though the word "bag," for example, has three phonological units, and correspondingly, three letters in print, it has only one pulse of sound: The three elements of the underlying phonological structure—the three phonemes—have been thoroughly overlapped and merged into that one sound—"bag." ... [Beginning readers] can understand, and properly take advantage of, the fact that the printed word *bag* has three letters, only if they are aware that the spoken word "*bag*" ... is divisible into three segments (1991, p. 6).

Figure 1.2. Learning phonics without phonological awareness.

phonics involves knowledge of how single letters or letter combinations (i.e., graphemes) are used to represent speech sounds. To learn to decode words using phonics rules, a child must have some phonological awareness or, more specifically, phonemic awareness. The child must also have letter–sound knowledge (i.e., sound–symbol correspondences). Trying to learn phonics without having some phonemic awareness is, for many children, a frustrating and unsuccessful endeavor (see Figure 1.2).

American English has 40–44 speech sounds, depending on the dialect of English spoken. In English writing, more than 240 graphemes are used to represent these 40–44 speech sounds (Moats, 2010). The complexity of representing speech sounds with graphemes is illustrated by considering the many ways that the speech sound /s/ is represented in print (see Table 1.2). Moats's (2010) book *Speech to Print, Second Edition,* written for educators, provides an accessible explanation of the sound structure of English and the representation of speech with print symbols.

Table 1.2. Some of the graphemes that are used to represent the speech sound /ʃ/

ship
chef
mi**ss**ion
ac**ti**on
sugar
gla**ci**er
o**c**ean

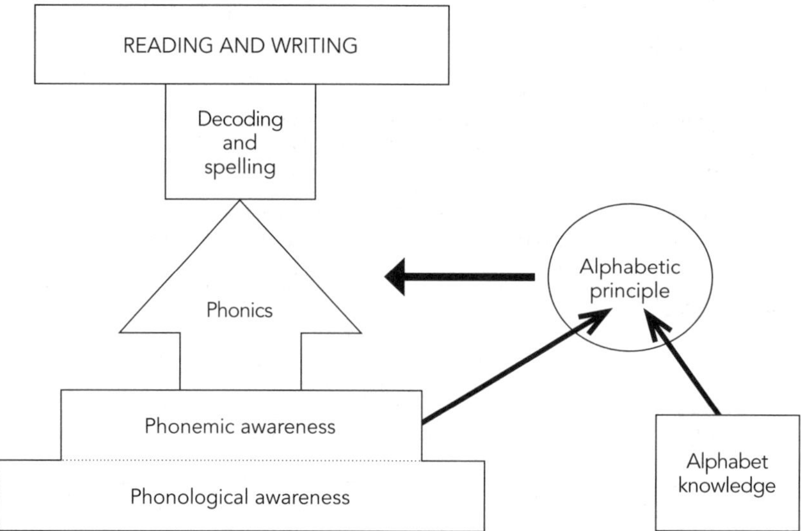

Figure 1.3. The relationship of phonological awareness to reading and writing.

WHAT IS THE RELATIONSHIP OF PHONOLOGICAL AWARENESS TO READING?

The simple view of reading (Hoover & Gough, 1990) suggests that "reading can be characterized as the product of skill in decoding and listening comprehension" (p. 127). Phonological awareness, and specifically phonemic awareness, is a strong predictor of the decoding aspect of early literacy proficiency (Stahl & Murray, 1994). Some researchers maintain that there is a causal connection between phonological awareness and word decoding (Bradley & Bryant, 1983). Literacy success in kindergarten through second grade relies heavily on children's ability to spell words and decode words and, thus, on children's phonemic awareness (Juel, 1996).

Figure 1.3 provides a simple illustration of the relation of phonological awareness to reading and writing. Children initially develop some phonological awareness skills that provide a foundation for developing phonemic awareness skills (blending and segmenting). At the same time, children learn letter names and letter sounds. Children's realization that letter symbols can be used to represent speech sounds is an insight labeled as the *alphabetic principle.* Once children have this insight, they learn the many graphemes that are used to represent speech sounds, and this knowledge is used to decode and spell words. The ability to spell and decode words sets the stage for proficient reading and writing. However, proficient reading and writing requires many skills other than spelling and decoding.

Children with strong phonological awareness tend to be good readers, and children with weak phonological awareness tend to be less proficient readers. Children who begin first grade with weak phonological awareness are unlikely to make progress in learning to decode words without explicit instruction in phonological awareness (Foorman, Francis, Fletcher, Schatschneider, & Mehta, 1998). When followed through fifth grade, children who had strong phonological awareness in first grade tend to be good readers, whereas children who had limited phonemic awareness in first grade tend to be poor readers (Torgesen & Mathes, 2000). Children who are the poorest readers in the elementary grades tend to remain the poorest readers throughout the school years. Furthermore, the majority of children who receive special education services for reading by the third grade will not exit special education before they graduate from high school (Francis, Shaywitz, Stuebing, Shaywitz, & Fletcher, 1996).

There is extensive empirical support that children can improve their phonological awareness skills through classroom instruction and specialized intervention (Bus & Van IJzendoorn, 1999; Ehri et al., 2001; Troia, 1999). These improvements are associated with improvements in reading, specifically word decoding. However, it is important to note that improvements in reading result not from just teaching pure phonological awareness. Once children have some ability to segment words into sounds, they must be taught to represent those sounds with letters (i.e., phonics or word decoding instruction). This can be provided to children in classroom instruction and also in supplemental interventions for struggling learners.

WHEN DOES PHONOLOGICAL AWARENESS BEGIN TO DEVELOP?

The development of phonological awareness begins in the preschool years for some, but not all, children (Lonigan, Burgess, Anthony, & Barker, 1998). Phonological awareness continues to develop in kindergarten and the early grade school years (Wagner et al., 1997). Although a foundation of phonological awareness is needed to initially learn to decode words, as children gain proficiency in reading, they continue to refine their phonological awareness.

To acquire phonological awareness, children must have experiences that focus their attention on the sounds of words. For some children, their preschool years are filled with experiences of this nature, both at home and at school, and these children begin kindergarten with a good foundation of phonological awareness. Some of these experiences involve letters and sounds, for example, reading alphabet books, watching television shows like *Word World* or *Sesame Street*, and playing literacy computer games (e.g., www.starfall.com). Other experiences may draw children's attention to the sounds of words: reading rhyme books or listening to nursery rhymes. These experiences often lead children to make comments about sounds in words or about letters and sounds at other times of their day. Adults often pick up on these comments and provide more information about sounds in words. In addition, many preschool curricula provide targeted phonological awareness instruction that influences children's development of phonological awareness.

WHEN SHOULD CHILDREN HAVE MASTERED PHONOLOGICAL AWARENESS?

Phonological awareness can continue to develop across the life span. A college course in phonetics will increase a student's phonological awareness. Reading *Speech to Print, Second Edition* (Moats, 2010), will increase an educator's phonological awareness. So rather than talking about a child mastering phonological awareness, it is more relevant to talk about a child's proficiency with specific phonological awareness skills important for developing word decoding and spelling—*segmenting* and *blending*. Although phonological awareness abilities can emerge in the preschool years, children typically are not proficient on many phonological awareness skills until kindergarten or first grade. The rate at which proficiency is achieved will relate to the amount of exposure or instruction children have had as well as to the learning abilities children bring to the table. Specifying the point at which children should have proficiency at blending and segmenting phonemes really relates to the curricular expectations children encounter. In many kindergarten classrooms, children are now learning to read simple books, particularly in the second half of kindergarten. Curricular expectations for reading and writing in first grade are far greater than expectations of even 10 or 20 years ago.

Given these expectations, we argue that by the end of kindergarten children need to be able to proficiently segment and blend CV, VC, and CVC words (C, consonant; V, vowel) with relative ease, and they need some proficiency in the segmentation and blending of words with consonant blends (CVCC, CCVC). The research literature places mastery for segmentation beyond late kindergarten and early first grade (e.g., see Table 8.2, p. 147, Moats, 2000). However, note that in these studies, children are tested in situations in which they receive no support and they often are given stimuli that tax their abilities (e.g., some phonemes or phoneme combinations are more difficult to segment; compare *warm* with *fast*). In contrast, in the classroom, children's performance is much more supported. Thus, it is likely that children would appear more proficient in the classroom than in research studies.

WHAT IS THE ROLE OF EXPERIENCE OR LEARNING OPPORTUNITIES IN THE DEVELOPMENT OF PHONOLOGICAL AWARENESS FOR INDIVIDUAL CHILDREN?

The development of phonological awareness is highly influenced by opportunity. All other things being equal (e.g., children's general ability level), differences in the quantity and quality of children's phonological awareness learning opportunities will lead to equivalent differences in outcome—that is, individual children's phonological awareness skills. Because children from more educated families tend to have more emergent literacy experiences, at school entry they typically have greater phonological awareness than children from less educated families (e.g., Lonigan, 1998).

Some groups of children, such as children with specific language impairment and children with a family history of dyslexia, seem to benefit less than expected from phonological awareness learning opportunities (Catts, Adlof, Hogan, & Ellis Weismer, 2005; Kamhi & Koenig, 1985; Kamhi, Lee, & Nelson, 1985; Warrick & Rubin, 1992). Despite the same or similar learning experiences as same-age peers, these children tend to have deficient phonological awareness skills (e.g., Boudreau & Hedberg, 1999). The research evidence suggests that these groups of children need more frequent and repetitive learning opportunities than their peers in order to acquire the same level of phonological awareness ability.

WHAT IS THE SEQUENCE OF DEVELOPMENT OR LEARNING FOR PHONOLOGICAL AWARENESS?

The development of phonological awareness is characterized by a child's growing ability to be successful on increasingly complex phonological awareness tasks. In Figure 1.4, we illustrate a general sequence of phonological awareness development using an illustration of a staircase. As they learn and move up the staircase, children are successful on increasingly complex phonological awareness tasks. The simpler phonological awareness tasks lead to proficiency on the more complex phonological awareness tasks. The work of Anthony and colleagues (2002, 2003) reminds educators that children do not master each step before they begin to develop skill at the next step. Rather some proficiency on one step enables a child to begin to gain proficiency on a more complex skill, all the while advancing proficiency on the less complex skill.

On each step of the staircase, we can further describe the sequence of development by considering how a child's skill within a particular area evolves. For example, on the rhyme step, a child is successful judging whether two words rhyme before the child is able to generate rhymes. Furthermore, within each task we can consider the sequence of development.

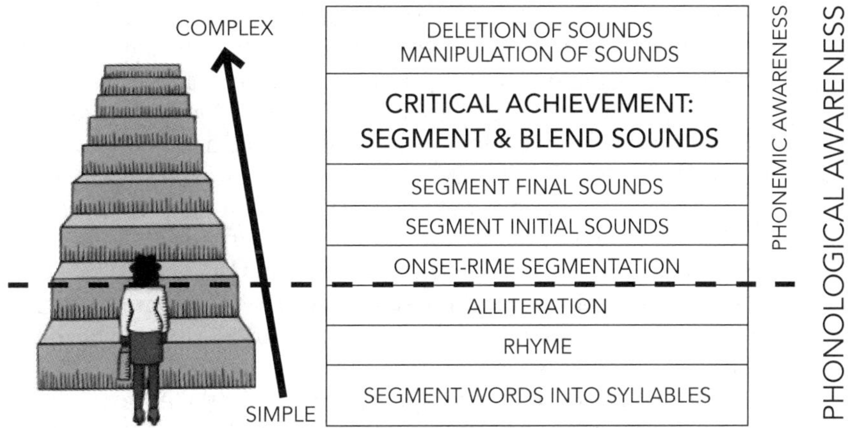

Figure 1.4. Illustration of the sequence of development of phonological awareness, with the critical achievement for learning to decode and spell identified as segmenting words into sounds and blending sounds into words.

A child will accurately judge rhyme pairs that are very different (e.g., *Do* cat *and* moon *rhyme?*) before rhyme pairs that are similar (e.g., *Do* cat *and* can *rhyme?*). The Intensive Phonological Awareness (IPA) Program intervention sequence, across the units, within each unit, and within each activity sequence, reflects this developmental evidence from research.

WHO HAS DIFFICULTY ACQUIRING PHONOLOGICAL AWARENESS?

Given good classroom instruction in phonological awareness, most children make consistent progress in preschool, kindergarten, and first grade. However, children who are not able to segment phonemes and blend phonemes by early first grade often fail to gain decoding and spelling skills in the early grades at the same rate as most of their peers. Many of these children are eventually identified as having a reading disability. Thus, a common characteristic of children with early reading difficulties is poor decoding with an underlying deficit in phonological awareness. Knowing which groups of children are likely to have difficulty acquiring phonological awareness can help educators provide differentiated instruction in the classroom and identify children for small-group interventions (i.e., Tier 2 in response to intervention [RTI] programs). Early intervention on phonological awareness is provided to reduce the likelihood of reading disability or to reduce the severity of reading disability.

The research is clear in some respects. First, children with oral language disabilities are likely to have reading disabilities, evident in decoding and comprehension, with deficiencies in phonological awareness evident in preschool and school-age children (Boudreau & Hedberg, 1999; Catts, 1993; Catts, Fey, Tomblin, & Zhang, 2002; Catts, Fey, Zhang, & Tomblin, 2001; Tomblin, Zhang, Buckwalter, & Catts, 2000). The work of Catts et al. (2002) demonstrated, in a population-based study of language and reading impairment, that 40% (specific language impairment) to 60% (nonspecific language impairment) of children with primary language impairment (i.e., nonverbal IQ above 70) had a reading disability. Rates of reading disability have been reported to be higher in clinically referred samples of children with language impairment (e.g., Stark et al., 1984). Second, children with isolated speech sound disorders are at no increased risk for reading disability, but spelling may be problematic. In contrast, children with moderate to severe speech sound disorders who also have concomitant spoken language disorders have the same risk of reading disability as a child with an isolated oral language disability (Larrivee & Catts, 1999; Lewis & Freebairn, 1992; Lewis, Freebairn, & Taylor, 2000, 2002; Raitano, Pennington, Tunick, Boada, & Shriberg, 2004). The challenge, of course, due to unintelligibility of connected speech, is obtaining a valid and reliability assessment of expressive language skills in children with speech sound disorders. Thus, it appears prudent to monitor the development of literacy skills, including phonological awareness, in children with speech sound disorders and intervene as appropriate. Third, the risk of reading disability in children with mild speech sound disorders (e.g., /r/, /l/, /s/) is not elevated above the risk for the general population (Catts, 1993). Fourth, children who have a family history of reading disability (or dyslexia) are at increased risk for reading disability (Scarborough & Dobrich, 1990). Although some of these children may have oral language problems, there is a sizable group of children with word decoding deficits that do not. Lastly, the average reading level of children from socioeconomically disadvantaged families is below the average reading level for children from middle and upper-middle income families (Walker, Greenwood, Hart, & Carta, 1994). Although comprehension often is a problem, likely related to reduced word knowledge and world knowledge, there are more children in this group than expected who have poor phonological awareness and poor decoding skills (see Sirin, 2010, for a review of socioeconomic status and academic achievement).

Thus, children more likely to have deficient phonological awareness include children with language impairments, and perhaps concomitant speech sound disorders, children with a family history of reading disability or dyslexia, and children from socioeconomically disadvantaged families. Any child who lags behind his or her peers in phonological awareness development should be considered at risk for reading disability.

DOES PHONOLOGICAL AWARENESS INTERVENTION IMPROVE PHONOLOGICAL AWARENESS AND READING OF ALL STRUGGLING LEARNERS?

The research evidence on group outcomes clearly demonstrates improvement in phonological awareness and word decoding after intervention. Nevertheless, examination of change for individual research participants indicates that there are children who fail to make progress despite intensive interventions in phonological awareness and word decoding. Al Otaiba and Fuchs (2002) reported that phonological awareness deficits were apparent in the majority of children who were "unresponsive to generally effective early literacy interventions" (p. 300). It is possible that these children have differing learning abilities that prevent them from gaining proficiency in word decoding and phonological awareness, or it is possible that even the research interventions have not been sufficiently intensive for these children.

2

Development of the Intensive Phonological Awareness Program

In 1998, we embarked on developing a phonological awareness intervention program. We were thinking about phonological awareness intervention that might be provided by speech-language pathologists (SLPs) for children who meet Individuals with Disabilities Education Act Amendments (IDEA) of 1997 (PL 105-17) eligibility for speech-language impairment (e.g., van Kleeck, Gillam, & McFadden, 1998; Warrick & Rubin, 1992; Warrick, Rubin, & Rowe-Walsh, 1993). Children with language impairments, some of whom have concomitant speech sound disorders, are at great risk for reading disability. Despite documentation of this risk as early as the late 1970s (Aram, Ekelman, & Nation, 1984; Aram & Nation, 1980; Hall & Tomblin, 1978; Stark et al., 1984) and the call from researchers to include phonological awareness as an intervention goal before children fail to learn to read (Catts & Kamhi, 1986; Schuele & van Kleeck, 1987; van Kleeck, 1994), even in 1998 it was not routine for SLPs to provide phonological awareness intervention to children on their caseloads. Our interactions with clinicians suggested that even when SLPs included phonological awareness as an individualized education program (IEP) goal, the intervention was not of sufficient intensity and scope to have a positive impact on children's literacy outcomes. We believed that SLPs would be in a better position to target phonological awareness if they had a treatment protocol to implement. Table 2.1 outlines some possible reasons for SLP practices at the time. Many of these reasons may still influence speech-language pathology practices as of 2014.

In 1998, educators had access to a variety of phonological awareness intervention and instructional materials. Although these materials provided activities at varying levels of complexity, what was missing was guidance on how to combine these materials to develop and implement a comprehensive and effective phonological awareness intervention for struggling learners. Although several successful phonological awareness intervention studies had been reported (e.g., Ball & Blachman, 1991; Torgesen, Morgan, & Davis, 1992; van Kleeck et al., 1998), the treatment protocols had not been published in sufficient detail for clinical replication (but see Blachman, Ball, Black, & Tangel, 2000).

We initially considered using commercially available materials to develop an intervention program to systematically develop phonological awareness. However, the characteristics of the materials we reviewed did not easily lend themselves to accomplishing this goal. In earlier iterations of the IPA Program, we incorporated some commercially available materials for some activities (Catts & Vartiainen, 1993; Robertson & Salter, 1995). However, in later iterations we developed unique stimulus materials for all activities in the IPA Program in order to control task difficulty and more thoroughly apply what is known about phonological awareness development to the IPA Program components.

Table 2.1. Hypothesized reasons speech-language pathologists did not routinely provide phonological awareness intervention

A belief that phonological awareness training is not within the professional practice domain of speech-language pathologists
Lack of training in how phonological awareness intervention benefits struggling readers, particularly those with language impairments
Belief that classroom instruction in phonological awareness is sufficient for all children, including children with language impairments
Lack of time to review materials available and organize the materials to provide effective, systematic, comprehensive intervention
Lack of understanding of the benefits of small group intervention for struggling learners
A belief that phonological awareness skills are an *extra*, to be targeted only *after* all other language or speech sound goals have been met
Lack of administrators' recognition of the potential contributions speech-language pathologists can make to literacy instruction and intervention

When we first distributed the IPA Program in 2000, we found that it had wide appeal for the diverse group of children who experience difficulty acquiring phonological awareness and for a variety of interventionists, including reading specialists and special educators as well as SLPs. Thus, the revision of the IPA Program as published in this book was guided by the expectation that the program would be implemented by a variety of interventionists and that intervention groups would include a diverse group of struggling learners with phonological awareness deficits.

We conducted three development studies, two in the university clinic at the University of Nevada, Reno (Dayton & Schuele, 1997; Schuele, Paul, & Mazzaferri, 1998), and one in a suburban public school in Ohio. Subsequently, we worked with the West Virginia Department of Education for 5 years as it implemented the IPA Program across the 54 counties in the state as part of statewide curricular reform (e.g., Justice, Schuele, Kingery, Knighton, & Lee, 2004; Schuele et al., 2008; Schuele, Justice, Knighton, & Kingery, 2002). The continued development of the IPA Program has been guided by our experience implementing the program, by feedback from SLPs, reading specialists, and special educators who have used the program, and by the literature on phonological awareness development and phonological awareness instruction and intervention. In addition, the changes in professional practice (American Speech-Language-Hearing Association [ASHA], 2002; International Reading Association, 1998, 2000) and in public policy (e.g., No Child Left Behind Act of 2001 [PL 107-110]; IDEA 2004 [PL 108-446]) have influenced our thoughts as we made revisions. The overall format of the program has remained the same. Our iterative changes have involved refinement of activities, refinement of teaching materials (e.g., word stimuli), and increased content in the session plans to allow interventionists to implement the program with fidelity.

FEDERAL POLICY INFLUENCES EDUCATION PRACTICES

Two years after we embarked on this project, the National Institute of Child Health and Human Development (NICHHD, 2000a, 2000b) published the *Report of the National Reading Panel* (NRP), a document that has had a far-reaching impact on education in the United States. The members of the NRP were charged by Congress to evaluate the research on literacy in reading to identify "what works." There are five sections of the report that are sometimes referred to as the key elements of literacy instruction: phonemic awareness, phonics, vocabulary, comprehension, and fluency. In the phonemic awareness section of the NRP report, several key findings were identified (see Table 2.2).

Many characteristics of the IPA Program were consistent with the guidelines and conclusions in the NRP Report: 1) blending and segmenting are taught, 2) total instruction is 18

Table 2.2. Important findings on phonemic awareness instruction and intervention

Phonemic awareness can be taught and learned. Small group instruction was most effective. Optimal length of instruction was 5–18 hours, but not all children reach proficiency with 18 hours of instruction. Struggling learners (at risk, with disabilities) made fewer gains than nonstruggling learners.
Phonemic awareness instruction helps children learn to read.
Phonemic awareness instruction helps children learn to spell.
Phonemic awareness instruction is most effective when children learn to segment and blend phonemes.
Phonemic awareness instruction and intervention is most effective when children also have opportunities to apply their ability to analyze the sounds of words to representing those sounds with graphemes.

Source: National Institute of Child Health and Human Development (2000a, 2000b).

hours, and 3) children have opportunities to apply their developing phonemic awareness to representing sounds with letters and letter combinations.

In 2004, the reauthorization of IDEA allowed for early intervening services. Concerned with increasing numbers of children being identified for special education services, Congress authorized the use of federal IDEA funds for prevention activities, before children were referred to or were found eligible for special education services. The provision for early intervening services set the stage for the development of RTI models (see Fuchs, Fuchs, & Vaughn, 2008; Mellard & Johnson, 2007; National Center on Response to Intervention, http://www.rti4success.org).

FEATURES OF THE IPA PROGRAM AND UNDERLYING RATIONALE

In this section, we explain much of the reasoning that underlies the development, format, and components of the IPA Program. We believe that interventionists who understand authors' perspectives on the development of intervention programs are in a better position to successfully implement those programs.

Standard Treatment Protocols

To a great extent in speech-language pathology, but perhaps to a lesser extent in remedial reading and special education, there has been an emphasis on intervention being individualized to meet each child's unique learning needs. Using the same intervention program for all children has been frowned upon because it is assumed that such programs cannot meet children's individual needs. However, a better understanding of the benefits of standard treatment protocols has come about in recent years with the development of RTI models (Fuchs & Fuchs, 2007). To efficiently and effectively provide intervention to children, educators need research-principled and empirically validated treatment protocols. If the interventionist must devise and plan an appropriate intervention protocol for each student's individual learning needs, then intervention becomes an overwhelming task at best. At worst, the intervention design is ineffective and insufficient to meet children's needs and to propel them to greater academic achievements.

Fuchs and Fuchs (2007) highlight several benefits of standard treatment protocols. Standard treatment protocols can be used as preventive interventions to address learning challenges that are common across children. Most preferred are standard treatment protocols that have been shown in randomized controlled studies to improve academic achievement for most struggling learners. Standard treatment protocols can provide more intensive instruction in Tier 2 interventions than can classroom instruction (Tier 1). One educator works with a small group of children on a consistent basis (3–4 times per week;

10–20 weeks) with the goal of improving achievement in a specific area (e.g., phonological awareness, spelling). Standard treatment protocols provide some level of scripted instruction (i.e., what interventionist says) and a high level of prescriptive guidance (e.g., instructional activities, instructional stimuli, time on task). The procedures for the development of standard treatment protocols—content experts and instructional experts iteratively developing the intervention, empirical validation of the program—mean that interventionists can feel confident that the intervention protocol or program will lead to improved performance and can focus their time and energy on the actual teaching rather than on the arduous task of planning treatment sessions.

The IPA Program is a standard treatment protocol. It is research-principled, in that the planning of the components of the program and the sequencing of those components were driven by the developmental and experimental literature. The selection and sequencing of stimuli were guided by the basic literature on phonological awareness that has explored how the linguistic features of words (e.g., nature of speech sounds, word length, syllable shape) influence children's success on phonological awareness tasks. The effectiveness of the IPA Program has been demonstrated in one published study (Schuele et al., 2008) and, thus, we would argue that there is initial evidence to view the IPA Program as a research-validated protocol. It is our hope that the publication of the IPA program will lead to additional rigorous evaluation beyond our own research efforts.

Developmentally Appropriate and Developmentally Sequenced

The teaching of phonological awareness must be developmentally sequenced, and teaching must be provided in activities that are developmentally and age appropriate. The IPA Program is designed to meet the needs of struggling learners in kindergarten and first grade. The activities are engaging for children of this age. The repetition in the activities allows children to focus their attention on the phonological awareness skills. The program teaches skills in the order that children typically learn these skills, moving from simple to complex. Repetition provides multiple learning opportunities, which is important for struggling learners. The sequence is consistent with research that indicates children do not necessarily fully master one skill before demonstrating emerging ability on more complex skills (Anthony et al., 2002).

The developmental sequence of phonological awareness is not captured when a letter-by-letter approach is taken, as in some early reading series (Smith et al., 2001). In these series, children are engaged simultaneously in many different phonological awareness activities that require different skill levels (e.g., rhyme *B* words, circle words that begin with *B*, segment words that include /b/). This nondevelopmental format of instruction may be counterproductive with struggling learners. What is essential is that a developmentally sequenced phonological awareness program moves from simple level skills such as rhyming to complex activities such as segmenting with a recognition that the linguistic features of words, not letters of the alphabet, influence difficulty. Adams, Foorman, Lundberg, and Beeler (1998) provide an excellent example of a developmentally-sequenced, classroom-based phonological awareness instruction.

Focus on Phonological Awareness

The IPA Program focuses primarily on developing children's phonological awareness, separate from developing alphabet knowledge. It begins intervention with activities that are phonological awareness activities but not phonemic awareness activities. Once children gain some experience and proficiency, phonemic awareness activities are targeted (e.g., segment initial sounds in the Initial Sound section, all activities in the Segmentation and Blending section). Although the NRP Report suggested that the most effective phonemic awareness instruction provides children with opportunities to represent sounds with letters, a careful examination of this recommendation provides practical guidelines for its implementation. The citation for this conclusion is the work of Blachman and her colleagues (e.g., Ball & Blachman, 1988, 1991). Examination of the studies clarifies that only after children were successful at segmentation of sounds were letters incorporated into segmentation activities (Blachman et al., 2000).

Thus, from its inception, the IPA Program has specifically focused on developing a foundation of phonological awareness separate from instruction that teaches children how speech sounds are represented with print symbols. We hypothesize that isolated phonological awareness instruction is the piece of classroom instruction that is insufficient for many struggling learners. In addition, we hypothesize that when all phonological awareness instruction or intervention includes representing sounds with letters, as may be done in the classroom or in some intervention programs, it is not truly phonological awareness instruction. More important, struggling learners can be overwhelmed because they are simultaneously trying to figure out the sound structure of words and the representation of that structure with print symbols. Furthermore, we argue that particularly for struggling learners, a foundation of phonological awareness is needed before children are asked to focus their attention on the details of figuring out word decoding. The IPA Program develops children's letter-sound knowledge alongside developing phonological awareness. Throughout the program, children have plenty of learning opportunities during which they are only asked to analyze the sound structure of words. Gradually, children are given opportunities within the Letter Activity to combine their ability to segment sounds with their ability to represent those sounds with letters. We assume that this foundation of phonological awareness and letter-sound knowledge allows children subsequently to benefit from the extensive word decoding and spelling instruction they receive in the classroom in kindergarten and first grade.

Comprehensive Focus on Phonological Awareness

In 1998, our review of the literature suggested that effective phonological awareness intervention needed to be sufficient in scope, intensity, and duration (see Warren, Fey, & Yoder, 2007) for a general discussion of treatment intensity). Intervention needed to be developmentally sequenced, targeting earlier developing skills (e.g., rhyme) before later developing skills (e.g., segment initial sounds) and culminating in teaching children to segment and blend phonemes. Within each step of the phonological intervention sequence, activities needed to move from simple to complex, and within individual activities, instructional stimuli needed to move from easy to difficult.

Therefore, we sought to develop a program that met these challenges and that developed the foundation of phonemic awareness needed to build initial word decoding and spelling skills—segmentation and blending of individual phonemes. The literature offers guidance on what constitutes this foundation, but nowhere do we find a definitive answer on the extent of phonemic awareness a child needs in order to decode and spell. Our hypothesis in the IPA Program is that this foundation involves proficiency in segmenting and blending CV, VC, and CVC words and an emerging ability to segment and blend CCVC and CVCC words. Thus, the intervention activities lead to proficiency at this level by the end of 12 weeks.

We begin the intervention program with the relatively simple phonological awareness task of rhyme, not because it is an essential skill for reading and writing but because it is a good place to begin intervention. Our inclusion of rhyme as the initially targeted skill was based on a simple idea: Children who have poor phonological awareness are often very reluctant to engage in phonological awareness instruction. They have figured out that these activities are difficult activities in which they experience a lot of failure. And who wants to keep at tasks that are very difficult and frustrating? Because it is easy to get children to experience success with rhyme, the IPA Program begins with rhyme and then moves to more difficult tasks that require children to isolate individual phonemes. We have found that children's success at rhyme provides motivation to try more complex tasks. Thus, rhyme is a good place to start to move children along the road to gaining segmentation and blending skills—the critical phonemic awareness skills when it comes to decoding and spelling.

From rhyme activities, the program moves to analysis of initial sounds and final sounds, and then sessions move to segmenting and blending sounds in words. Because children have had experience with analysis of initial and final sounds, segmentation activities initially only require one new step: segmentation of the vowel sound in monosyllabic words. Once children have success with VC, CV, and CVC words, they are asked to segment words with blends (CCVC, CVCC).

The session focus skill is taught and practiced in one or two activities per session. In the last session of each week, the specific skill focused upon in the following week is introduced. (This plan is altered somewhat in the last 3 weeks of the program.) In this way, children know what they will be learning next. Skills taught in previous weeks are reinforced in subsequent weeks of training. For example, rhyme is taught initially in Weeks 1–3 and then reviewed in Weeks 4–6 when initial segmentation is taught. This review allows for additional practice to strengthen established skills. Further, the simultaneous focus on two skills (e.g., rhyme and initial sounds) develops flexibility in children's ability to perform phonological awareness tasks. Lastly, the review activities allow for important learning opportunities for children who do not firmly establish skills during the initial instructional weeks. Given that the IPA Program is designed to be used with kindergarten and first grade struggling learners, the skills being targeted in the IPA Program are likely being taught and practiced in the classroom as well.

Phonological Awareness Skills Not Included in the IPA Program

The hierarchy of phonological awareness development suggests that children are first successful at segmenting words into syllables. We did not include activities at this level in the IPA Program but presumed that children would have ability at this level. If that is not the case, syllable segmentation skills could be developed by using activities from Adams et al. (1998)?

The IPA Program does not develop phoneme manipulation or phoneme deletion (e.g., *Say cat without the /k/)* as these skills are not considered foundational phonemic awareness skills. Some researchers argue that phoneme deletion and manipulation are skills that develop as a result of learning to read rather than being skills helpful for initial learning to decode and spell (Wagner, Torgesen, & Rashotte, 1994).

Letter-Sound Knowledge

Although the primary goal of the IPA Program is to establish a foundation of phonemic awareness skills (blending, segmenting), children need letter-sound knowledge to make use of their phonemic awareness skills in decoding and spelling words. It is our experience that struggling learners frequently fail to learn letter names and sounds at the same pace as their classmates. We included a Letter Activity in each session to assure that alphabet knowledge is well-established when children finish the IPA Program. Our experience has been that the repetitive and concentrated practice on letters and sounds in the IPA Program is effective. Letter of the week frameworks used in many kindergarten and first grade classrooms fail to provide sufficient repetitive practice for struggling learners.

Repetition of Activities

The learning of children who are struggling to master particular content may be enhanced when the children are able to focus their attention and resources on the critical skills of interest. Intervention may be less effective for children when learning activities require children to figure out the rules of a game or activity and figure out the targeted skill. Thus, to maximize focus on learning phonological awareness simultaneously, we use the same learning activities across the first three units of the IPA Program; the activities stay the same, the target skill changes. In the Rhyme, Initial Sounds, and Final Sounds section, the repetition of learning activities allows children to focus on the targeted phonological awareness skill. In the Rhyme section (Weeks 1–3), children are asked to judge whether two words rhyme (judgment), then to choose which of three words does not rhyme (odd-one-out), then to match rhyming words, and then to generate rhymes. This same sequence of activities is used in Initial Sounds (Weeks 4–6) and Final Sounds (Weeks 7–9). These activities were not amenable to teaching phoneme segmentation and blending; thus, different activities are used in Weeks 10–12.

Instructional Stimuli

There has been some suggestion that phonological awareness is best taught when children are asked to analyze words that are firmly established in their lexicons (Metsala & Walley, 1998; Walley, Metsala, & Garlock, 2003). In the IPA Program units of Rhyme, Initial Sounds, and Final Sounds, nearly all instructional stimuli are monosyllabic words that are likely to be familiar to kindergarten and first-grade children. (There may be words that are not familiar to English language learners.) Many of the instructional stimuli words are used across the units and appear in multiple activities (see Appendix A). We hypothesize that this repetition of words facilitates learning. For example, children might first analyze *cat* in learning to rhyme, and then in learning to segment initial sounds, then final sounds, and lastly, in learning to segment all the sounds in words. When words are repeated across activities and units, task complexity is reduced. Furthermore, interventionists can refer back to previous activities as a means to scaffold children's success: *Tell me a word that rhymes with cat. Remember when we matched rhyming words? Do you remember a word that rhymed with cat?*

Complexity

In the IPA Program activities, complexity increases in three ways. First, the overall complexity of phonological awareness skills increases requiring increasingly sophisticated phonological awareness ability, moving from rhyme, to analysis of initial sounds, to analysis of final sounds, and lastly to blending and segmentation of whole words. Second, within each target area, activities move from simple to complex. In the more simple activities, children have a greater chance of being successful than in the more complex activities. For example, in the judgment tasks, chance-level performance is 50%, but in odd-one-out, chance level performance is 33%. Third, within each activity, session plans provide guidance for beginning with stimuli that are likely to be easier for children. For example, segmentation of initial continuants (e.g., /f/, /s/) is likely to be easier than segmentation of initial stops (e.g., /d/, /k/).

Intensity and Duration of Intervention

Our initial development studies of the IPA Program were conducted in a university setting where a semester calendar guides what is accomplished. We chose 12 weeks of intervention because it fit neatly within the university semester calendar. When we began to implement the IPA Program in school settings, we found that the 12-week framework fit well into the school calendar as well, where the winter break essentially is a mid-year break and a point in kindergarten where children who are struggling may be identified for a Tier 2 or specialized intervention. We chose three 30-minute sessions each week because our impression was that this amount of time provided consistent and sufficient learning opportunities for many struggling learners. The intensity and duration of the IPA Program is consistent with the NRP recommendations (NICHHD, 2000b) and other phonological awareness interventions (Blachman et al., 2000; van Kleeck et al., 1998).

Interventionist

In 1998 we developed the session plans with a SLP as the presumed interventionist. When we began to field-test the program in schools in West Virginia, some schools wanted to use a broader range of interventionists, for example, special educators or reading specialists. Furthermore, in some schools, the SLP and reading specialist worked as a team to implement the program. Some days both conducted the intervention, and other days, just one person conducted the intervention. This collaborative effort worked well with individual SLP and teacher schedules in some schools. Furthermore, the SLPs and teachers reported that the collaboration enhanced their knowledge and skills beyond what they would have achieved by implementing the program as the sole interventionist. Thus, in the current version we have revised the session plans to provide implementation support for interventionists with varying levels of expertise in phonological awareness (Spencer, Schuele, Guillot, & Lee, 2008).

Children in IPA Program Intervention Groups

Because phonological awareness instruction is now included in most, if not all, kindergarten classrooms, the IPA Program is appropriate for those children who have failed to make adequate progress in classroom instruction. We recommend that children participate in the program in the second half of kindergarten or early in first grade, before they fail at learning to read (i.e., prevention). The program may be appropriate for children beyond first grade who are in need of remediation or for older children with intellectual disabilities when they are ready to benefit from phonological awareness intervention.

In our development studies and in the statewide implementation of the IPA Program in West Virginia schools, our intervention groups typically had six children, sometimes as few as four, and never more than eight. A group of six children allows for sufficient practice by children and for interactive learning opportunities across the group. More than eight children in a group no longer provides a small-group learning experience. Our groups included children solely in general education as well as children who were eligible for special education (e.g., learning disability, speech-language impairment) and had IEPs. In some schools children with hearing loss or children with intellectual disabilities were included in the intervention groups.

Our suggestion is that when more than one IPA Program intervention group is implemented at a school, the intervention groups not be formed by grouping children according to ability (e.g., lowest children in one group, higher children in another group). We have found that a mix of initial skill levels provides an excellent learning environment for all children. It is impossible to predict the rate of learning for children and so a child who begins as the least proficient in the group may be the child with the strongest phonological awareness skills at the end of the program. Also, the more proficient children provide excellent models for the less proficient children. Having a range of ability within the group allows for very valuable observational learning opportunities for all children.

Group Intervention

Individual intervention often is considered to be the ideal and best learning context to remediate children's deficits. It might be argued to be optimal because all learning interchanges can be highly focused to address a child's individual needs. However, perhaps because individual intervention can be cost prohibitive, the typical context for addressing children's speech, language, and learning deficits in the schools is small-group intervention. Although financial considerations may drive the selection of group therapy, our experience with the IPA Program has led us to believe that small-group intervention may be the preferred context to develop children's phonological awareness skills. The NRP found small-group phonological awareness intervention more effective than individual intervention (NICHHD, 2000b). The group learning context allows children to learn from interactions in which they are active participants and from observational learning as well. The pressure to perform is much less in small-group intervention than in individual intervention.

The IPA Program provides group intervention, not intervention in a group. Children are selected to participate in the intervention because they have a common deficit—weak phonological awareness skills. They are engaged in 12 weeks of small-group intervention to improve their phonological awareness skills. All children are engaged in the same activities for the same reason—ultimately, to acquire the ability to segment and blend sounds in order to use these skills to develop initial decoding and spelling proficiency.

Group therapy is familiar to most SLPs. But much of the group intervention that SLPs provide can be best characterized as "therapy in a group" rather than "group therapy." Therapy in a group occurs when the group aspect is limited to a group of children working with the SLP at the same time. Although the children are seen in the same block of time, each child is working on his or her own goals, and goals across the group of children are often quite disparate (e.g., articulation of /s/, vocabulary development, production of past tense markers). Therapy in a group is conducted for time efficiency, not for learning efficiency. In this context, children only benefit from their own turns in the session. Thus, within a thirty minute session with three children, at best each child receives 10 minutes of intervention, albeit spread across 30 minutes.

The IPA program is group therapy, not therapy in a group. Group therapy, or group intervention, involves a group of children working on developing the same skills or knowledge. Although children may be at varying levels of proficiency and scaffolding varies across children, all instructional interchanges are manipulated to enable each child to benefit. Sometimes a child benefits from directly responding, other times a child benefits from observational learning. Thus, at the end of a 30-minute session, each child has benefited from the entire 30 minutes of intervention.

Individualized Instruction Through Scaffolding

Group intervention can effectively meet the needs of children who are functioning at varying levels of proficiency. The IPA Program standard treatment protocol lays out a developmentally driven sequence of intervention activities that gradually builds children's proficiency. Although teaching can be individualized within each session, the overall program is not individualized to each child's strengths and needs. The implementation of the sessions proceeds in a lock-step fashion. The sessions are implemented sequentially across 36 days, regardless of children's performances in a particular session. Session plan 1 is implemented on the first day of intervention, session plan 2 on the second day, and so forth until all 36 session plans are implemented. The reality of this format means that one child in an intervention group may begin the program with the ability to rhyme but will engage in that set of learning activities nevertheless. Or regardless of whether each child masters rhyming in the first 3 weeks of the program, the group moves on to initial sounds at the beginning of the fourth week of the program.

Although the session plans are prescribed and not individualized, interventionists individualize at the level of support that is provided to each child as each session occurs. The interventionist scaffolds children's participation in the activities. The goal is for each child to achieve success and the interventionist's task is to provide the scaffolding needed to make this success happen. For example, if the session activity requires children to segment initial sounds, interventionists may need to simplify the task for some children. One child may easily respond /s/ when asked *What is the first sound in sun?* Another child may need the interventionist to make the initial sound salient by stretching the sound out (e.g., *sssssun*). Another child may need the interventionist to segment the word at the level of onset rhyme: *What is the first sound in sun? Listen ssssun. What is the first sound in ssss [pause] un*?

Response to Intervention

Small-group interventions with standard treatment protocols are often provided in the context of RTI models (see Fuchs et al., 2008; Mellard & Johnson, 2007). Within these models, Tier 1 instruction involves excellent classroom instruction with some form of progress monitoring so as to identify children who are not making adequate progress. In the West Virginia project (Schuele et al., 2008), we used the *Phonemic Awareness in Young Children: A Classroom Curriculum* (Adams et al., 1998) as the Tier 1 instruction. Tier 2 intervention is provided to children who fail to make adequate progress with classroom instruction alone. The IPA Program can be used as a Tier 2 intervention in an RTI model. The assumption within an RTI model is that many, but not all, children will make sufficient progress on the targeted skill(s) after participation in the Tier 2 intervention. For those children who do not make adequate progress at Tier 2 (treatment resisters or nonresponders), individualized intervention, perhaps one to one, is provided as a Tier 3 intervention.

3

Implementing the Intensive Phonological Awareness Program

This chapter provides guidance on implementing the IPA program. Three forms are used to document the implementation of the program (see Figure 3.1). In combination these forms provide an easy and convenient means to document child session attendance (see Figure 3. 2), to note the date and duration of individual sessions (see Figure 3.5), to summarize child attendance within each unit and for the entire program (see Figure 3.5), and to record notes about the implementation of individual sessions (Figure 3.3 and Figure 3.4). Blank versions of each form are available on the accompanying CD and as downloads. For each group, the interventionist will need one copy of the *IPA Program Child Attendance Record* and one copy of the *IPA Program Implementation Record* as well as 36 copies of the *IPA Program Daily Implementation Record.*

Child attendance is recorded so that the interventionist has an accurate record of the amount of intervention time for each child (see Figure 3.2). Child attendance can be summarized in the *IPA Program Implementation Record* (Figure 3.5). The IPA Program sessions include a good bit of redundancy, as we developed the program realizing that individual children miss days of school. We included the redundancy in the session plans to eliminate the need for interventionists to "catch children up" on sessions that were missed. When a child misses a particular session, the subsequent sessions should provide adequate learning opportunities for children. Trying to find time to work individually with specific children to catch up on missed sessions can be very difficult. In addition, such catch-up sessions would involve only the child(ren) who missed a particular session and, thus, the learning environ-

IPA Program Child Attendance Record

Use this form to track children's daily attendance at the sessions.

IPA Program Implementation Record

This form provides a place to note the date each lesson is conducted, to note the length of the lesson, and to summarize the child attendance across the segments or units of the program.

IPA Program Daily Implementation Record

This form allows you to document the implementation of each individual session or lesson plan. Make 36 copies of this page and insert the individual session numbers at the top of each form. Store these pages in a binder for ease of reference throughout program implementation. Remove an individual page each day to record notes.

Figure 3.1. Three forms that can be used to record the implementation of the *Intensive Phonological Awareness (IPA) Program.*

CHILD ATTENDANCE RECORD (✓ for attended, A for absent)

	Rhyme									Initial Sounds								
Child Names	1	2	3	4	5	6	7	8	9	10	11	12	13	14	15	16	17	18
Melissa W.	✓	✓	✓	✓	✓	✓	✓	✓	✓	✓	✓	✓	✓	✓	✓	✓	✓	✓
Anne F.	✓	✓	✓	✓	✓	✓	✓	✓	✓	✓	✓	✓	✓	✓	✓	✓	✓	✓
Daniel L.	✓	✓	✓	✓	✓	✓	✓	✓	✓	✓	✓	✓	✓	✓	✓	✓	✓	✓
Isaac S.	✓		✓	✓	✓	✓	✓	A	✓	✓	✓	✓	✓	✓	✓	✓	✓	✓
Austin P.	✓	✓	✓	✓	✓	✓	✓	A	✓	✓	✓	✓	✓	✓	✓	✓	✓	✓
Bella K.	✓	✓	✓	A	✓	A	✓	A	✓	A	✓	✓	✓	✓	✓	✓	✓	✓

	Final Sounds									Segmentation and Blending								
Child Names	19	20	21	22	23	24	25	26	27	28	29	30	31	32	33	34	35	36

Figure 3.2. Sample IPA Program Child Attendance Record.

ment may be quite different than the typical IPA Program learning environment. Hence, we recommend that interventionists not schedule "catch-up sessions" for individual children. Clearly when a child misses multiple sessions within a week (e.g., child is absent from school for an entire week), the interventionist will have to weigh the possible benefit and plausibility of catch-up lessons.

As a standard treatment protocol, the IPA Program is planned for sequential implementation of the 36 sessions (i.e., all sessions, in the order specified). Each week three sessions are conducted with each session 30 minutes in length. Within each session plan there is a suggested time length for each activity. Sufficient repetition within activities should be done so that each activity lasts the suggested time and the entire session lasts 30 minutes. Note that the length of IPA Program sessions are time driven, not activity driven. Thus, a session should never be finished "early" because all the activities were completed in less than 30 minutes.

We know that interventionists may have to deviate from the protocol sequence occasionally, typically due to events outside the control of the interventionist (e.g., a fire drill during the session, days off, snow/weather days). Deviations in the length of a session can be noted on the *Program Implementation Record.* Scheduled or unscheduled schools days off sometimes make it impossible to have three sessions within a week. Our preference has been to make adjustments so that we conduct two 45-minute sessions in 1 week rather than interrupt the weekly structure of the IPA Program.

Our experience suggests that recording individual responses from children (e.g., to calculate a percent correct) during the implementation of the IPA Program sessions is counterproductive for several reasons. First, recording individual child responses in group intervention is very difficult to do. Creating an atmosphere where all children are focused on the instructional dialogue and each turn in the intervention interchange and where learning is appropriately scaffolded requires the interventionist's complete attention. Providing a sufficient focus to the learning situation leaves little time for an interventionist to record individual child responses. Second, the recording of individual responses often results in meaningless data. Child responses are rarely simply correct or incorrect, except in testing situations. Rather, the accuracy of a child's response is a function of the scaffolding provided. Within intervention sessions that appropriately scaffold children's learning, the interventionist's goal is to support each child's performance to elicit an accurate response from each child. Less proficient children will be provided far more scaffolding than more proficient children. Thus, calculating percent correct across responses often ignores that each re-

Scope of activities implemented:
Able to get through about half of the rhyme generation stimuli. Repeat initial stimuli several times to help some of the children catch on.

Comments on individual child performance (list child's first name and comments):
Sam: *Able to generate rhyme words with no assistance. Seems to have mastered this skill.*
John Harold: *Not able to generate rhyming words. Had to provide choice options and walk him through both choices—for example, "What rhymes with cat? Let's see if it would be rat or gum."*
Antoine: *Last time needed choice to generate rhyme word but today when given an initial sound cue could usually come up with rhyme word.*

Problems or challenges encountered in implementation of today's lesson plan:
Two children missed last session. Did not provide enough orientation at the outset of the session to help them understand what we were doing. Next time child misses, take a minute at beginning to introduce activity so everyone understands what is going on.

Figure 3.3. Excerpt from a sample IPA Program Daily Implementation Record.

Daily Implementation Record

Complete this form after each session.

Session number *24* Today's date *3-3-14*

Start time *2:00* End time *2:28* Total minutes of lesson *28*

Child attendance: Were any children absent from today's session? Yes (No)

List the names of the children who were absent:

Melissa
Anne

Deviations from and/or modifications to today's session plan:

None

Scope of activities implemented:

Letter Activity - finished all letters

Final Sound Matching - did all puzzles, children able to quickly match puzzles

Final Sound Sorting - only got through 1/2 pix

Comments on individual child performance (list child's first name and comments):

Daniel & Isaac able to do tasks today with little support. Isaac seems to be catching on.

Austin - final sound sorting - hard time. Needed me to iterate/stretch sounds several times before he could sort.

Problems or challenges encountered in implementation of today's session plan:

Anne had hard time with puzzles previous session - may need to scaffold more for her next time since she was absent today.

Lost a couple of minutes of time because fire alarm went off.

Figure 3.4. Sample IPA Program Daily Implementation Record.

sponse was obtained under a particular level of scaffolding and that scaffolding varied from one response to the next. Third, recording percent correct may focus the interventionist on individual child accuracy rather than the levels of scaffolding individual children need to be successful. We have found that when interventionists focus on eliciting accurate responses from all children, their awareness of scaffolding increases and it becomes far easier to appropriately scaffold children's learning within and across sessions. Although SLPs are accustomed to documenting progress within intervention sessions on a response-by-response basis, this process is not routine for reading specialists, special educators, or classroom teachers. Consider that in classrooms a large amount of instruction occurs under conditions where there is little consideration to grading. Assignment of a grade or a determination of whether a skill has been achieved is left to unit testing, for example.

The *Daily Implementation Record* provides a one-page form for the interventionist to document relevant details of each individual session. Prior to the session, the interventionist should note, at the top of the form, the session number, the date, and the time that the session begins. Attendance can be recorded just as the session begins. The rest of this form is set up so that interventionists have a place a) to note any deviations or modifications to the day's session (e.g., less time spent on an activity than planned), b) to note anything relevant about the scope of activities implemented (e.g., only five rhyme pairs were practice), c) to comment on individual child performance, including scaffolding that individual children needed to be successful, and d) to note any general or overall problems or challenges encountered. At the end of the session, the interventionist should record the ending time and calculate the total minutes. If the session time of 30 minutes is not routinely maintained, fidelity to the protocol is not being maintained (see Kaderavek & Justice, 2010).

Typically there is not much time within an individual session to record anything but cursory notes on the *Daily Implementation Record*. See Figure 3.4 for an example of a completed *Daily Implementation Record*. These cursory notes can be expanded on and added to after the session. We recommend that interventionists plan to allot 5–10 minutes immediately following each session to complete this form. Waiting until the middle of the day or end of the day to record such information will likely result in information that is not maximally informative to implementing subsequent sessions. Types of comments that clinicians will find helpful to guiding their implementation of the IPA Program include descriptions of the scaffolding that individual children need, descriptions of changes in child proficiency and child confidence, examples of child errors, and so on. Taking time at the end of each week to review the *Daily Implementation Records* will guide interventionists to consider how children are progressing and changes in scaffolding that might be needed in subsequent sessions.

Intensive Phonemic Awareness (IPA) Program Implementation Record

Site *Bertram Elem.* Dates implemented *1-7-14*

SESSION IMPLEMENTATION

Note date each session implemented and the length of the session in minutes.

Rhyme	Initial Sounds	Final Sounds	Segment and Blend
Session 1 Date: *1-7* Minutes: *30*	Session 10 Date: *1-28* Minutes: *30*	Session 19 Date: Minutes:	Session 28 Date: Minutes:
Session 2 Date: *1-8* Minutes: *30*	Session 11 Date: *1-29* Minutes: *30*	Session 20 Date: Minutes:	Session 29 Date: Minutes:
Session 3 Date: *1-9* Minutes: *30*	Session 12 Date: *1-31* Minutes: *30*	Session 21 Date: Minutes:	Session 30 Date: Minutes:
Session 4 Date: *1-14* Minutes: *30*	Session 13 Date: *2-4* Minutes: *30*	Session 22 Date: Minutes:	Session 31 Date: Minutes:
Session 5 Date: *1-15* Minutes: *30*	Session 14 Date: *2-6* Minutes: *25*	Session 23 Date: Minutes:	Session 32 Date: Minutes:
Session 6 Date: *1-16* Minutes: *25*	Session 15 Date: *2-7* Minutes: *30*	Session 24 Date: Minutes:	Session 33 Date: Minutes:
Session 7 Date: *1-21* Minutes: *30*	Session 16 Date: *2-11* Minutes: *30*	Session 25 Date: Minutes:	Session 34 Date: Minutes:
Session 8 Date: *1-22* Minutes: *30*	Session 17 Date: *2-12* Minutes: *30*	Session 26 Date: Minutes:	Session 35 Date: Minutes:
Session 9 Date: *1-24* Minutes: *32*	Session 18 Date: *2-13* Minutes: *26*	Session 27 Date: Minutes:	Session 36 Date: Minutes:

ATTENDANCE SUMMARY

Indicate the number of sessions each child missed in each segment of the program.

Child name	Number of sessions missed				Total Missed
	Rhyme Weeks 1–3	Initial Sounds Weeks 4–6	Final Sounds Weeks 7–9	Segment and Blend Weeks 10–12	
Melissa W.	*0*	*0*			
Anne F.	*0*	*0*			
Daniel L.	*0*	*0*			
Isaac S.	*2*	*0*			
Austin P.	*1*	*0*			
Bella K.	*2*	*0*			

Figure 3.5. Sample Intensive Phonemic Awareness (IPA) Program Implementation Record.

II

Session Plans

WEEK 1

OVERVIEW

Session 1 Focus: Introduction of Rhyme and Rhyme Judgment

Session 2 Focus: Rhyme Judgment and Rhyme Odd-One-Out

Session 3 Focus: Rhyme Odd-One-Out and Introduction to Rhyme Matching

Materials Needed

- ➜ Alphabet cards (uppercase)
- ➜ Game board and game pieces
- ➜ Optional: Mirror
- ➜ Rhyme Judgment Cards
- ➜ Rhyme Generation Cards—subset
  ape grape
  bat cat hat mat
  bug rug
  cake snake
  car star
  three tree knee bee
- ➜ Rhyme Odd-One-Out Cards
- ➜ Rhyme Puzzle Cards—subset
  bed head
  stop cop
  night light
  drum gum

Intervention Notes

____

____

____

____

____

____

____

____

WEEK 1 → SESSION 1

Session Focus: Introduction of Rhyme and Rhyme Judgment

ACTIVITY

Letter Activity (3–5 minutes)

Note: Letter activity at the beginning of each session should take no more than 3–5 minutes.

Materials: None

Directions: Singing ABCs as a group. The clinician leads the group in singing the ABC song, being careful to clearly enunciate each letter, especially *l-m-n-o-p*.

→ **Teaching strategies:** This is a good first day warm-up activity. Sing the song multiple times within this block of time. Encourage but don't require children to join in. Children who do not know their ABCs are less likely to be intimidated by group singing than by a focus on individual children. Depending on child skill level, vary the pace of the singing. Less proficient children will benefit from a slower presentation that allows them to repeat or chime in. Use child skill level to guide the level of support provided.

ACTIVITY

Introduction of Rhyme

(5–10 minutes)

Materials: None

Directions: Explanation with group participation. Children repeat rhyming pairs as modeled by the clinician:

top–mop
cat–bat
back–sack

There are no pictures for this introductory activity.

→ **Teaching strategies:** ***We're going to talk about words that rhyme today. Words that rhyme are words that sound the same at the end, like top and mop, tOP–mOP*** (emphasize the end of the words, i.e., the rime). ***Do you hear how there is an OP at the end of top and an OP at the end of mop? Listen again: top–mop, t-op, m-op. Now you try saying them. Remember, rhyming words sound the same. And my mouth does the same thing! Watch my mouth! top–mop.*** Have children in unison repeat the rhyme pairs; then have a few individual children repeat the rhyme pairs. Go through this explanation for each of the three rhyme pairs, calling the children's attention to how the words sound and how the words are produced in the mouth.

ACTIVITY

Rhyme Judgment (15–20 minutes)

Materials: Rhyme Judgment Cards, game board and game pieces

Directions: Each child picks a card; there are two pictures on each card. The child says aloud the names of the pictures and tells whether the pair rhymes. The group can provide feedback on accuracy of the responses. Initially and as needed, the clinician can model how to complete the task with the first card. Repeat model with other picture pairs as needed. At the end of the turn, the child can move one square forward on the game board after providing a correct answer.

→ **Teaching strategies:** ***We're going to play a game. We'll decide if two words rhyme. All these cards have two pictures on them. On some cards, the words for the two pictures rhyme. But on other cards, the words for the pictures do not rhyme. We are going to take turns picking the cards, saying the names of the pictures, and deciding if the words rhyme. Remember, for each one, you have to decide: Do the words [word 1] and [word 2] sound the same at the end? Does my mouth do the same thing?*** Whether or not the child provides a correct answer, have the child and the group consider these guiding questions for each word pair.

If a child does not provide an answer, prompt with ***Do the words rhyme? Do ___ and ___ rhyme? Do they sound the same at the end? Does your mouth do the same thing?*** It is important that each child says the words aloud himself or herself. After a child responds, the group can repeat the word pair aloud in unison and answer as a group regarding whether the words rhyme. The clinician should provide sufficient cues and scaffolding support so the target child eventually is able to answer correctly and move forward on the game board. At the end of each turn, the clinician can provide summative feedback by repeating the word pair, repeating the words segmented by onset-rime (e.g., *m-op, c-at*), and saying whether or not the words rhyme. This feedback assures that all children clearly recognize the correct answer for each word pair.

Session Focus: Introduction of Rhyme and Rhyme Judgment

SESSION STIMULI

Rhyme Judgment Cards

Pairs that Do Rhyme

cone	phone
moon	spoon
sun	one
cane	train
ice	dice
house	mouse
race	vase
glove	dove
ring	king
rope	soap
cape	tape
book	hook
gate	skate
chair	bear
snow	bow
red	bed
bag	flag
duck	truck

Pairs that Don't Rhyme

mop	cake
house	phone
moon	tooth
fan	drum
bug	match
foot	nose
duck	lamb
cat	fish
comb	house
cap	bus

Examples

Easier pairs: cape–tape, mop–cake, cat–fish, cane–train

More difficult pairs: snow–bow, fan–drum

Most difficult: cap–can, house–rose, bat–foot

IMPLEMENTATION SUGGESTIONS

Choosing Stimuli

- Some word pairs may be easier than others for children. For children with little proficiency, building initial success may be best accomplished with rhyme pairs that have final sounds that are visible (e.g., *cape–tape, rope–soap*) and nonrhyme pairs that have final sounds that are maximally different (e.g., not *fan–drum,* but *duck–lamb*).
- When words are associated on some conceptual level, it may be more difficult for a child to focus on the sound structure of the words. Thus it may be more difficult to judge whether *nose–foot* rhyme than whether *rose–foot* rhyme. Therefore, the word pairs in the Rhyme Judgment Cards are for the most part unrelated.
- Words that end with consonants (e.g., consonant–vowel–consonant, or CVC) may be easier than words that end in vowels (consonant–vowel, or CV). Children may be able to use the articulatory placement cues of the final consonant sounds to facilitate their rhyme judgment. Thus only one rhyme pair in this game includes CV stimuli (*snow, bow*). Subsequent sessions include more words that end in vowels.

RHYME-GUIDING QUESTIONS

Do [word 1] and [word 2] sound the same at the end?

Does my mouth do the same thing?

More on Teaching Strategies

- When modeling rhymes, the clinician should emphasize the ending segment (i.e., rime) of each spoken word (e.g., put stress on the final segment, tOP, mOP, or repeat and emphasize the rime, tOP, mOP).
- Have children say the words while looking in a mirror so that they can see themselves articulate the words and can use that articulatory information to focus their attention on speech sounds.
- It is *not* important that children use particular words to label the pictures. Have the child judge the two spoken words he or she uses to label the two pictures. If some children use alternate labels, the group can judge that pair of spoken words as well. The focus is judging any rhyme pair, not judging particular spoken word pairs.

Session Focus: Rhyme Judgment and Rhyme Odd-One-Out

ACTIVITY

Letter Activity (3–5 minutes)

Materials: Alphabet cards

Directions: Children take turns picking a card and holding it up for the group. All children together say the name and the sound in the sentence frame "This is ___ and ___ says ___" (e.g., *This is* S, *and* S *says* /s/). Complete about half of the alphabet cards.

→ **Teaching strategies:** The clinician says the name and the sound along with the children. Children are not expected to perform independently but rather in unison with the clinician or by repeating the clinician's model (e.g., the clinician says, then the clinician says in unison with the children). Move quickly through the deck to do about half of the cards within the allotted time. Typically, for vowel sounds, introduce with long vowel sounds first. With the exception of *U*, the name of the letter and the vowel sound will be the same. The clinician can decide whether to do the letters in order or out of order; with less proficient children, order may be easier because children can use their rote knowledge of the alphabet song as a scaffold.

ACTIVITY

Brief Reminder of Rhymes

Materials: None

Directions: Explanation with group participation

→ **Teaching strategies:** ***Does everyone remember what rhyme words are? They're words that have the same sounds at the end, like dog and log. Does everyone hear the OG sound at the end of both dog and log? dog–log. d-OG, l-OG. My mouth does the same thing and they sound the same. dog–log.*** Repeat with a few additional pairs, and perhaps pair the children's names with a (real or nonsense) rhyme word.

ACTIVITY

Rhyme Judgment (10–12 minutes)

Materials: Rhyme Judgment Cards

Directions: Each child picks a card with two pictures. The child says aloud the names of the pictures and tells whether the pair rhymes. Children can separate cards into "rhyme" and "don't rhyme" piles.

→ **Teaching strategies:** Children should be familiar with at least some of the word pairs from the previous session. Begin the session with those pairs, particularly if some children are not catching on to judging rhymes. Throughout the activity, review the cards in the separate piles. ***None of these words rhyme.*** [Say pairs in the "don't rhyme" pile.] ***But these words rhyme.*** [Say pairs in the "rhyme" pile.] This repetition provides models for the children struggling with the rhyme concept.

For each pair, have children answer guiding questions (see Session 1).

ACTIVITY

Rhyme Odd-One-Out

(10–12 minutes)

Materials: Subset of Rhyme Generation Cards

Directions: The clinician chooses sets of three cards (two rhyme, one does not rhyme) as the activity proceeds, repeating card sets as needed to facilitate success.

Three children are each given one picture card, two rhyme, one does not (e.g., *cake, snake, hat*). Each child names the picture on his or her card. The remaining children judge which of the three children should stand up because his or her picture does not rhyme with the other two.

→ **Teaching strategies:** ***We're going to play a new kind of game. See these picture cards? There are three pictures. We need to figure out the word that does not rhyme.*** The clinician guides children to the right answer. Have the group repeat the words aloud, emphasizing the rime. Guide the children to compare each pair of words within the set of three to find the word that does not rhyme. If children provide labels that do not lead to an odd-one-out (i.e., none of the words rhyme), first compare all pairs to determine that there are no rhyming pairs. Then help children think about alternate labels for one or more pictures that might yield a rhyme pair and odd-one-out (e.g., *ape–grape–hat* labeled as *monkey–grape–hat*). Alternatively, the clinician can offer a different label for one or more pictures.

Session Focus: Rhyme Judgment and Rhyme Odd-One-Out

SESSION STIMULI

Rhyme Judgment Cards

Pairs that Do Rhyme

cone	phone	cape	tape
moon	spoon	book	hook
sun	one	gate	skate
cane	train	chair	bear
ice	dice	snow	bow
house	mouse	red	bed
race	vase	bag	flag
glove	dove	duck	truck
ring	king		
rope	soap		

Pairs that Don't Rhyme

mop	cake
house	phone
moon	tooth
fan	drum
bug	match
foot	nose
duck	lamb
cat	fish
comb	house
cap	bus

Rhyme Generation Cards—Subset

ape	grape		
bat	cat	hat	mat
bug	rug		
cake	snake		
car	star		
three	tree	knee	bee

IMPLEMENTATION SUGGESTIONS

More on Teaching Strategies

- Letter Sounds:
  - Be sure to produce continuant consonants as an elongated or stretched-out production. That is, do not add a schwa sound for letters that represent continuant sounds: "This is *N*, and *N* says */n/*," but not "This is *n*, and *n* says *nuh*."
  - Be sure to produce stop consonant sounds with a minimized vowel; that is, a brief schwa /ə/, as in *a̲bout*, rather than a /ʌ/, as in *cu̲p*.
  - There is some ambiguity in the educational literature on the sounds associated with the letter *u*. The short *u* sound is always that in *cup*. However, the long *u* sound is sometimes taught as the vowel in *tune* but also may be taught as the first "sound" in *use*. Phonetically, *use* actually begins with the consonant /j/ as in *yes* with the second sound being /u/. We prefer to teach the vowel match for the letter *u* as the vowel in *tune*, but individual clinicians may wish to follow their phonics or word-decoding curricula. See Moats (2010) for further explanation.
- For some children, drawing attention to the place of articulation for final sounds may be helpful. The clinician can provide placement feedback. For example, *mop–cake*. "Watch my mouth: *mop*, that ends with a sound made with my lips; *cake*, that ends with a sound at the back of my mouth. *Mop* and *cake* do not rhyme. My mouth does not do the same thing; *mop* and *cake* do not sound the same."
- For children with little proficiency on rhyme, responses may be driven by guessing rather than an understanding of rhyme. For these children's turns, the clinician may present a stimulus card that was practiced in a previous session or one that was already practiced in the current session (e.g., a word pair that is in the "rhyme" or "not rhyme" piles). The clinician presents this word pair to the child in order to use the child's memory to scaffold his or her learning. For children who are struggling, initial learning may be a process of memorizing some rhyme pairs that provides a basis on which to figure out or intuit the concept of rhyme.

WEEK 1 → SESSION 3

Session Focus: Rhyme Odd-One-Out and Introduction to Rhyme Matching

Note: In the last session of each week, the skill for the next week is introduced. This activity should occupy the last 5 minutes of the session and is marked in the session plan by "Introduction."

ACTIVITY

Letter Activity (3–5 minutes)

Materials: Alphabet cards

Directions: Continue from previous session and complete the alphabet cards.

→ **Teaching strategies:** The clinician says name and sound along with the children: ***This is S, and S says /s/.*** The children can imitate. Group responding allows less skilled children to blend in with the group. Less skilled children may naturally repeat the responses just after the rest of the group.

ACTIVITY

Rhyme Odd-One-Out (20 minutes)

Materials: Rhyme Odd-One-Out Cards, game board and game pieces

Directions: Each child picks a card with three pictures, names the pictures, and decides which picture does not rhyme with the other two. Support each child with group assistance to figure out the answer and check the answer. Each child moves game piece forward on game board at end of turn.

→ **Teaching strategies:** ***We're going to play the same game we did yesterday. But today we have cards with three pictures. We'll say the name of each picture. Then we have to find the word that does not rhyme.*** Make sure the child(ren) says the names of the pictures aloud. The clinician can repeat the names of pictures, emphasizing the rime and providing a cue of onset-rime segmentation, emphasizing the rime. Cue the child: ***Listen and watch my mouth. bug–rug–five. b-ug, r-ug, f-ive. Which one does not rhyme? Listen to the ends of the word. bUG–rUG, bUG–fIVE, rUG–fIVE. Which one does not rhyme?*** Present each pair sequentially, helping children decide whether the two words rhyme. Guide the child to judge each pair. Have children answer guiding questions. For struggling children, (1) ask a more competent child to perform task, then have target child imitate, or (2) have the child select a word card that already has been practiced in today's session. Have the target child provide a response and then have the group check the response. ***Mary says five does not rhyme. Is she right? Let's see. Does bug rhyme with rug? Yes, you're right! Does bug rhyme with five? No! Does rug rhyme with five? No! You are right! Five does not rhyme.***

ACTIVITY

Introduction to Rhyme Matching (5 minutes)

Materials: Subset of Rhyme Puzzle Cards

Directions: Half of each puzzle is taped to the wall so that all children can easily see the pieces. The other half of each puzzle is placed on the table. Each child chooses a picture on the table and tries to find the rhyming match on the wall. Complete introduction with only three or four matches at most.

→ **Teaching strategies:** ***Next time we are going to play a new game. We'll be matching pictures that rhyme. Today we'll practice the new game for a few minutes.*** The clinician should provide maximal assistance and support to ensure that children are successful. The purpose here is simply to introduce the new activity and help children have some success. Narrow choices for the child or suggest a particular picture to try. Demonstrate the process of trial and error by systematically pairing the child's picture with each picture on the wall. ***Let's do the first one together. You have bed. b-ed. b-ED. We need to find the picture that rhymes with bed. Let's try each picture on the wall. The first picture on the wall is cop. bed–cop. Does that rhyme? b-ed, c-op. Do they sound the same? b-ed, c-op. Does your mouth do the same thing? No! bed–gum. b-ed, g-um. Does that rhyme? No! bed–head. b-ed, h-ead. They sound the same at the end. Does your mouth do the same thing? Yes! We figured it out. bed–head. Those words rhyme, and look, the pieces match. They fit together.*** Complete the other puzzles in the same way.

Session Focus: Rhyme Odd-One-Out and Introduction to Rhyme Matching

SESSION STIMULI

Rhyme Odd-One-Out Cards

goose	**leaf**	moose
pen	ten	**comb**
pig	ham	lamb
chime	dime	**fish**
cat	mice	dice
keys	**witch**	cheese
pan	class	gas
vase	face	**cap**
fan	**book**	van

snake	rain	cane
bone	phone	**tree**
gum	**cake**	thumb
mop	hat	cat
boat	**cup**	goat
bug	rug	**five**
bed	**king**	sled
cap	map	**duck**
sock	clock	**tub**

stove	cake	rake
fox	**pig**	box
frog	dog	**kite**
plant	**mouse**	ant
nose	top	cop
light	pie	tie
sun	tool	stool

*Bold words are the non-rhymes

Rhyme Puzzle Cards—Subset

Note: Suggested subset of puzzle cards to use in today's session. All puzzle cards will be used in the next session. Use of a subset often will be used with new activities/skills.

bed	head
stop	cop
night	light
drum	gum

IMPLEMENTATION SUGGESTIONS

RHYME-GUIDING QUESTIONS

Do [word 1] and [word 2] sound the same at the end?

Does my mouth do the same thing?

Choosing Stimuli

- For the rhyme odd-one-out activity, easier items may include those cards that include words used in the Rhyme Judgment Cards. See Appendix A for a listing of words used in each activity. Thus, clinicians can easily determine the stimuli that repeat across activities and units. *A printable/downloadable version also is available on the accompanying CD and among the downloads.*
- For the rhyme odd-one-out activity, easier items may include those cards for which the rime of the nonrhyming word is maximally different from the rime of the two words that rhyme; for example, *gum–cake–thumb* may be easier than *pen–ten–comb.*
- With today's session, words that end with a vowel–consonant–consonant (VCC) rime are included (*fox, box*). We will include more of these in subsequent sessions. The VCC rime words may be more challenging.

More on Teaching Strategies

- If some of the children need an explanation of rhymes, repeat the "Brief Reminder of Rhymes" from Session 2.
- Continue to use rhyme-guiding questions to facilitate learning.
- Question correct responses as well as error responses. For example, *goose, leaf, moose.* "Are you sure *leaf* is the word that does not rhyme? Let's check it out. *goose–leaf.* Do they rhyme? Did your mouth do the same thing? *g-oose, l-eaf?* No, my mouth did not do the same thing. *Leaf–moose. l-eaf, m-oose.* Do they rhyme? Do they sound the same at the end? *l-eaf, m-oose.* Nope. What about *goose–moose? g-oose, m-oose.* Does your mouth do the same thing? [Let children answer.] You're right. Yes. Do they sound the same? *goose–moose* [Let children answer.] Yes, they sound the same. So what word does not rhyme? *Leaf* does not rhyme. *Moose* and *goose* rhyme."
- In introducing the activity for the following week, the purpose is for children to experience some success with the next level of tasks and to set up an anticipation of what is to come. Only 5 minutes will be spent on the Introduction activity. It may be beneficial to do group turns rather than have individual turns on the Introduction activity. When introducing rhyme matching, children will have visual access to both halves of the puzzle and can use puzzle shape to scaffold selection of correct responses. Repeat pairs if necessary to use the full 5 minutes.

WEEK 2

OVERVIEW

Session 4 Focus: Rhyme Matching and Rhyme Odd-One-Out

Session 5 Focus: Rhyme Matching and Rhyme Sorting

Session 6 Focus: Rhyme Sorting and Introduction to Rhyme Generation

Materials Needed

- ➜ Alphabet cards (lowercase)
- ➜ Small paper bag (unmarked)
- ➜ Rhyme Puzzle Cards
- ➜ Rhyme Cards for Sorting
- ➜ Rhyme Odd-One-Out Cards
- ➜ Rhyme Generation Cards—subset
  bug
  cake
  cat
  drum
  hat
  phone

Intervention Notes

WEEK 2 → SESSION 4

Session Focus: Rhyme Matching and Rhyme Odd-One-Out

ACTIVITY

Letter Activity (3–5 minutes)

Materials: Alphabet cards

Directions: The clinician shows the letter to group and prompts children to respond as a group: *This is __ and __ says __.*

→ **Teaching strategies:** Complete about half the alphabet. The clinician can let the children respond as a group and should provide letter names/sounds only when children don't provide a correct answer. If some children do not respond the first time, then the entire group can repeat with all children responding. ***Let's do that one again. Everyone together.***

ACTIVITY

Rhyme Matching

(15 minutes)

Materials: Rhyme Puzzle Cards

Directions: Place half of the puzzle cards in a pile on the table and tape the other half to the wall. A child picks a card and matches it to its rhyming pair taped on the wall. The group can be asked to decide whether they agree with the child's response. As rhymes are located, take the corresponding cards down from the wall to fit the puzzle pieces together.

→ **Teaching strategies:** Begin by selecting a small set of the puzzle cards, depending on the skill level of the group (e.g., a smaller number for less-skilled children). After completing that small set, choose a larger set in the next round. If children are struggling, in a subsequent round mix some of the rhyme puzzles just completed with some new puzzles.

Remember the new game I showed you at the end of last week? We're going to play that matching game again. We're going to look for words that rhyme today. Remember words that rhyme sound the same at the end. Children take turns finding matches. If needed, the clinician can suggest a picture to try: ***Look, Billy put kite and light together. Do those rhyme? Let's say them together and see if they rhyme.*** Use the guiding questions with children.

Children may discover the strategy of matching the puzzle pieces to identify the rhymes. This strategy is appropriate for today's lesson. The clinician can then model to show that indeed the words rhyme. The clinician also can demonstrate a trial-and-error strategy by saying the word/picture the child has with each word/picture on the wall. Have the child say the words aloud and help the child judge each time. Use the guiding questions.

ACTIVITY

Rhyme Odd-One-Out

(10 minutes)

Materials: Rhyme Odd-One-Out Cards, game board, and game pieces

Directions: Each child picks a card with three pictures, names the pictures, and decides which picture does not rhyme with the other two. Support the child with group assistance to figure out the answer and check the answer. The child moves the game piece forward on game board at the end of his or her turn.

→ **Teaching strategies:** Typically, once a new activity is introduced, we will not return to previous activities. But here we provide one more opportunity for children to have practice with the Rhyme Odd-One-Out Cards. ***Let's play this rhyme game one last time. Remember, we have three pictures on the cards, and we have to find the picture that does not rhyme. We have about 10 minutes. Maybe we can finish all these cards.*** If child proficiency allows, move children quickly through the cards and finish the whole set of Odd-One-Out Cards. Adjust scaffolding to individual child needs.

Session Focus: Rhyme Matching and Rhyme Odd-One-Out

SESSION STIMULI

Rhyme Puzzle Cards

bear	pear	fan	pan	night	light
bed	head	fish	dish	shoe	two
bell	well	gate	eight	sink	drink
bone	phone	hat	cat	skate	plate
car	star	hook	book	stop	cop
coat	boat	house	mouse	train	rain
dog	frog	jug	rug	tree	bee
door	four	moon	spoon		
drum	gum	mop	top		

Examples

Easier: When set to match only includes pairs with unique final phonemes.

More difficult: When set to match includes multiple pairs with the same ending phoneme (e.g., *moon–spoon, bone–phone*).

Rhyme Odd-One-Out Cards

goose	**leaf**	moose	boat	**cup**	goat
pen	ten	**comb**	bug	rug	**five**
pig	ham	lamb	bed	**king**	sled
chime	dime	**fish**	cap	map	**duck**
cat	mice	dice	sock	clock	**tub**
keys	**witch**	cheese	**stove**	cake	rake
pan	class	gas	fox	**pig**	box
vase	face	**cap**	frog	dog	**kite**
fan	**book**	van	plant	**mouse**	ant
snake	**rain**	cane	**nose**	top	cop
bone	phone	**tree**	**light**	pie	tie
gum	**cake**	thumb	**sun**	tool	stool
mop	hat	cat			

IMPLEMENTATION SUGGESTIONS

Choosing Stimuli

- Select matching sets based on child proficiency. There are multiple matches that end with the same phoneme. Less proficient children will need matching sets that only include puzzles with unique final consonants.
- There are a few pairs that include the same rime (e.g., *mop–top, stop–cop*). If children find a match that rhymes, but the puzzle pieces don't fit, encourage the child to look for another possible rhyme. "You are right, *mop* and *cop* rhyme. But those puzzle pieces don't fit. Hmm, maybe that means there is another picture that rhymes with *mop*. Let's check the other pictures."

More on Teaching Strategies

- As in the previous rhyme sessions, emphasize the ending segment of each spoken word (e.g., put stress on the final segment, cAT, hAT, or highlight the final segment by repeating it, cat-at, hat-at; "Do those sound the same at the end?"). Highlighting can be accomplished by saying the rime more loudly than the onset, repeating the rime, or elongating the sounds in the rime, which will be easiest when the final phoneme is a continuant.
- For children struggling with rhyme or for those who are reluctant to participate, it may be necessary to facilitate answers by providing additional cues. For example, the clinician may want to use some form of self-talk to demonstrate how a student might problem solve a rhyme judgment task of which he or she is unsure (e.g., "Let me think...*tree-ee, bee-ee*. Do those two make my mouth do the same thing? *Tree...Bee*. Yes, I think I hear the same sound. What do you think, Sarah?"). The clinician may initially want to cue a child by nodding or shaking his or her head as the two words are produced (e.g., "I don't know, *tree, cat*. I'm not sure they rhyme." The clinician shakes her head. "What do you think, Sarah?").
- Remember that the goal is to individualize at the level of teaching, rather than at the level of the session plan. Tailor teaching strategies to meet the learning needs of individual children within the group.

Session Focus: Rhyme Matching and Rhyme Sorting

ACTIVITY

Letter Activity (3–5 minutes)

Materials: Alphabet cards

Directions: The clinician leads children in completing the sentence frame and the question as a group: *This is the letter ___. What sound does ___ make?*

➜ **Teaching strategies:** Continue with the half of the alphabet not completed in the previous session.

For individual children who cannot produce particular letter-sound correspondences quickly, ask that child along with a skilled child to repeat in unison that letter-sound correspondence in the sentence frame used in previous session: ***This is __ and __ says ___.***

ACTIVITY

Rhyme Matching (10–15 minutes)

Materials: Rhyme Puzzle Cards

Directions: A child picks a card, says the name of the picture, and gives the card to the clinician. The child finds the rhyme match on the wall; the clinician gives the card to the child and the child checks whether the choice is correct by seeing if the puzzle pieces fit together. If the child is wrong, then he or she makes another attempt to find the matching puzzle. The group can indicate agreement/disagreement with the responses by using the rhyme-guiding questions.

➜ **Teaching strategies:** ***We're going to look for words that rhyme today. Look, Billy, put kite and light together. Do those rhyme? Let's say them together to see if they rhyme.*** In this session, children do not initially have the visual cue of matching the puzzle pieces because the clinician holds the card. The clinician can narrow the range of choices or suggest choices to direct the child to the correct answer if the child initially fails. Other children can provide suggestions of word(s) to try.

Even after children have identified the correct answer, sometimes guide the child(ren) to check the other puzzle pieces to assure that the correct picture was chosen. Use this strategy as well when the child is incorrect without explicitly telling the child he or she is incorrect. ***Bone–gum. You think those rhyme. Well let's check these other two pictures and see if we are right.*** The clinician would then guide the child to check the remaining picture, helping the child to discover his or her error without being explicitly told he or she is wrong.

ACTIVITY

Rhyme Sorting (10–15 minutes)

Materials: Rhyme Sorting Cards

Directions: Place three pictures on the table: *three, cat, snake.* Put the remaining cards in a pile face down on the table. Each child picks a card and determines the picture on the table it belongs with. Add the picture to the picture on the table to create three columns of rhyming pictures. The group determines whether the answer is right or wrong.

➜ **Teaching strategies:** ***We have three pictures on the table. We also have this pile of cards. We need to sort this pile of cards and find the picture on the table that rhymes with each card in this pile. Let's say the names of these pictures on the table: three, cat, snake. Now let's say them again and break the word apart so that we can hear the part that will rhyme or sound like the other words: thr-EE, c-AT, sn-AKE.*** The clinician can say onset-rime segments and children repeat. ***Now let's sort the pictures. Pick the one at the top of the pile and say the name for everyone.*** As the cards are sorted, the clinician can lead the children to name the pictures in each column, saying each word and emphasizing the rime in each word.

If a child responds incorrectly, the clinician can model each pair and have the child repeat (e.g., *rake–hat, cat–hat*) or another more proficient child can provide the model. ***Hmm, do you hear the same sound at the end of rake and cat? Let's listen: rake, ake, -ake, cat, -at, -at. Do those sound the same at the end?***

There should be sufficient time to repeat this activity a couple of times. This repetition may be very beneficial for children who are struggling or who are not confident in their rhyme skills.

Session Focus: Rhyme Matching and Rhyme Sorting

SESSION STIMULI

Rhyme Puzzle Cards

bear	pear	fan	pan	night	light
bed	head	fish	dish	shoe	two
bell	well	gate	eight	sink	drink
bone	phone	hat	cat	skate	plate
car	star	hook	book	stop	cop
coat	boat	house	mouse	train	rain
dog	frog	jug	rug	tree	bee
door	four	moon	spoon		
drum	gum	mop	top		

Examples

Easier pairs: stop–cop, tree–moon, shoe–gum

More difficult pairs: boat–night, four–pear, hook–sink

Rhyme Sorting Cards—Subset

cat	bat	hat	mat
snake	cake	lake	rake
three	bee	tree	knee

IMPLEMENTATION SUGGESTIONS

More on Teaching Strategies

- The visual cue of the matching puzzle piece is not immediately available in this session. Therefore, describing the way the sounds look/feel in the mouth as a means to help students decide whether or not a pair of words rhyme is an important cueing strategy.
- For students struggling with rhyme or for those who are reluctant to participate, it may be necessary to facilitate answers by providing additional cues. In this session, students who are struggling may need to hold the puzzle piece and match it to its pair on the wall to be successful. Children more adept at rhyming should be challenged and asked to find the rhyme without using the shape of the puzzle as a cue.
- Vary the level of difficulty by the number of puzzle pieces to choose from. More skilled children can take turns when more puzzle pieces are available, and less skilled children can take turns when there are fewer puzzle pieces to choose from.
- In the rhyme-sorting activity, if the child calls the word by a different label than intended, let the child first discover that there is nowhere to place the picture. Then guide the child to think of an alternate label. Provide the correct label if needed.

RHYME-GUIDING QUESTIONS

Do [word 1] and [word 2] sound the same at the end?

Does my mouth do the same thing?

WEEK 2 ➔ SESSION 6

Session Focus: Rhyme Sorting and Introduction to Rhyme Generation

ACTIVITY

Letter Activity (5 minutes)

Materials: Alphabet cards

Directions: Children name the letter that corresponds to the sound given by the clinician. For each letter, the clinician shows the picture on the alphabet cards and asks individual children; for example, *What letter says* /b/ *like in* b-b-ball? and so on. Complete as many cards as possible in 5 minutes.

➔ **Teaching strategies:** After the child responds, the clinician turns the card over to show the letter on the back for the child to determine whether the correct answer was given. If the child gives an incorrect answer, then the clinician should provide the correct answer and re-present the question. ***Joey says R is the letter that says /b/ like in ball. Let's look. Looks like B is the letter that says /b/.*** (Flip card back over and show the picture.) ***Let's try again. Which letter says /b/ like in b-b-bear?*** [child response] ***That's right, B says /b/. Great job. Let's try another one.*** Task difficulty can be varied by showing the picture or showing the letter when re-asking the question. If a child does not respond, encourage the child to provide a best guess. ***If you aren't sure, give me your best guess.*** Or show the child the letter and have the child name the letter (or repeat the name of the letter as provided by the clinician or another child). Then re-present the question to the child. Or have another child respond and have the target child repeat the answer.

ACTIVITY

Rhyme Sorting (20 minutes)

Materials: Rhyme Sorting Cards

Directions: Randomly select one picture from each rhyme set and place face up on the table. Place the remaining cards face down in a pile on the table. A child picks a card and lines it up with the rhyming picture on the table, creating columns of pictures. The group provides feedback regarding whether or not the choice is correct.

➔ **Teaching strategies:** Decide how many sets to sort at one time based on child proficiency. Repeat the game with more sets. Remind the children to pay attention to sounds at the ends of the words. For some turns, despite the correct sort, have the children check the choice by saying the picture with each of the other pictures on the table. Have children repeat words aloud. Lead the children in splitting the words into onset-rime. If a child responds incorrectly, lead the child through trial and error by saying the picture with each of the pictures on the table (e.g., ***mat–cake, NO; mat–bat, YES; mat–rose, NO***). Or have another child provide assistance by suggesting another answer. Have children explore all possibilities before making a decision.

ACTIVITY

Introduction to Rhyme Generation (5 minutes)

Materials: Bag, subset of Rhyme Generation Cards: *bug, cake, cat, drum, hat, phone*

Directions: Children divide into two groups; one group draws a card out of a bag and names it. The other group tries to think of a word that rhymes with the one given. Picture cards are from previous matching games.

➔ **Teaching strategies:** ***We're going to play a rhyming game. Team 1, you will try to think of a word that rhymes with the word Team 2 finds in the bag. Each team will have a turn to think of rhyming words and each team will have a turn to pick a word from the bag.*** The clinician should give maximal assistance to the group generating rhymes. Because the pictures are from previous activities, children may remember a rhyming word from previous experience. This will increase success at the initial stages of rhyme generation. As group members suggest options, the clinician should help children to check the response by saying the two words aloud and using the rhyme-guiding questions. If the children cannot think of a rhyming word, provide a choice of two words to try ***(What about rug or shoe?).*** This is only an introduction; independent skill is not expected. If the response is a rhyme that is not a real word, comment that the child is correct and that the rhyme is not a real word.

Session Focus: Rhyme Sorting and Introduction to Rhyme Generation

SESSION STIMULI

Rhyme Sorting Cards

cat	bat	hat	mat
snake	cake	lake	rake
three	bee	tree	knee
bug	mug	jug	rug
hose	nose	toes	rose
top	cop	stop	mop
clock	rock	lock	sock

Rhyme Generation Cards—Subset

bug
cake
cat
drum
hat
phone

IMPLEMENTATION SUGGESTIONS

Choosing Stimuli

The rhyme sorting activity can include up to seven sets of words, depending on the proficiency of the group. The first six sets above have unique rimes; there are no repeats in the vowels or consonants across the rimes of these sets. The last set, however, repeats the vowel (*clock* set and *top* set have same vowel) and the consonant (*snake* set and *clock* set have the same final consonant). Thus, if these latter sets are included, the activity is more difficult.

RHYME-GUIDING QUESTIONS

Do [word 1] and [word 2] sound the same at the end?

Does my mouth do the same thing?

More on Teaching Strategies

- In the sorting activity, narrow the options for less proficient children. "*I think your picture belongs with one of the first three pictures. Let's just try these first* (point to pictures to try for sorting)."
- When introducing the rhyme generation activity, be prepared to provide maximal scaffolding so that children are successful. Some children will be able to generate rhymes with little support. Other children will need the clinician to structure the task quite a bit to generate a rhyme. For example: "*Cat.* Jimmy needs to think of a word that rhymes with *cat.* Everyone say the word out loud with Jimmy. *cat. c-at.* Jimmy, what's a word that rhymes with *cat?*" Some cues the clinician might provide are:
  - Provide a sound cue: "What rhymes with *cat? c-at.* ffffff?"
  - Provide a semantic cue: "Hmm, we're trying to think of a word that rhymes with *cat. Cat, c-at.* Can you think of another word that ends with *-at,* that rhymes with *cat?* What about that wooden thing you use to play baseball?"
  - Provide a choice cue: "What rhymes with *cat?* Is it *fat* or *house?*"
  - Engage the other children in modeling a correct response: "Okay, team, let's think. What word ends with that *-at* sound and rhymes with *cat?* Jimmy, the team is saying *bat* rhymes with *cat.* What do you think?"
  - Help the child use his or her memory of past games: "In our other games, we found words that rhyme with *cat.* Can you remember a word that rhymes with *cat?*"

WEEK 3

OVERVIEW

Session 7 Focus: Rhyme Generation

Session 8 Focus: Rhyme Generation

Session 9 Focus: Rhyme Generation and Introduction to Initial Sound Judgment

Materials Needed

- ➜ Letter puzzle (uppercase)
- ➜ Alphabet cards (uppercase)
- ➜ Game board and game pieces
- ➜ Small paper bag (unmarked)
- ➜ Paper
- ➜ Marker
- ➜ Rhyme Generation Cards
- ➜ Initial Sound Judgment Cards—subset

mouse	mail
net	knee
sun	soap
ball	box
bike	girl
pig	pie
face	sink
moon	gate

Intervention Notes

Session Focus: Rhyme Generation

ACTIVITY

Letter Activity (5 minutes)

Materials: Letter puzzle, small paper bag

Directions: Children take turns pulling a letter out of the bag, giving a name and sound for the letter before putting the letter in the puzzle. *This is* B, *and* B *says* /b/. Complete as much as possible in 3–5 minutes. If the puzzle is not complete, continue in the next session.

➔ **Teaching strategies:** If unsure or incorrect, the child may enlist the help of the group. The clinician should question some correct responses as well as incorrect responses. ***Are you sure S says /s/? Are you sure that H says /tʃ/?***

ACTIVITY

Rhyme Generation (25 minutes)

Materials: Rhyme Generation Cards, small paper bag, game board and game pieces

Directions: A child picks a card from the bag and gives a word that rhymes with the picture on the card. The group determines whether the answer is right or wrong. After giving a word that rhymes, the child moves his or her game piece forward on the game board. The child puts the card back in the bag.

➔ **Teaching strategies:** Make sure the individual child and then the group name the picture chosen. Expect children to have difficulty generating rhymes and on this first day; expect to provide lots of scaffolding. Clinician should give the maximal assistance needed to individual children generating the rhyme; vary level of scaffolding based on individual child ability. ***Sam, which word did you choose? Oh, nose. Everybody say nose. Great. Hmm, nose, N-OSE. Everyone say that with me, N-OSE. Sam, can you tell me a word that rhymes with nose? What is a word that sounds the same at the end?*** When a child provides a response, use guiding questions for the child to check his or her answer. ***You think toes rhymes with nose? Everyone, say those two words together and we'll listen for the rhyme. Nose–toes. Did your mouth do the same thing? N-OSE–T-OES. Do they sound the same at the end? Yes, toes rhymes with nose.***

If a child cannot generate a rhyme, there is a range of scaffolds that can be provided. We illustrate a few here and further illustrate in the "More on Teaching Strategies" section on the opposite page and in the session plans that follow. Have other children suggest a rhyme. Have the target child repeat the suggested word and picture card word and then judge whether or not the words rhyme, using the guiding questions. Provide a choice of two words to try ***(What about rose or shoe?)***, or provide a semantic cue of a rhyme ***(I'm thinking of a flower that grows in the garden.)***. Put the picture cards back in the bag after each turn. The repetition of pictures may help some children catch on. The clinician can then also reference previous answers, as appropriate. ***Remember, Sue picked cat. What word did she say rhymed with cat? Let's think of another one.*** For children who are less proficient, accepting a previous response for a particular card may be appropriate rather than prompting for a unique response.

SESSION STIMULI

Rhyme Generation Cards

ape	drum	pie
bat	duck	pig
bed	face	rain
bee	fish	ring
bell	frog	rug
book	grape	shoe
box	hat	skate
bug	hoe	snake
cake	jack	sock
cap	knee	star
car	lamp	stop
cat	light	sun
chair	mat	ten
cheese	moon	train
chin	nose	tree
coat	phone	van

Pictures in the Rhyme Generation Cards that have a rhyme match

Note: To decrease redundancy, only include one card from each of the word groups below in the Rhyme Generation activities.

ape	grape		
bat	cat	hat	mat
bug	rug		
cake	snake		
car	star		
three	tree	knee	bee

IMPLEMENTATION SUGGESTIONS

More on Teaching Strategies

RHYME-GUIDING QUESTIONS

Do [word 1] and [word 2] sound the same at the end?

Does my mouth do the same thing?

- As in the previous rhyme sessions, emphasize the ending segment or rime of the word the student is attempting to rhyme.
- Continue to emphasize the way the sounds look/feel in the mouth as a means to help students decide whether or not a pair of words rhyme.
- Several scaffolding options can be used to help children generate rhymes. These scaffolds can be used to assist children from the outset of their turn or can be used when children are unable to generate a rhyme or generate a word that does not rhyme with the chosen picture. This scaffolding is arranged in a hypothesized order of stronger to weaker scaffolds. Here we present strong scaffolds. In the next lesson we present weaker scaffolds. After providing the scaffold, assist the child in using the rhyme-guiding questions to check whether the two words rhyme. If the words do not rhyme, provide additional scaffolding for the child to generate another possible rhyme.
    - Give answer: "I think *light* rhymes with *kite*. Say those with me: *light–kite*. It rhymes! What rhymes with *kite*?" Continue with guiding questions.
    - Provide an option that rhymes: "You picked *light*. Can you think of a word that rhymes with *light*? What about *kite*? See if *kite–light* rhyme." Continue with guiding questions.
    - Provide two choices, one that rhymes and one that does not rhyme: "Which rhymes with *light: kite* or *book*?" Assist the child to compare each with the target word, as was done in the sound judgment activities.
    - Provide a narrow semantic cue: "*Kite*. What rhymes with *kite*? Let's see. I am thinking of something you turn on when it is dark in your house. *Light*. Great! Let's figure out if *light* rhymes with *kite*."
    - Provide a broad semantic cue (i.e., the child will think of a couple of possibilities and then covertly select among the possibilities): "*Cat*. Let's see. I'm thinking about something you wear on your head." The child may think of *hat, cap, scarf,* or *helmet* and will have to select among those for the answer.

Session Focus: Rhyme Generation

ACTIVITY

Letter Activity (5 minutes)

Materials: Letter puzzle, small paper bag

Directions: Children take turns pulling a letter out of the bag and then giving a name and sound for the letter before putting the letter in the puzzle. *This is* B, *and* B *says* /b/.

➔ **Teaching strategies:** Complete puzzle from previous session, and then repeat as time allows. ***We didn't finish this puzzle last time. Let's finish the puzzle, and we might have time to do the puzzle again.*** If unsure of the letter name and sound, the child may enlist the help of the group. Provide the group an opportunity to catch incorrect responses. ***Today I'm not telling you when someone gives the wrong answer. I want you to listen and decide whether the answers are right or wrong. If you hear an answer that you don't think is right, raise your hand.*** Let the target child try to correct the response. Provide the necessary scaffolding for each child to ultimately provide the correct letter name and sound for his or her turn.

ACTIVITY

Rhyme Generation (25 minutes)

Materials: Rhyme Generation Cards, small paper bag

Directions: Divide children into two small groups. One group draws a card out of the bag and names it as the other group tries to think of a word that rhymes with the picture chosen. The group who chose the card is asked to judge the accuracy of the answer provided by the other group. Don't put cards back in the bag.

➔ **Teaching strategies:** Children should be increasing their skill. As children become more proficient, adjust the level of support as appropriate. But be sure to provide sufficient support to individual children so that everyone is able to complete their turn by generating a rhyming word.

The picture cards provided for rhyme generation include several sets of words that rhyme (see Session 7). These rhymes can be used to support children's success. For example, refer to a word previously selected. ***You picked bug. Sam just had a word that rhymed with bug. Do you remember the word that Sam picked? Yes, he had rug. Let's see if that rhymes: bUG–rUG. Or pull pictures out of the set to scaffold success. You picked cake. Hmm, I have two pictures here: snake and tree. Do you think either of these rhyme with cake?*** To make the task more difficult for the children, include only one picture of each of these rhyming sets in the bag. Thus every picture a child picks will require the generation of a rhyme unique from other turns. Be sure to repeat the rhyme at the end of each turn to make the rhyme pair clear to children. ***Okay, we are done with that one: bug, rug. Bug rhymes with rug. Let's pick another picture.***

Remember, the goal is for children to generate rhyming words, not to rhyme particular words. So although we suggest a label for each picture (i.e., list of picture names on opposite page), it does not matter if a child uses that label or another label. So if the child said *seat* for *chair,* then help the child generate a rhyme for *seat.* If the child generates a multisyllabic label, it may be easier to provide an alternate label or guide the child to an alternate label. ***Hmm, gorilla. That's a long word. Let's think of a shorter word for that picture. How about ape? Can you think of a word that rhymes with ape?***

SESSION STIMULI

Rhyme Generation Cards

ape	drum	pie
bat	duck	pig
bed	face	rain
bee	fish	ring
bell	frog	rug
book	grape	shoe
box	hat	skate
bug	hoe	snake
cake	jack	sock
cap	knee	star
car	lamp	stop
cat	light	sun
chair	mat	ten
cheese	moon	train
chin	nose	tree
coat	phone	van

IMPLEMENTATION SUGGESTIONS

More on Teaching Strategies

- More ideas on scaffolds are provided here. The scaffolds presented on this page are hypothesized to provide less support than those presented in the previous session. The scaffolds are presented below in order of decreasing level of support. Help the child use the guiding questions to check whether the word generated rhymes with the picture chosen.
    - Produce the onset and rime of the target word followed by the onset and rime of a rhyming word. The child then needs only to blend the onset and rime to produce a rhyming word. "*Fish, ffffff* [pause] *iiiishsh*. What rhymes with *fish*? How about *d-d-d-d-d* [pause] *iiiiishshsh*. Put those sounds together, *d-d-d-d-d* [pause] *iiiiishsh*. What word rhymes with *fish*?" Providing a continuant onset may be easier than a stop onset (e. g., for *bat*, prompt with *ffff* [pause] *at*).
    - Repeat the target word by emphasizing the rime and then provide an onset as cue: "Let me help you. *Cat. c-AT.* (or *cat, AT*). Now try *ssss*. What's the word? Yep, *sat*. Does *sat* rhyme with *cat*?" Continuant sounds may be easier for the child than stop sounds.
    - Produce the stimulus word and then produce the word again with a pause between the onset and rime. Optionally elongate or iterate the rime and onset. "*Fish, ffffff* [pause] *iiiishsh*. What word rhymes with *fish*?"
    - Repeat the target word as an onset and rime: Follow with the onset of a plausible rhyme. "*Cat, c [pause] at*. What rhymes with *cat, c-at*? What rhymes with *cat*? Let me give you a hint: */s/~*" The child needs to access the rime and blend the onset provided with the rime.
    - Give the initial sound of a plausible rhyme: "You picked *cat*. What rhymes with *cat*? */s/~*"
- Cues or scaffolds can be combined to provide further help to children. For example, combine a sound cue and a semantic cue: "Let's see. *Cat, c-AT.* I'm thinking of something you play baseball with. *b-b-b-b~*"
- Children may generate nonsense words as rhymes. Nonsense rhymes actually are the best evidence that a child can rhyme because we are sure that the child is not relying on his or her memory to generate a rhyme. It may be helpful, however, to point out that the rhyme is not a real word. "*Dish–bish*. You are right! Those two words sound the same at the end. They rhyme. *Dish* is a real word. But *bish* is a made-up word. It is not a real word."
- Some words are harder than others for children to generate a rhyme. If a child is having substantial difficulty with a particular word, then give the child a different card, one that provides a better teaching opportunity or will be easier for the child to be successful. "Oh, I do not like that picture you picked. Let me look in the bag and find you a different picture. Here. Try this one."

* tilde (~) is used to indicate that an adult uses an intonation that indicates the child should respond (e.g., slightly rising intonation).

Session Focus: Rhyme Generation and Introduction to Initial Sound Judgment

ACTIVITY

Letter Activity (5 minutes)

Materials: Alphabet cards

Directions: The clinician provides the initial sound for a picture, and children give the letter for the sound. The clinician holds up a picture, names the picture, and says the sound. The group or an individual child says the letter that makes the sound. The clinician turns the card over to show the group whether they're right or wrong.

➜ **Teaching strategies:** ***I am going to show you a picture and tell you the first sound in the picture. You then tell me what letter goes with the sound I give. Let's do a few together and then we'll have each person take their own turn. Here's our first picture: sun, ssssun. /s/ is the first sound in sun. What letter goes with /s/? Yes, you are right, S.***

Incorrect responses can be kept separate to review or placed back in the pile for a second try. If one child responds incorrectly, whereas others provide a correct response, then have that child repeat the correct response.

ACTIVITY

Rhyme Generation

(20 minutes)

Materials: Rhyme Generation Cards, marker, paper

Directions: Teams are assigned points for the number of rhymes they are able to generate for a single picture.

One group draws a card and attempts to come up with as many words that rhyme with the picture on the card as possible. The other team judges whether or not the responses are correct rhymes. Children can keep score on paper using hash marks that can be totaled at the end of the game.

➜ **Teaching strategies:** Most children should be somewhat proficient with this skill at this point in the program. However, some children may still be unable to rhyme or have difficulty. Provide assistance to those still having difficulty. Use responses of skilled peers to assist less skilled peers. Provide semantic cues, onset-rime, and sound cues as needed. Provide reminders to children about how much they have learned about rhymes in the first 3 weeks of the program. ***Remember when you didn't know any rhyming words? We all know so much more about rhyming words. Rhyming words are so much easier for us now!***

Use a second timer or egg timer to set time limits if needed. Or limit each group to a preset number of words that they can generate (e.g., three). Within teams, let children take individual turns, but engage the entire group so that all children are engaged in the game. Use guiding questions with the team that is judging the response. At the end of each word, have all children repeat the responses. ***Okay, great. That team gave three words that rhyme with stop: cop, mop, and drop. Let's all say those words together.***

ACTIVITY

Introduction to Initial Sound Judgment

(5 minutes)

Materials: Subset of Initial Sound Judgment Cards

Directions: Children choose a card from the pile. The child names pictures aloud and says whether the two words begin with the same sound. Each child can have a chance to do one card.

➜ **Teaching strategies:** ***We've been talking about rhyming words. Rhyming words sound the same at the end of the word. Now we are going to talk about the sounds at the beginning of words. Words like b-b-ball and b-b-bat: both begin with the /b/ sound. Or fffffish and fffffan: both begin with the /f/ sound. I want you to decide if the pictures on your card start with the same sound or with different sounds. I'll do the first one.***

Provide maximal assistance to assure children are successful. Have a child say words aloud. The clinician repeats the words and elongates or iterates the initial sounds, as illustrated above. Give the child a chance to respond. If no response or an incorrect response is given, then repeat the words aloud, and ask, ***Do they sound the same at the beginning?*** while simultaneously prompting the correct response by nodding your head "yes" or shaking your head "no." If children have a hard time, do the same card over and over several times before moving on to the next card.

Session Focus: Rhyme Generation and Introduction to Initial Sound Judgment

SESSION STIMULI

Rhyme Generation Cards—Subset

Subset that only includes unique rimes

bat	drum	pig
bed	duck	rain
bee	face	ring
bell	fish	shoe
box	frog	skate
book	grape	snake
bug	hoe	sock
cake	jack	stop
cap	lamp	sun
car	light	train
chair	moon	ten
cheese	nose	van
chin	phone	
coat	pie	

Initial Sound Judgment Cards—Subset

mouse	mail	*(continuants, same sound)*
net	knee	*(continuants, same sound)*
sun	soap	*(continuants, same sound)*
face	sink	*(continuants, different sounds)*
ball	box	*(stops, same sound)*
pig	pie	*(stops, same sound)*
moon	gate	*(continuant and stop, different sounds)*
bike	girl	*(stops, different sounds)*

IMPLEMENTATION SUGGESTIONS

More on Teaching Strategies

- For the rhyme generation activity, use the subset of Rhyme Generation Cards (i.e., only unique rimes).
- The stimuli are limited to words that can be easily pictured (nouns). But the clinician can help children think of words from other grammatical categories when generating rhyming words. "*Cheese*. What word rhymes with *cheese*? I am thinking about something you always say when you ask for something."
- For the initial sound judgment activity, remember the goal is to familiarize the children with the new task and assure some success. The word pairs that include continuants may be easier for children because initial sounds can be made more salient by stretching the sounds out for a long period of time. At the end of each turn, have all children repeat the words and the response. "Okay, now everyone say it with me. *mmmmouse, mmmmail*. Yes, those words start with the same sound." If this task is quite challenging for the children, introduce only a few word cards and do each one a couple of times. For this introduction, the clinician can focus on demonstrating elongating and iterating the initial sound and modeling how to figure out the answer rather than explicit teaching.
- Continuant sounds (e.g., /f/, /s/) can be elongated or stretched out. Stop sounds cannot be elongated but can be iterated (i.e., quickly repeated). When iterating a stop sound, minimize the schwa vowel as the sound is repeated (i.e., *don't* say buh-buh-ball but do say bababall [ə as in *a*bout]).

WEEK 4

OVERVIEW

Session 10 Focus: Initial Sound Judgment

Session 11 Focus: Initial Sound Judgment and Initial Sound Odd-One-Out

Session 12 Focus: Initial Sound Odd-One-Out and Introduction to Initial Sound Matching

Materials Needed

- ABC magnets (lowercase)
- Letter puzzle (lowercase)
- Alphabet cards (lowercase)
- Metal board (or other surface for magnets to stick to)
- Two small paper bags (one marked "Same Sounds," other marked "Different Sounds")
- Small paper bag (unmarked)
- Game board and game pieces
- Initial Sound Judgment Cards
- Initial Sound Odd-One-Out Cards
- Initial Sound Puzzle Cards—subset

fan	fox
lamp	leg
match	moon
nest	nail
sock	seven
shoe	ship
vase	van

Intervention Notes

Session Focus: Initial Sound Judgment

ACTIVITY

Letter Activity (5 minutes)

Materials: ABC magnets, metal board, small paper bag

Directions: Each child pulls a letter out of the bag, names it, and provides the sound for the letter before putting it up on the metal board.

➜ **Teaching strategies:** Children should be rather proficient at this task by now. However, some children may need assistance, particularly with certain letters/sounds. The clinician can use the strategies previously introduced. For letters/sounds that children continue to miss, have all children repeat the name and sound in unison or in sequence. Place the challenging letters off to the side of the board and review these at the end of this activity.

ACTIVITY

Initial Sound Judgment (25 minutes)

Materials: Initial Sound Judgment Cards, two bags (one marked "Same Sounds" and the other marked "Different Sounds")

Directions: Each child draws a card and decides whether the words on the card begin with the same sound or with different sounds. He or she places the card in either the "Same Sounds" bag or the "Different Sounds" bag. Other children in the group can indicate whether they agree with the target child's response.

➜ **Teaching strategies:** In this first full session of initial sounds, provide maximal support to assure success at judging initial sounds. Continuants may be easier to judge because children can elongate those sounds, thereby making them more salient than stop sounds. Have children say the words aloud. Teach them to elongate (***ffffffish***) or iterate (***b-b-b-ball***) the initial sound. To elongate the sound, hold out the production of the initial sound; use this strategy with initial continuant sounds. To iterate a sound, repeat the initial sound a few times with a brief schwa; use this strategy with initial stop sounds.

Begin activity by demonstrating the task of judging initial sounds. It might help to demonstrate one pair with continuants and another pair with stops.

Today we are going to pay attention to the sounds at the beginning of words. Remember to pay attention to what your mouth is doing when you start to say the word.

We have these cards with two pictures on the card. We'll decide if the words begin with the same sound or different sounds. Then we'll sort the cards into these two bags. This bag says "Same Sounds." This bag says "Different Sounds."

I'll do a couple of cards to show you. You can say the words after me. (Have children repeat.) ***Fish, four, ffffish, fffour. Now you say the words with me: ffffish, ffffour. Do fish and four start with the same sound? I think those have the same sound. My mouth does the same thing when I start to say each word. I would put this card in the "Same Sounds" bag. Do fffish and fffour begin with the same sound? Yes, I'll put the card in this bag.***

Okay, let's do one more together. This card has moon and gate, mmmmoon, g-g-g-gate. You say those words with me: moon, gate, mmmoon, g-g-gate. Do those start with the same sound? Does your mouth do the same thing at the beginning of the words? (Shake head "no" to prompt children.) ***Right, they don't start with the same sound. They start with different sounds. Let's put the moon–gate card in the "Different Sounds" bag. Now it's your turn.***

Provide children with the necessary support to be successful. Occasionally stop the turns and pull the cards from each bag and review. Repetition helps children catch on. ***Let's look at all the cards in the "Same Sounds" bag.*** Say each pair of words and reinforce that the two words begin with the same sounds. Do the same with the different sounds bag.

SESSION STIMULI

Initial Sound Judgment Cards

Same Initial Sound

fish	flower	box	ball
fox	finger	dog	dish
mouse	mail	cat	cow
mop	moon	pig	pie
nut	nail	top	tail
net	knee	goat	girl
sun	soap	cheese	cherry
seven	sink	two	tent
shoe	ship	kite	car
light	lips	bus	boy

Different Initial Sound

face	sink
nose	one
bike	girl
key	sheep
cake	wolf
book	table
door	bag
tape	pan
moon	gate

INITIAL SOUND JUDGMENT GUIDING QUESTIONS

Do [word 1]and [word 2] start with the same sound?

Does my mouth do the same thing at the beginning of [word 1] and [word 2]?

PROCESS FOR INITIAL SOUND ACTIVITIES

Say the word. [typical prosody and intonation]

Stretch the beginning sound or bounce (i.e., iterate) the beginning sound.

Perform task (e.g., judge sounds, segment sound).

IMPLEMENTATION SUGGESTIONS

Choosing Stimuli

- Continuants will be easier for children than stops. The above lists are organized with continuant pairs listed first.
- No words that begin with vowels are included in the initial sound sessions. For this task vowels are challenging for two possible reasons. Vowels do not provide articulatory feedback. When stretching a vowel, any shift in mouth shape will change the vowel sound. Thus we target vowel segmentation in the last 3 weeks (blending and segmentation) when children have obtained some initial proficiency with sound segmentation.

More on Teaching Strategies

- During this initial session with initial sound judgment, it may be necessary to emphasize and remind children that the focus is now on the sound at the *beginning* of words rather than the final sounds they were focused on during the weeks of rhyme practice. "The last few times we've met we were listening to the sounds at the *end* of words. Now, we're going to be listening for the sound at the *beginning* of words. Like *mmmmop* and *mmmmeat*. Those words start with */m/*. Or like *b-b-ball* and *b-b-box*. Those words both start with */b/*." The clinician may model initial sounds in isolation but should not expect children to segment initial sounds in the initial sound judgment task. Don't explain the difference between rhymes and initial sounds; just refocus children's attention on initial sounds.
- Prompt correct response with gesture/facial expression: "Do *sssun* and *sssoap* start with the same sound?" The clinician nods and smiles when asking question. "Do *b-b-bike* and *g-g-girl* start with the same sound?" The clinician shakes head and furrows brow when asking question.
- Always have children use the "Process for Initial Sounds" presented in the above box. Repeat this process for all words. Have the target child complete each step in the process, with the rest of the children repeating. Because *iterate* is not a word in children's vocabulary, use the word *bounce* instead.
- If some children are having a hard time, after doing about six cards, pull those cards out of the bags and re-do those cards. Then try some new cards.

Session Focus: Initial Sound Judgment and Initial Sound Odd-One-Out

ACTIVITY

Letter Activity (5 minutes)

Materials: Alphabet cards

Directions: The clinician shows a picture, says the name of the picture with the initial sound elongated or iterated, and then produces the initial sound in isolation. The children raise their hands to repeat the initial sound and letter name for the sound.

→ **Teaching strategies:** ***Look, here is a picture of a goat. Listen closely and then I want you to tell me the first sound in goat, g-g-goat. /g/. What's the first sound in goat? Yes, /g/. What letter goes with the /g/ sound?*** If the target child provides a wrong response, ask another child to provide a response. Then re-ask the target child: ***Hmm, Seth, I'm not sure that /b/ goes with the letter D. What do you think, Billy? What letter do you think goes with /b/? Yep, B. Seth, now you tell me; what letter makes the /b/ sound?***

ACTIVITY

Initial Sound Judgment (5 minutes)

Materials: Initial Sound Judgment Cards

Directions: Each child draws a card and decides whether the words on the card begin with the same sound or with different sounds. Place the card face down in a "finished" pile after the turn. The group can indicate whether they agree with the target child's response.

→ **Teaching strategies:** This activity may be relatively easy, especially if all cards were practiced in the previous session. If the children are proficient, go through the activity quickly. Occasionally stop the game to review the "finished" pile. ***Okay, let's quickly do these cards again. Everyone together. I'll show the picture, and everyone say the names of the pictures. Let's say the words and then say the words with the first sound stretched or bounced. And then you tell me "same sound" or "different sounds." Let's see how fast we can do these.*** Pay attention to children who are not able to quickly do this task and who are not keeping up with the group; they need more scaffolding.

ACTIVITY

Initial Sound Odd-One-Out (20 minutes)

Materials: Initial Sound Odd-One-Out Cards, game board and game pieces

Directions: The target child draws a card, names the three pictures aloud, and chooses the picture that does not begin with the same sound as the other two. Other children in the group can indicate whether they agree with the response given. Children move their game piece forward when completing their turn.

→ **Teaching strategies:** Model or demonstrate the activity, letting the children know they played this activity with Rhyme Cards. ***We have cards with three pictures. We need to find the picture that does not have the same sound at the beginning. Do you remember when we played this game with the Rhyme Cards? We found the word that did not rhyme. Now we are going to find the word that does not begin with the same sound. Let's try this one: foot, fox, sun. ffffoot, fffox, sssun. Now everyone say the words and be sure to stretch out the sound at the beginning of each word. Okay, now let's figure out which one does not start with the same sound: fffoot, fffox. Say those. FFFoot, FFFox. Do fffoot and fffox start with the same sound? Watch my mouth. Does my mouth do the same thing at the beginning? Yes, those have the same sounds at the beginning. Remember, we are trying to find the word with the different sound. Fox, sun, fffox, sssun. Those have different sounds! Foot, sun, fffoot, sssun. Those have different sounds. Which word does not have the same sound: fffoot, fffox, sssun. Yes, sun. Foot and fox begin with /f/, but sun begins with /s/.*** Use this last statement to give children feedback on what is to come—segmenting initial sounds. Do not expect them to segment sounds yet.

Sequence stimuli by first presenting cards with all continuant initial sounds. Practice these several times and then move on to other cards. Always have children iterate and/or elongate initial sounds as they repeat the words. Difficult cards can be placed back in the pile to be drawn again later in the activity. To reinforce the target skill, review completed cards by repeating words and indicating the odd word.

Session Focus: Initial Sound Judgment and Initial Sound Odd-One-Out

SESSION STIMULI

Initial Sound Judgment Cards

Same Initial Sound

fish	flower	box	ball
fox	finger	dog	dish
mouse	mail	cat	cow
mop	moon	pig	pie
nut	nail	top	tail
net	knee	goat	girl
sun	soap	cheese	cherry
seven	sink	two	tent
shoe	ship	kite	car
light	lips	bus	boy

Different Initial Sound

face	girl
nose	table
bike	wolf
key	bag
cake	sink
book	sheep
door	gate
tape	one
moon	pan

Initial Sound Odd-One-Out Cards

foot	fox	**sun**	cat	cane	**box**	light	leaf	**sink**
four	moon	monkey	chair	**wolf**	cherry	mouse	**bus**	mop
sheep	**nest**	shoe	dish	**cake**	dog	nose	night	**pear**
sun	sock	**mouse**	fan	phone	**nail**	rake	**gum**	rain
face	bus	box	four	**gas**	fish	ten	tub	**leaf**
van	**foot**	vase	gate	**table**	girl	tire	toes	**pig**
ball	chain	cheese	**goose**	key	king	**two**	ball	boy
cake	coat	**moon**	king	**shoe**	corn			
cap	pie	pin	lamp	light	**book**			

IMPLEMENTATION SUGGESTIONS

Choosing Stimuli

Initial Sound Odd-One-Out Cards: The first six cards in the above list include only words that begin with continuants, followed by words with some continuant initial sound words, and then words with all initial stop sounds.

PROCESS FOR INITIAL SOUND ACTIVITIES

Say the word. [typical prosody and intonation]

Stretch the beginning sound or bounce (i.e., iterate) the beginning sound.

Perform task (e.g., judge sounds, segment sound).

More on Teaching Strategies

- For odd-one-out, if the children generate picture labels that all begin with different sounds, pair the words and help children judge that none of the words have the same sound. Then help the children generate an alternate label for one of the pictures so that there will be two words that begin with the same sound. Then guide the children to pair the words to find the word that does not begin with the same sound (e.g., for *foot, fox, sun*, if child generates *toes, fox, sun*, then compare *toes–fox, fox–sun, toes–sun*).
- Scaffolding strategies: Use separately or combined. Tailor scaffolding to child's proficiency level, fading prompts and scaffolding for individual students based on their success and learning.
    - Exaggerate and elongate the initial sound to highlight the similarity or difference between the two initial sounds: "*ssssun, ssssoap*. Do those words both start with the same sound? Does your mouth do the same thing at the beginning when you say *sssun* and *sssoap*?" Teach children to elongate and iterate initial sounds.
    - Provide the answer and re-ask the question. "I think I hear the same sound at the beginning of *sssun* and *sssoap*. Watch my mouth. What do you think, Seth?" Ask the group to assist. "What do we think, do *sssun* and *sssoap* start with the same sound?"

WEEK 4 ➜ SESSION 12

Session Focus: Initial Sound Odd-One-Out and Introduction to Initial Sound Matching

ACTIVITY

Letter Activity (5 minutes)

Materials: Letter puzzle, small paper bag

Directions: Each child pulls a letter out of the bag, names it, and gives the sound the letter makes before putting it into the puzzle.

➜ **Teaching strategies:** If unsure, the child may enlist the help of the group or call on a peer to provide assistance. If the child responds incorrectly, provide a second opportunity or have a peer provide the answer. Have the child repeat the correct answer. There may be a few letters that continue to be problematic for children. Provide repeated practice on these.

ACTIVITY

Initial Sound Odd-One-Out (20 minutes)

Materials: Initial Sound Odd-One-Out Cards

Directions: The clinician chooses a card and shows it to the children. Have three children each say the name of one picture on the card. The child with the odd-one-out stands up. Have the other children in the group decide which child should stand up.

➜ **Teaching strategies:** The children not naming the pictures decide which child needs to stand up because his or her picture does not have the same initial sound. Encourage children to use iteration (e.g., ***b-b-b-ball***) and elongation (e.g., ***fffffish***). ***We played with these cards the last time. But today we are going to play the game a little bit differently. I'll choose the card, and three of you will name the pictures. We'll have one person say the name of each picture. Remember to say the name of the picture and then stretch the first sound or bounce the first sound. The rest of the group will decide which picture does not begin with the same sound. We'll tell the person with the picture with the different sound to stand up.***

ACTIVITY

Introduction to Initial Sound Matching (5 minutes)

Materials: Subset of Initial Sound Puzzle Cards

Directions: Place half of each pair on opposite sides of the table. The children match pictures with the same initial sound. Put as many pairs on the table as children in the group.

➜ **Teaching strategies:** The purpose of this introduction is simply to give children a feel for the next activity that will be introduced. Use the subset of cards that begin with continuant sounds. The children will see the card shape and can use the card shape to match the pictures that begin with the same sounds. ***We have puzzles to play with for a few minutes today. We'll play this game again next time. Let's find the picture on this side of the table that begins with the same sound as fan, ffffan. What card matches with fan? Let's see if the pictures fit together. Yes. Let's try the other pictures to make sure you are correct.*** Once a child selects a picture, repeat the words and elongate the initial sounds. Then show the children how to check themselves by making sure that the picture does not start with the same sound as any other picture.

ACTIVITY

Review Rhyme During Initial Sound Matching

Materials: None

Directions: Each child should be given an opportunity to generate a rhyming word for one of the words in the initial sound matching task.

➜ **Teaching strategies:** ***Okay, you matched those two words, fan–fox. They start with the same sound. Now, can you tell me a word that rhymes with fan?*** Use peer assistance if difficulties or errors arise. Have the child choose a friend to help. Summarize at the end of each turn. ***Fan and fox start with the same sound. f-an, f-ox. And we decided that pan rhymes with fan. f-an, p-an. Great job!***

Session Focus: Initial Sound Odd-One-Out and Introduction to Initial Sound Matching

SESSION STIMULI

Initial Sound Odd-One-Out Cards

foot	fox	**sun**	cat	cane	**box**	light	leaf	**sink**
four	moon	monkey	chair	**wolf**	cherry	mouse	**bus**	mop
sheep	**nest**	shoe	dish	**cake**	dog	nose	night	**pear**
sun	sock	**mouse**	fan	phone	**nail**	rake	**gum**	rain
face	bus	box	four	**gas**	fish	ten	time	**leaf**
van	**foot**	vase	gate	**table**	girl	tire	toes	**pig**
ball	chain	cheese	**goose**	key	king	**two**	ball	boy
cake	coat	**moon**	king	**shoe**	corn			
cap	pie	pin	lamp	light	**book**			

Initial Sound Puzzle Cards—Subset

fan	fox
lamp	leg
match	moon
nest	nail
sock	seven
shoe	ship
vase	van

IMPLEMENTATION SUGGESTIONS

More on Teaching Strategies

- For the matching task, vary the level of support to individual needs. Use child performance on previous sessions and previous turns to guide the level of support provided. With each child, plan to provide less support than in previous turns. But remember that the goal is for each child to have success on each turn. So if a child struggles to generate a response or generates an incorrect answer, increase the level of support to assure that in the end the child experiences success.
- End each child's turn with restating the correct response. This information will assure that all children are clear on the correct responses. The interchange of teaching can confuse children regarding the correct response. "We figured it out. *Boy* and *ball* start with the same sound." Or "James thought that *pig* and *boy* started with the same sound. But that wasn't right. We figured out that *boy* and *ball* start with the same sound. Everyone say those words with me: *boy, ball. b-b-boy, b-b-ball. boy–ball.*"
- Another scaffolding strategy: Isolate the beginning sound as a cue. "*Fish, four; ffffish, fffour. Fish* starts with */f/. Four* starts with */f/*. Do *fish* and *four* start with the same sound? [child response] Yes, they do. They start with */f/*." Some children may spontaneously catch on to segmenting initial sounds, but don't expect or require children to be able to segment initial sounds at this point in the program.

PROCESS FOR INITIAL SOUND ACTIVITIES

Say the word. [typical prosody and intonation]

Stretch the beginning sound or bounce (i.e., iterate) the beginning sound.

Perform task (e.g., judge sounds, segment sound)

WEEK 5

OVERVIEW

Session 13 Focus: Initial Sound Matching

Session 14 Focus: Initial Sound Matching and Initial Sound Sorting

Session 15 Focus: Initial Sound Matching and Initial Sound Sorting and Introduction to Initial Sound Segmentation

Materials Needed

- ABC magnets (uppercase)
- Letter puzzle (uppercase)
- Alphabet cards (lowercase)
- Metal board
- Dry erase markers
- Tape
- Dry erase board
- Three small paper bags with *M, K* and *C, G* written on the bag
- Small paper bag (unmarked)
- Initial Sound Puzzle Cards
- Initial Sound Cards
- Initial Sound Sorting Cards
- Initial Sound Segmentation Subset

Intervention Notes

Session Focus: Initial Sound Matching

ACTIVITY

Letter Activity (3–5 minutes)

Materials: Alphabet magnets, metal board, small paper bag

Directions: Each child pulls a letter out of the bag, names it, and provides the sound for the letter before putting it up on the metal board. Ask the child to provide a word that begins with that sound or select the word with that sound.

→ **Teaching strategies:** After a child provides the letter sound, present two words and ask the child to choose the word that goes with the letter sound. ***Good, you said M says /m/. What starts with /m/, milk or fun?*** For some letters, ask the child to generate a word for the letter sound. Some children may be able to do this, and others may do it by relying on memory. Likely they have memorized some words that go with particular letters. Reinforce accurate words by having all children repeat the word. ***Samantha picked the letter l and said it makes the /l/ sound. She says that lion starts with /l/: llllion. Everyone say that: lion, llllion, /l/.***

ACTIVITY

Initial Sound Matching

(15 minutes)

Materials: Initial Sound Puzzle Cards, tape

Directions: Tape half of the puzzle to the wall. Place the other half of each puzzle on the table. Children choose a picture on the table and match to a picture on the wall. Use group participation to decide whether an answer is right or wrong. Check the accuracy of an answer by matching the puzzle shapes.

Note that there are several pairs for some beginning sounds. Today, in each set practiced, only include one pair per sound (e.g., *ball–bear,* but not also *bed–bug*). When children finish with one set, compose a new set of puzzles to practice. Include a greater number of puzzle pairs in the practice set as children get more proficient.

→ **Teaching strategies:** Begin with a small set of cards with a few continuant pairs and a few stop pairs. If children are struggling, begin only with continuants. ***We have some puzzles to put together. We played this game with the Rhyming Cards a while ago. Now we're going to match the cards that begin with the same sound. Remember both words have to start with the same sound. Look at the cards. Let's try to find the picture that goes with mmmatch. Which picture on the table starts with the same sound as mmmatch?*** For the word(s) children choose, say the words together to help children determine whether they have the same first sound. ***Someone said moon and someone said dog. Let's try each of those and see which one matches. Say these after me: mmatch, d-d-dog. Hmm. Do we all think that those two words start with the same sound? Did your mouth do the same thing? No! Okay, mmmatch, mmmmoon. Do we think those words start with the same sound? Did your mouth do the same thing? Yes! Now let's put the puzzles together and see if they fit.*** All cards in the practice set should be displayed for children so that they can use the shape of the puzzle as a cue. If a child makes an incorrect choice, provide another chance to find the match. Take suggestions from the other children as needed to help the target child.

ACTIVITY

Initial Sound Matching

(10–15 minutes)

Materials: Initial Sound Cards, dry erase markers, dry erase board, tape

Directions: Select pairs of pictures with the same initial sound from the Initial Sound Cards. Tape one card from each pair randomly on opposite sides of the dry erase board so that each picture on the left side has a match on the right side with the same initial sound. For each turn, a child chooses a picture on the left side and finds the picture with the same initial sound on the right side. The child then draws a line to connect the pictures.

→ **Teaching strategies:** Teach the process of pairing to find a match. Label the picture in the right column and then repeat the word emphasizing the initial sound (***ball, b-b-ball***). Demonstrate pairing that word/picture with pictures/words on the right side until a match is found. Then check a few more pictures. (***b-b-ball, mmmop; b-b-ball, b-b-boy; b-b-ball, sssock; b-b-ball, k-k-king***). Segment the initial sound to highlight and isolate the initial sound of each word. ***Car, cat. Melissa, do those start with the same sound? Listen, c-c-car, c-c-cat. c*** [pause] ***ar, c*** [pause] ***at. Say those words. Does your mouth do the same thing?***

Depending on the level of the group, vary the number of picture pairs. For less proficient groups, five or six pairs may be plenty, whereas more proficient groups can handle more. Perhaps begin with six pairs and then practice again with a larger set of pairs.

Session Focus: Initial Sound Matching

SESSION STIMULI

Initial Sound Puzzle Cards

fan fox
match moon
nest nail
nose nut
sail sink
sock seven
shoe ship
vase van

lamp leg
ball bear
bed bug
bee book
chain chair
corn king
door dog
duck dice

gate girl
house hat
pie pin
pot pool
rain rake
tack tent
wing one

Initial Sound Cards

ball boy
car cat
chicken cheese
clown dog
dime fan
four flower
game goat
heart hat
jar jam
king lake
log map
moon mop
mouse nose
net pen
pig rake
rat rug
sheep shoe
snail sky
sock sun
table ten
tooth vase
van

IMPLEMENTATION SUGGESTIONS

Choosing Stimuli

- Continuants are likely to be easier than stops. The continuant sound puzzles are listed first in the above list.
- Initial sounds are easier to segment in CCVC (*spoon, snail*) words than CVC words. No words that begin with blends are included in the puzzle cards. Very few blend words are included in the Initial Sound Cards (only *clown, flower, sky*). Present these blend words only to more proficient children.

More on Teaching Strategies

- Question correct responses and incorrect responses.
- Have the group repeat the words after the target child. For all stimuli, have children complete the "Process of Initial Sound Activities" presented in previous sessions.
- Model segmentation of initial sounds by producing initial sounds in isolation. But do not expect children to perform this skill at this point in the program.
- For children who continue to struggle, have another child model the answer and have the target child imitate the response.
- When composing new practice sets, include some puzzles from a previously practiced set. Let children who are struggling do these puzzles.
- Review completed pictures within each activity to reinforce the target skill.

Session Focus: Initial Sound Matching and Initial Sound Sorting

ACTIVITY

Letter Activity (3–5 minutes)

Materials: Letter puzzle, small paper bag

Directions: Each child pulls a letter out of the bag, gives the letter names and sounds, and puts the letter in the puzzle. Ask some children to provide a word that begins with the letter sound.

➔ **Teaching strategies:** Children should be quite proficient at this task of naming letters and sounds. If a child is having difficulty with particular letter names or sounds, then the clinician should reinforce these names/sounds with that child. For example, have the child repeat another child's response for that letter.

If a child cannot generate a word for his or her letter, enlist help from the group.

ACTIVITY

Initial Sound Matching

(10 minutes)

Materials: Initial Sound Puzzle Cards

Directions: Place half of each picture puzzle on the table. The clinician keeps the other half, chooses a card, and says the picture name for the child. The child repeats the word and looks for a match on the table. Once the child has made a choice, the clinician gives the child the puzzle piece to match. Compose practice sets with more than one pair with the same initial sounds (e.g., include *ball–bear* as well as *bed–bug*).

➔ **Teaching strategies:** Begin with six puzzles. If child proficiency allows, add new puzzles as children complete puzzles and increase to more than six puzzles. Have more proficient children go first when there are more puzzles, and have less proficient children take a turn when there are fewer puzzles. The clinician should try to prevent the child from using the puzzle shape as a hint, except as a last resort. Make sure the child says the names of the pictures aloud and uses iteration/elongation. Where there is more than one possible matching picture, guide the child to try to find another picture that might work to find the puzzle pieces that fit together. After completing a puzzle, have all children say the pair words together—say words, elongate/iterate, say words. Or have individual children repeat the pair. ***Jennifer, say the words that Thomas matched. cat–cow. Those start with the same sound. You say those words. Remember say the words, bounce the first sound in each word, and say the words again.***

ACTIVITY

Initial Sound Sorting

(15 minutes)

Materials: Initial Sound Sorting Cards, small paper bags with letters (M, G, K and C) on the front, tape.

Directions: Tape a picture to each bag under the letter(s): *car, gate, moon.* Each child draws a card from the pile and decides which bag the card goes in. Have children say the two words together. Then have the child produce the initial sound in isolation using the letter on the bag as a cue.

➔ **Teaching strategies:** ***Here's a new game to play. We are still going to pay attention to the beginning sound in each word. We have a pile of cards and three bags. Let's say the sound for each letter on the bags and name the picture. The letter m says /m/, like moon; g says /g/ like in gate, and k and c say /k/ like in car. I'll do the first one. I chose key. Key, k-k-key, k*** [pause] ***ey. Key–car, key has the same beginning sound as car. Let's put key in the K bag. Key, /k/. That's the sound at the beginning of key. Key does not have the same beginning sound as gate or moon. Now it's your turn. Pick a card. You decide if this picture starts with the same sound as car, gate, or moon. Remember to stretch or bounce the sound.***

This task provides some challenges. /k/ and /g/ differ only in voicing. Children have to pay attention to all features (place, manner, voicing) of the sounds. Stimuli include a few multisyllabic words; judging initial sounds is more challenging in longer than shorter words.

ACTIVITY

Review Rhyme During Initial Sound Sorting Task

Materials: None

Directions: After children have decided what bag to place the cards in, sometimes ask children to give a rhyme.

➔ **Teaching strategies:** When asking students to also generate a rhyme during the initial sound segmentation task, give clear directions and expectations for rhyming. ***Now I want you to think of a word that rhymes with coat. Remember, words that rhyme are words that sound the same at the end, like cat–hat.*** Only request rhymes for monosyllabic words.

Session Focus: Initial Sound Matching and Initial Sound Sorting

SESSION STIMULI

Initial Sound Puzzle Cards

fan	fox	lamp	leg	gate	girl
match	moon	ball	bear	house	hat
nest	nail	bed	bug	pie	pin
nose	nut	bee	book	pot	pool
sail	sink	chain	chair	rain	rake
sock	seven	corn	king	tack	tent
shoe	ship	door	dog	wing	one
vase	van	duck	dice		

Initial Sound Sorting Cards: /k/ /g/ /m/

can	candy	car
carrot	cat	caterpillar
clock	clown	coat
comb	computer	corn
cow	cowboy	crown
kangaroo	key	kick
kids	king	kitchen
kite	game	garbage
gate	ghost	girl
goat	golf	gorilla
guitar	gumball	mail
man	map	mask
match	meat	menu
milk	money	monkey
moon	mountain	mouth
muffin		

IMPLEMENTATION SUGGESTIONS

More on Teaching Strategies

PROCESS FOR INITIAL SOUND ACTIVITIES

Say the word. [typical prosody and intonation]

Stretch the beginning sound or bounce (i.e., iterate) the beginning sound.

Perform task (e.g., judge sounds, segment sound)

- There is no need to complete all stimulus cards in the sound-sorting task. Instead, focus on getting children proficient on a subset of pictures. Occasionally, pause the activity and take the pictures out of each bag and have children say each word, elongating or stretching the sound and repeating the clinician's model of the initial sound in isolation. "Let's pull all these *g* pictures out of this bag and say them quickly. You say it after me. *Goat, g-g-goat, /g/. Guitar, g-g-g-guitar, /g/.* All these words begin with the */g/* sound. The letter *G* says */g/*".
- In the initial sound sorting task, provide children with the opportunity to segment the initial sound. "What sound does game start with?" Some children may be able to do this; others will rely on the letter cue to produce the sound in isolation. Either is appropriate. Although segmenting sounds is not expected at this point, using the letter cues may enable the child to produce the sound in isolation. This process also provides the clinician with the opportunity to model segmentation of initial sounds before expecting proficiency in this skill in later sessions (e.g., game starts with /g/.)
- Provide initial sound cues and semantic cues when needed to help children generate rhyme.

WEEK 5 ➜ SESSION 15

Session Focus: Initial Sound Matching and Initial Sound Sorting and Introduction to Initial Sound Segmentation

ACTIVITY

Letter Activity (3–5 minutes)

Materials: Alphabet cards

Directions: The clinician shows the picture side of the alphabet cards, asks the group what sound each word starts with and what letter says that sound, and then flips the card over to show the answer.

➜ **Teaching strategies:** The clinician should elongate or iterate the initial sound of the words. If children still cannot segment the initial sound, the clinician can re-ask the question, saying the word twice, the second time with a pause between the initial sound and the rest of the word. Kite. ***What's the first sound and letter? k*** [pause] ***ite*** (minimize the release of the vowel after the /k/, do not say "kuh").

ACTIVITY

Initial Sound Matching

(10–12 minutes)

Materials: Initial Sound Cards, dry erase markers, dry erase board, tape

Directions: Select pairs of pictures with the same initial sound from the set of Initial Sound Cards. Tape one card from each pair randomly on opposite sides of the dry erase board so that each picture on the left side has a match on the right side with the same initial sound. Split the group into teams. Give a team 1 minute to see how many matches they can identify. Review matches after 1 minute.

➜ **Teaching strategies:** Include eight pairs each time. ***We played this game before, but today we are going to play the game a little bit differently. We are going to have teams. You three will be on Team A, and you three will be on Team B. Okay, I have the board set up for Team A. I have eight pictures on this side and eight pictures on this side. Team A, you have 1 minute to match the pictures. Remember, you need to find the pictures that start with the same sound. On your mark, get set, go.*** Give the group 1 minute***. Let's look at the lines you drew. We'll say the two words together and make sure the words begin with the same sounds. Let's put a check mark if your team was right. Team A says the words first, and then Team B repeats. Remember to stretch or bounce the sounds.***

After Team A finishes, set the board up for Team B. Repeat as time allows.

ACTIVITY

Initial Sound Sorting

(10 minutes)

Materials: Initial Sound Sorting Cards, small paper bags with letters (M, G, K and C) on the front; tape.

Directions: Tape a picture to each bag along with the letter: *car, gate, moon.* Each child draws a card from the pile and decides into which bag the card goes.

➜ **Teaching strategies:** Have the child say the name of the card selected and the name of the card on the bag. Then have the child produce the initial sound in isolation using the letter on the bag as a cue. ***We'll play this game again today. Remember we have to sort the pictures into these three bags. Let's see if we can do this whole pile of cards. Choose a picture. Cow. C-c-cow. You think that cow goes in the car bag with the letter c, /k/. Okay say those words together: c-c-cow, c-c-car. Do those words have the same sound at the beginning? Yes, you are right.***

ACTIVITY

Introduction to Initial Sound Segmentation

(5 minutes)

Materials: Subset of Initial Sound Cards

Directions: Each child draws a card from the pile and orally segments the initial sound. Select a small set of cards for this introduction. See guidance under "choosing stimuli".

➜ **Teaching strategies:** Because this is just the introduction of this task, the clinician should provide maximal assistance to assure success. ***We have this pile of pictures. We are going to do something different. After we bounce or stretch the first sound, we'll say just the first sound for each picture. I'll do the first one. mouse, mmmmmouse, m*** [pause] ***ous. The first sound in mouse is /m/.*** Give each child a turn, and provide support for the child to have success. After each child's turn, repeat the cards already completed. This strategy provides many opportunities for children to clearly understand the segmentation process. ***Let's look at the ones we just did. I'll say each one and then you all say it after me. fffour. f*** [pause] ***our, fffour. Now you tell me. What sound does four start with? /f/, that's right.*** Continue through the pile.

Session Focus: Initial Sound Matching and Initial Sound Sorting and Introduction to Initial Sound Segmentation

SESSION STIMULI

Initial Sound Cards

ball	flower	moon	shoe
boy	game	mop	snail
car	goat	mouse	sky
cat	heart	nose	sock
chicken	hat	net	sun
cheese	jar	pen	table
clown	jam	pig	ten
dog	king	rake	tooth
dime	lake	rat	vase
fan	log	rug	van
four	map	sheep	

Initial Sound Sorting Cards /k/ /g/ /m/

can	kangaroo	game	mail
candy	key	garbage	man
car	kick	gate	map
carrot	kids	ghost	mask
cat	king	girl	match
caterpillar	kitchen	goat	meat
clock	kite	golf	menu
clown		gorilla	milk
coat		guitar	money
comb		gumball	monkey
computer			moon
corn			mountain
cow			mouth
cowboy			muffin
crown			

IMPLEMENTATION SUGGESTIONS

Choosing Stimuli

For the Introduction of Initial Sound Segmentation, use a subset of cards. Begin with continuant sounds and then use stop sounds if children are successful.

mouse
nose
sock
vase
sheep
king
dog
pig

PROCESS FOR INITIAL SOUND ACTIVITIES

Say the word. [typical prosody and intonation]

Stretch the beginning sound or bounce (i.e., iterate) the beginning sound.

Perform task (e.g., judge sounds, segment sound)

WEEK 6

OVERVIEW

Session 16 Focus: Initial Sound Segmentation

Session 17 Focus: Initial Sound Segmentation and Initial Sound Generation

Session 18 Focus: Initial Sound Generation and Introduction to Final Sound Judgment

Materials Needed

- ABC magnets (lowercase)
- Metal board
- Two large pieces of paper
- Marker
- Box with slots
- Game board and game pieces
- "Busy" picture books, such as "Where's Waldo" books or "All About Town"
- Initial Sound Cards
- Initial Sound Sticks
- Rhyme Generation Cards
- Final Sound Judgment Cards—subset

dish	brush
wolf	leaf
drum	ham
ten	moon
cap	tape
book	horse
mop	duck
rope	milk

Intervention Notes

Session Focus: Initial Sound Segmentation

ACTIVITY

Letter Activity (5 minutes)

Materials: Large piece of paper, marker

Directions: The clinician asks, *What letter says ___?* Select a child to say the letter and write the letter on the large piece of paper. Ask the child to give a word for that letter and sound. Complete about half of the alphabet, randomly selecting sounds to present.

→ **Teaching strategies:** If a child provides a wrong answer, the clinician says the sound again and asks for the letter name. ***No, listen again. What letter says /t/?*** Elicit assistance from peers in response to further errors. Peers can provide assistance to think of a word for the sound. Also, the clinician can give a semantic cue as a hint for words. ***It's a word that starts with /t/ and it's something you play with.*** Children also can be prompted to recall the picture for the letter on the alphabet picture cards.

Children can write uppercase or lowercase letters.

ACTIVITY

Initial Sound Segmentation (10–12 minutes)

Materials: Initial Sound Cards

Directions: One child serves as the quizzer and asks one of the other children what sound a given word starts with. The quizzer picks a picture card and then chooses a target child: *[child name], what does ___ start with?* When the target child provides the correct sound, he or she keeps that card.

→ **Teaching strategies:** Have the target child repeat the word, elongating or iterating the initial sound. The clinician can model. If the target child provides an incorrect answer, scaffold the child to provide the correct answer. Start with a weaker prompt, and provide a stronger prompt if the child is not successful. The strongest prompt is asking the child to repeat the correct answer. ***George says that dog begins with /f/. fffdog. ffffd-d-dog. Nope, dog does not begin with /f/. George, let's see if we can figure out what sound dog begins with. Dog, d-d-dog. You say that; pay attention to your mouth.*** Follow with a stronger prompt if needed. ***Dog, d-d-dog. d*** [pause] ***og. Listen for this first sound and say it like me. d-d-dog, d*** [pause] ***og. Now tell me the first sound in dog.***

Pause the game occasionally to have one or more children go through their cards and quickly say the first sound for each word in their pile of cards.

ACTIVITY

Initial Sound Segmentation (15 minutes)

Materials: Initial Sound Sticks, box with slots

Directions: A child points to a picture, names the picture aloud, provides the initial sound for that picture, and then determines what letter makes that sound before being allowed to pull the stick out of the box to see if he or she is correct by checking the letter.

→ **Teaching strategies:** If a child cannot segment the initial sound, the clinician can prompt by elongating, iterating, and, lastly, producing the word with a slight pause between the first sound and the rest of the word. If a child provides the letter ***name*** rather than the sound, remind the child that you want to know the sound. ***Oops, you gave me a letter name. Now tell me the sound that kite starts with, and then tell me the letter.*** After the target child provides a response, have the other children repeat the response and indicate whether they agree with the child's response.

ACTIVITY

Review Rhyme During Initial Sound Segmentation

Materials: None

Directions: Children give a rhyming word for one of the words they give in the initial sound generation activity.

→ **Teaching strategies:** For the first initial sound segmentation activity, occasionally ask a child to provide a rhyme for the word, after the initial sound is segmented. If this is difficult, provide clear instructions regarding what type of response is needed (rhyme, particular initial sound). Continued practice will develop flexibility in children's skills.

Session Focus: Initial Sound Segmentation

SESSION STIMULI

Initial Sound Cards

ball	boy	car	cat
chicken	cheese	clown	dog
dime	fan	four	flower
game	goat	heart	hat
jar	jam	king	lake
log	map	moon	mop
mouse	nose	net	pen
pig	rake	rat	rug
sheep	shoe	snail	sky
sock	sun	table	ten
tooth	vase	van	

Initial Sound Sticks

ball	bed	bus	cat
cheese	coat	dog	duck
fan	goat	hook	jar
kite	leaf	mop	mouse
pie	shell	sock	sun
three	tire		

IMPLEMENTATION SUGGESTIONS

More on Teaching Strategies

INITIAL SOUND SEGMENTATION GUIDING QUESTIONS/PROCESS

Say the word and stretch or bounce the sounds.

Produce the word with onset-rime segmentation. Say initial sound.

What sound does your mouth make at the beginning of the word?

- For the letter activity, students may need assistance generating a word that starts with the target sound. Providing choices (e.g., "Which starts with /t/? *b-b-ball* or *t-t-toy*?") or semantic cues (e.g., "I think the things you play with start with a /t/ sound.") may initially give reluctant students more success generating words independently.
- When segmenting words, have children complete these steps: Say the word, say the word again and elongate or iterate the first sound, and segment the sound. "*Cheese, ch-ch-cheese, /ch/.*"
- If children have a hard time segmenting the first sound, play freeze tag. "Okay, I want you to say the word. Now say the word and stretch the first sound. Now say it again. When I say *freeze*, don't move your mouth." While the child is stretching the initial sound, say "Freeze. Tell me the sound your mouth is making." Prompt the child by beginning to produce the sound yourself.
- During the initial sound segmentation activity with the sticks, it is important that the students provide the initial *sound* of the word before they pull the stick out of the box to reveal the letter. Clinicians may want to present this task in a game show–like format. "Ladies and gentlemen, our next contestant is Tommy. Tommy, what sound does the word *leaf* begin with? Take your time, Tommy. Remember, we're looking for the *sound*, not the letter. Audience, Tommy has answered */l/*. What letter goes with */l/*? Tommy says letter *L*. Let's see if he's correct! Let's pull the stick out."

WEEK 6 ➜ SESSION 17

Session Focus: Initial Sound Segmentation and Initial Sound Generation

ACTIVITY

Letter Activity (3–5 minutes)

Materials: Large piece of paper, marker

Directions: The clinician asks, *What letter says ___?* Select a child to say the letter and write the letter on the large piece of paper. Ask the child to give a word for that letter and sound. Complete remaining letters from the previous session.

➜ **Teaching strategies:** If a child provides a wrong answer, the clinician says the sound again and asks for the letter name. ***No, listen again. What letter says /t/?*** Elicit assistance from peers in response to further errors. Peers can provide assistance to think of a word for the sound. Also, the clinician can give a semantic cue as a hint for words.

Children can write uppercase or lowercase letters.

ACTIVITY

Initial Sound Segmentation (15–17 minutes)

Materials: Initial Sound Cards, game board and game pieces

Directions: A child selects a card, says the word, elongates or iterates the first sound when saying the word, and segments the sound. Move one space forward at the end of the turn after a correct response.

➜ **Teaching strategies:** ***Let's see if we can figure out the first sound in all of the pictures in this pile. We'll take turns.*** Remember, say the word, stretch or bounce the first sound while you say the word, then say the initial sound. Question correct responses as well as incorrect responses. Stop turns a couple of times and repeat pictures completed. ***Let's do these again, as fast as we can. I'll say the word and you tell me the sound. What is the first sound in ball? That's right, /b/. Say it together: b-b-ball, /b/. Now the next one.*** If the set is completed in less than 10 minutes, play again.

ACTIVITY

Initial Sound Generation (10 minutes)

Materials: Large pieces of paper, marker

Directions: Tell the group that they are going to try to name all of the words they can that start with a certain sound and that they will then count up the words to see which sounds they were able to generate the most words for. The clinician gives the group a sound and the group determines which letter(s) make that sound. The clinician writes the letter(s) at the top of the page and writes the words that the group provides.

➜ **Teaching strategies:** Give the children a time limit if you wish. Encourage each child to provide at least one word for each target letter sound. If one or more children do not provide many (any) responses, other children can be prompted to provide assistance. Children who are more proficient at this task can be enlisted to provide "clues" or semantic cues to children who are struggling. If a child provides a word that does not begin with the target sound, have that child or another child say the word aloud and segment the initial sound to show that it is incorrect. A few times the clinician can question a correct response: ***Hmm, pig, I'm not sure if that starts with /p/. Can someone show me what sound pig starts with?*** Children then can demonstrate segmentation of the initial sound.

ACTIVITY

Review Rhyme During Initial Sound Segmentation

Materials: None

Directions: Children are asked to determine a rhyming word for some of the words in the initial sound segmentation task.

➜ **Teaching strategies:** Elicit peer assistance if a child cannot generate a rhyming word, or provide an initial sound cue: ***Tell me a word that rhymes with sun. /f/~***

Session Focus: Initial Sound Segmentation and Initial Sound Generation

SESSION STIMULI

Initial Sound Cards

ball	boy	car	cat
chicken	cheese	clown	dog
dime	fan	four	flower
game	goat	heart	hat
jar	jam	king	lake
log	map	moon	mop
mouse	nose	net	pen
pig	rake	rat	rug
sheep	shoe	snail	sky
sock	sun	table	ten
tooth	vase	van	

There are no stimuli pictures for the initial sound generation task.

IMPLEMENTATION SUGGESTIONS

More on Teaching Strategies

- For the letter activity and initial sound generation task, children may need assistance generating a word that starts with the target sound. Providing choices (e.g., "Which starts with *t? b-b-ball* or *t-t-toy?*") or semantic cues (e.g., "I think the things you play with start with a *t* sound.") may initially give reluctant students more success generating words independently.
- For the initial sound generation task, do not use the vowel letters, the letter *q*, or the letter *x*. But the clinician can present the sounds /ʤ/ for CH, and the sound /ʃ/ for SH. There are not many words for TH, so this sound can probably be skipped. Children can generate monosyllabic or multisyllabic words.
- Scaffolding strategies for initial sound generation:
  - Provide choices. "Which starts with *t? b-b-ball* or *t-t-toy?*"
  - Provide semantic cues. "What are the things you play with that start with */t/?*"
  - Provide a picture or book to search for pictures of items beginning with the target sound. Use pictures that have lots of things in the picture (e.g., picture of a scene). Demonstrate how to use the pictures to generate words with specific beginning sounds. "Let's look at this picture for some things that start with */t/*. Does *k-k-kitchen* start with */t/*? No. How about *t-t-table?* I think I hear a */t/* sound at the beginning of *t-t-table*. How about you?"
  - Use facial expressions and gestures to cue a correct response. "Do you hear a */t/* sound at the beginning of *t-t-table* [clinician lifts eyebrows and nods head]?" "Yeah? I think I hear that sound, too!"

Session Focus: Initial Sound Generation and Introduction to Final Sound Judgment

ACTIVITY

Letter Activity (3–5 minutes)

Materials: ABC magnets, metal board

Directions: The clinician shows the group a letter and asks what that letter is and what sound it makes. The child who answers first puts the letter on the metal board.

➜ **Teaching strategies:** ***We are going to see how fast you know letter names and sounds. I'll show you a letter, and whoever knows the answer, say it as fast as you can.*** The clinician may want to make some responses a race between two children. Have the group repeat the letter name and sound as the magnet is placed on the metal board.

ACTIVITY

Initial Sound Generation

(20–22 minutes)

Materials: Rhyme Generation Cards

Directions: Segment initial sounds of words, generate words for sounds, and generate rhymes. The children sit in a circle. The clinician starts the game by drawing a picture from the bag and naming it. The child to the right provides a word that rhymes with that word. The next child to the right segments the initial sound of the rhyming word and provides another word that begins with that same sound. The next child to the right provides a rhyming word. The next child to the right segments the initial sound of the rhyming word and provides another word that begins with that same sound, and so on. After each child has taken a turn, allow another child to choose a picture and start again.

➜ **Teaching strategies:** ***Today we're going to play a game where we rhyme and we try to figure out the first sound in a word. Let's pick a picture from the bag. Bed. Tommy, can you think of a word that rhymes with bed? red? bed–red. Sounds like a rhyme to me. Now Ella, can you tell us what sound the word red starts with? What do you hear at the beginning of rrrred? /r/ That's right! Ella, can you also give us another word that starts with /r/? race? Yes, I hear /r/ at the beginning of rrrrace. rrr*** [pause] ***ace, race. Great! Now Jacob, can you think of a word that rhymes with race? Face? race, face, that's a great rhyme. Wow, you guys are really getting this!***

Prompt the child for the type of response needed (segmented sound and additional word *or* rhyme).

Provide initial sound cues for rhymes. Provide semantic cues for word generation. Assist with elongation or iteration for initial sound segmentation.

ACTIVITY

Introduction to Final Sound Judgment (5 minutes)

Materials: Subset of Final Sound Judgment Cards

Directions: Introduce the activity with a small set of Final Sound Judgment Cards. Give each child a chance to provide a response.

➜ **Teaching strategies:** ***We have been talking about sounds that words start with. Next week we're going to be talking about sounds that words end with. So we'll be listening for the sound at the end of a word. Let's try a few right now. I have these pictures. Let's say the name of the pictures and figure out if the words end with the same sound or different sounds.***

Provide maximal assistance to assure children are successful. Model and have a child repeat words and say the words again with the final sound elongated or iterated. Give the child a chance to respond. If no response or an incorrect response is given, repeat the words aloud, asking, ***Do they sound the same at the end?*** and prompt child's response by nodding your head "yes" or shaking your head "no."

ACTIVITY

Review Rhyme Embedded in Initial Sound Generation

➜ See Initial Sound Generation Activity above.

Session Focus: Initial Sound Generation and Introduction to Final Sound Judgment

SESSION STIMULI

Rhyme Generation Cards

ape	bat	bed	bee
bell	bug	cake	cap
car	cat	chair	cow
drum	fish	frog	grape
hat	lamp	light	mat
mop	nose	phone	pie
ring	rug	see	shoe
skate	snake	star	stop
ten	three	tree	van

Final Sound Judgment Cards—Subset

Same Final Sound

dish	brush
wolf	leaf
drum	ham
ten	moon
cap	tape

Different Final Sound

book	horse
mop	duck
rope	milk

IMPLEMENTATION SUGGESTIONS

More on Teaching Strategies

- At this point, the letter name/sound task should be fairly automatic. If naming letters and their corresponding sounds continues to be difficult for some students, cues such as providing choices, enlisting assistance from other students, or using facial expressions/head nodding to elicit a correct response may be necessary.
- Switching between rhyming, generating the initial sound in a word, and providing a word given an initial sound may be confusing to some children. Provide each child with clear information about what is expected during his or her turn. "Now for your turn we need a word that *rhymes* with *book.* Remember, words that rhyme are words that sound the same or make your mouth do the same thing at the end, like *cat–hat.* Now it's your turn to tell me the first sound in the word. Now you need to tell me another word that begins with */k/.*"
- Again, the purpose of the introduction activity is to familiarize children with the skill that will be targeted in the following week. There is no need to do all picture cards, but rather it is important that children have some success, even if it is necessary to have the child repeat the correct response. As always, children should repeat words, and then repeat words with the final sounds iterated or elongated. Children may be more successful with continuants. Begin with word cards that end in continuant sounds (*dish-brush, wolf-leaf, drum-ham, ten-moon*).

WEEK 7

OVERVIEW

Session 19 Focus: Final Sound Judgment

Session 20 Focus: Final Sound Judgment and Final Sound Odd-One-Out

Session 21 Focus: Final Sound Odd-One-Out and Introduction to Final Sound Matching

Materials Needed

- Alphabet cards (uppercase)
- ABC magnets (uppercase)
- Two small paper bags (one marked "Same Sounds," other marked "Different Sounds")
- Final Sound Judgment Cards
- Final Sound Odd-One-Out Cards
- Final Sound Puzzle Cards—subset

stove	five
fish	brush
bed	sled
egg	flag

Intervention Notes

Session Focus: Final Sound Judgment

ACTIVITY

Letter Activity (5 minutes)

Materials: Alphabet cards

Directions: Show picture on back of alphabet card. The clinician asks, *What sound does __ start with? What letter makes the __ sound?* Choose a child to respond. The child says the sound and letter name. Try to complete the entire set of alphabet cards.

→ **Teaching strategies:** If a child is unsuccessful, the clinician can elongate or iterate the initial sound. Another child may also produce the word with elongation or iteration. Difficult or error cards may be set aside and quickly reviewed at the end of the activity.

ACTIVITY

Final Sound Judgment

(25 minutes)

Materials: Final Sound Judgment Cards, two small paper bags (one marked "Same Sounds," other marked "Different Sounds")

Children: Children each draw a card and determine whether the two pictures on the card both end in the same sound. If the pictures end in the same sound they go into the "Same Sounds" bag; if not, they go in the "Different Sounds" bag. Group assistance can be solicited, as well as group judgment of the response.

→ **Teaching strategies:** Because this is the first week of final sounds, provide maximal support to ensure success. Model with final sounds elongated or iterated. Also, highlight the final sound by segmenting the final sound from the remainder of word. ***Do stove and rice have the same sound at the end? sto*** [pause] ***ve, ri*** [pause] ***ce*** (i.e., /v/ and /s/, respectively). Model the correct response. Provide a head shake prompt (described previously). Have the children attend to articulatory cues. Looking in the mirror while producing words may help some children.

Throughout the activity, review cards in each bag; quickly name the two pictures on each card, noting that they have the same ending sound or they end with different ending sounds.

Today we are only going to think about final sounds in our game. We are going to pay attention to the last sound in each word, the last sound your mouth makes. We've played this game before with rhymes and initial sounds. Now we are playing with final sounds. I'll do the first one. Look, my card has two pictures on it, dish and brush. I am going to stretch the last sound in each word. Dishshsh, brushshsh. Hmm, do those words end with the same sound or different sounds? Dishshsh, brushshsh. They end with the same sound. I made the /ʃ/ sound at the end of each word. I'll put this card in the "Same Sounds" bag. Review, having the whole group repeat the clinician's model. ***Let's do the next one together. Say these pictures with me. phone, fish. Now let's stretch that last sound. phonnnnne, fishshsh.*** Continue and have the children repeat after the clinician. ***Do phone and fish have the same sound at the end? Does your mouth make the same sound at the end?*** Continue the activity, providing the support necessary to make each child successful.

Children likely will need reminding to focus on the final sound of each word. If they provide an answer that focuses on the initial sound in the word, refocus their attention. ***Oops, you paid attention to the beginning of the word. Pay attention to the ending sound in the word. Pay attention to the last sound.***

ACTIVITY

Review Initial Sounds Embedded in Letter Activity

→ See Letter Activity above.

SESSION STIMULI

Final Sound Judgment Cards

Same Final Sound		Different Final Sound	
dish	brush	stove	rice
wolf	leaf	fan	lamb
drum	ham	phone	fish
ten	moon	mouse	ring
bus	face	cup	tooth
hen	sun	book	horse
nose	keys	mop	duck
house	vase	sled	bag
comb	dime	bed	foot
witch	match	rope	cake
bridge	cage	book	bag
hat	coat		
cap	tape		
light	gate		
rake	truck		
bug	egg		
book	cake		
bike	duck		
bed	hand		

IMPLEMENTATION SUGGESTIONS

Choosing Stimuli

- Words that end in continuants may be easier to judge than words that end in stops. In the above lists, continuant pairs are listed first. Words with final blends are more difficult than CVC words. We have included only a few words with final blends throughout this unit. Have the children with the most skill respond to the stimuli with final blends.
- In this section, only words that have consonants at the end are included. Again, vowels are harder to judge and segment because of lack of articulatory feedback.

FINAL SOUND GUIDING QUESTIONS

Say the word. Stretch or bounce the last sound.

Does your mouth do the same thing at the end of [word 1] and [word 2]?

More on Teaching Strategies

- Make sure children are saying the words and then saying the words again with the final sound of each word elongated or iterated before they make their judgment.
- It is not necessary to get through all the word cards. Rather it is important that children catch on to the notion of analyzing final sounds in words. Lots of repetition with the same cards will establish this skill. Repeat practice on a small set of cards and then move to new cards. Take the cards out of each bag and review. "Let's say all these again that have the same sounds at the end. We'll say the words together and remember to stretch or bounce the last sound in each word." Repeat for picture cards in the "Different Sounds" bag.
- Scaffolding strategies include the following:
  - Iterate or elongate the final sound in each word. "Let's listen. Do *wolf* and *leaf* end with the same sound? *wolffffff, leaffffff.* Do you hear the same sound at the end of those words? Let's listen: *boat-t-t, cup-p-p.* Do you hear the same sound at the end of those words?"
  - Segment the final sound to highlight the sound. "Do you hear the same sound at the end of *boat* and *cup? boa* [pause] *t, cu* [pause] *p.* Does your mouth do the same thing at the end of those words?" Don't expect children to be able to segment final sounds at this point of the program. But model segmentation of final sounds to highlight the final sounds for children.
  - Facial expression/head nod or shake: "You think you hear the same sound at the end of *wolf* and *leaf* [clinician nods]?"

WEEK 7 ➜ SESSION 20

Session Focus: Final Sound Judgment and Final Sound Odd-One-Out

ACTIVITY

Letter Activity (5 minutes)

Materials: ABC magnets, small paper bag

Directions: A child pulls a letter out of the bag, names it, and provides the sound that the letter makes, as well as a word that begins with that sound. The clinician may also ask for each child to provide a word that rhymes with the word generated for the initial sound. Complete half of the magnetic letters.

➜ **Teaching strategies:** The clinician may need to prompt responses. ***What is that letter? What sound does that letter make? Tell me a word that begins with that sound. Now tell me a word that rhymes with ___.*** Ask another child to judge the accuracy of responses and correct error responses. Occasionally question or challenge a correct response.

ACTIVITY

Final Sound Judgment

(10 minutes)

Materials: Final Sound Judgment Cards

Directions: A child chooses a picture card and tells whether the two words end in the same sound or different sounds. Place completed cards in two piles ("Same Sounds," "Different Sounds").

➜ **Teaching strategies:** Begin with the cards completed in the previous session. Children should be able to do these cards quickly. For each picture card, make sure children say the words, and then say the words again with the final sounds elongated or iterated. When completing each picture card, the clinician should provide final feedback by saying the words again, repeating the answer, and then saying the words with the final sound segmented. ***Bridge, cage; those words have the same sound at the end. Bri*** [pause] ***dge, ca*** [pause] ***ge. Those words have /ʤ/at the end.***

ACTIVITY

Final Sound Odd-One-Out (15 minutes)

Materials: Final Sound Odd-One-Out Cards, small paper bag

Directions: A child pulls a picture card from the bag and determines which of the pictures doesn't end in the same sound as the other two pictures.

➜ **Teaching strategies:** ***These cards have three pictures on them. We've played this game before; we have to find the one that does not belong. Today we need to find the word that does not have the same sound at the end. Remember, we are paying attention to the sound at the end of the words. Let's do this first one together.*** The clinician models how to figure out the answer, and the children imitate.

Have the child responding name the pictures and then repeat the words using elongation or iteration of final sounds. Because children have played this game before, they may be able to determine the answer without pairing the words. But if children have difficulty, pair the words and have the child repeat. Guide the child to judge each pair as a means to determine the odd-one-out. Have the group indicate agreement or disagreement with the child's response. Place the cards that are challenging or difficult back in the pile to repeat later. For less proficient children, have them complete two cards in sequence—first a card that has been practiced previously today and then a new card.

ACTIVITY

Review Rhyme and Review Initial Sounds Embedded in Letter Activity

➜ See Letter Activity above.

Session Focus: Final Sound Judgment and Final Sound Odd-One-Out

SESSION STIMULI

Final Sound Judgment Cards

Same Final Sound

dish	brush	bridge	cage
wolf	leaf	hat	coat
drum	ham	cap	tape
ten	moon	light	gate
bus	face	rake	truck
hen	sun	bug	egg
nose	keys	book	cake
house	vase	bike	duck
comb	dime	bed	hand
witch	match		

Different Final Sound

stove	rice
fan	lamb
phone	fish
mouse	ring
cup	tooth
book	horse
mop	duck
sled	bag
bed	foot
rope	cake
book	bag

Final Sound Odd-One-Out Cards

fish	brush	**van**	glass	vase	**cat**	hook	**gate**	bike
horse	drum	lamb	keys	**ship**	rose	rake	sock	**bag**
van	**dime**	clown	cab	tub	**boat**	dog	bag	**fan**
calf	**house**	wolf	sheep	mop	**rain**	**skate**	pig	frog
ring	mouse	grass	map	**book**	rope	witch	couch	**bike**
corn	bone	**hat**	**drum**	kite	hat	**book**	tooth	moth
leg	roof	leaf	foot	**snake**	cat	bridge	cage	**brush**
king	five	stove	bed	road	**mice**			
gas	bus	**egg**	cloud	**feet**	sand			

IMPLEMENTATION SUGGESTIONS

Choosing Stimuli

- Cards with all continuant ending sounds may be easier. These are listed first in the lists above.
- The more similar the final sound in the odd word to the final sound in the other words, the more difficult the card may be.

PROCESS FOR FINAL SOUND ACTIVITIES

Say the word. [typical prosody and intonation]

Stretch or bounce the ending sound.
Perform the task (e.g., judge sounds, segment sounds).

More on Teaching Strategies

- Have the children say the words while looking in the mirror. Or watch another child say the words. This strategy may help the children pay attention to articulatory cues. "MarySue has to figure out which word does not belong: *dog, bag, fan.* Everyone say those words with MarySue. Now say them again and remember to bounce or stretch the sound at the end. Look at your friend's mouth and watch him or her say the words. Does his or her mouth do the same thing at the end of the word?"
- Continue using cueing strategies highlighted in earlier sessions, but fade these supports as students begin demonstrating the ability to judge final sounds independently.
- Encourage struggling students to use peer feedback when they are unable to determine the word ending in a different sound than the other two (e.g., "Jimmy, if you'd like, you could ask someone in the group if they think *drum* is the word that ends with a different sound. Jimmy, say all three words aloud and see if Grace thinks *drum* is the answer. Make sure you stretch the final sounds in the words.")
- There is no need to get through all the cards in the odd-one-out task. As needed, repeat the cards to provide repeated success, especially for less proficient students.

Session Focus: Final Sound Odd-One-Out and Introduction to Final Sound Matching

ACTIVITY

Letter Activity (5 minutes)

Materials: ABC magnets, small paper bag

Directions: Children pull a letter out of the bag, name it, and provide the sound that the letter makes, as well as a word that begins with that sound. The clinician may also ask for each child to provide a word that rhymes with one they've generated. Complete the remainder of the alphabet from the previous session.

➜ **Teaching strategies:** The clinician may need to prompt responses. ***What is that letter? What sound does that letter make? Tell me a word that begins with that sound. Now tell me a word that rhymes with ___.*** Ask another child to judge the accuracy of and correct error responses. Occasionally question or challenge a correct response.

ACTIVITY

Final Sound Odd-One-Out (20 minutes)

Materials: Final Sound Odd-One-Out Cards, small paper bag, game board and game pieces

Directions: A child pulls a picture card from a bag, names the pictures aloud, and determines which of the choices doesn't end in the same sound as the other two. The child moves his or her piece on the game board after finishing the turn.

➜ **Teaching strategies:** ***We played this game last time. We're going to play again today, and we'll have some new cards today. Maybe Terrance can show us how to figure out the answer. Pick a card, Terrance, and show us how you figure out the answer.*** Pick a child who can easily do this task. ***Great. He remembered to say the words. Then he said the words again and bounced and stretched the ending sounds. And then he told us the word that did not belong. It has a different sound at the end. The other two words have the same sound at the end.***

Begin with a few of the cards from the previous session. If children are catching on, focus mostly on the cards not practiced in the last session. Place the cards that are challenging for children back in the pile to repeat later. Use more proficient children to model for less proficient children.

ACTIVITY

Introduction to Final Sound Matching (5 minutes)

Materials: Subset of Final Sound Puzzle Cards, small paper bag

Directions: Divide the group into two teams. Place one piece of each puzzle pair in a bag and lay the remaining piece of each pair on the table. Begin with four puzzles. One team will pull half of a puzzle pair out of the bag, show the card, and name the picture. Then the clinician says, *We're looking for a picture that ends with the same sound as [picture name].* The other team suggests an answer. The group with the original half of the puzzle pair determines whether or not the answer is correct by determining whether the two pieces match.

➜ **Teaching strategies:** Remember that the goal today is to introduce the activity and have the children experience some success. Because this is the first time children are doing this activity, the pairs in the subset have different final sounds and thus, there is only one possible answer for each puzzle. Limiting the puzzles to four makes the task easier by limiting the choices children have.

Because children can see puzzle pieces, they can use the shape of the puzzle as a hint. For each answer suggested, have the children repeat pairs of words aloud to determine whether they think the two pieces will match. Make sure they say the words, and then say the words again with the final sounds elongated or iterated. Then have the group with the puzzle piece match the pieces to check the response.

Provide feedback at the end of each puzzle. ***Stove and five end with the same sound. Stove and five end with the /v/ sound.***

Repeat puzzles as time allows.

ACTIVITY

Review Rhyme and Initial Sounds Embedded in Letter Activity

➜ See Letter Activity above.

Session Focus: Final Sound Odd-One-Out and Introduction to Final Sound Matching

SESSION STIMULI

Final Sound Odd-One-Out Cards

fish	brush	**van**	glass	vase	**cat**	hook	**gate**	bike
horse	drum	lamb	keys	**ship**	rose	rake	sock	**bag**
van	**time**	clown	cab	tub	**boat**	dog	bag	**fan**
calf	**house**	wolf	sheep	mop	**rain**	**skate**	pig	frog
ring	mouse	grass	map	**book**	rope	witch	couch	**bike**
corn	bone	**hat**	**drum**	kite	hat	**book**	tooth	moth
leg	roof	leaf	foot	**snake**	cat	bridge	cage	**brush**
king	five	stove	bed	road	**mice**			
gas	bus	**egg**	cloud	**feet**	sand			

Final Sound Puzzle Cards—Subset

stove	five
fish	brush
bed	sled
egg	flag

IMPLEMENTATION SUGGESTIONS

More on Teaching Strategies

FINAL SOUND GUIDING QUESTIONS

Say the word. Stretch or bounce the last sound.

Does your mouth do the same thing at the end of [word 1] and [word 2]?

- At this point, students should be having some success with judging final sounds. For those who continue to struggle, use scaffolding strategies highlighted in earlier sessions:
  - Segmentation. "Which word ends with a different sound: *dru...m, ki...te, ha...t?*"
  - Facial expression along with modeling. Have the child repeat your models. "Which word ends with a different sound: *drum, kite, hat?* Let me see: *drum-mmm, kite-t-t, hat-t-t.* Do you hear a different sound at the end of *kite and hat* (shake head no)? No? I think you're right. I hear the *same* sound at the end of *kite* and *hat.* I hear a */t/* sound at the end of both those words. What about *drum?* Do you hear a *different* sound at the end of *drum* (nod head yes). Me too! I think *drum* ends in a *different* sound than *kite* and *hat.* Great work!"
  - Have the child say the three words in pairs to compare all possibilities. This support initially reduces the task to a judgment task. Then ask the child to tell the odd-one-out.
- At the completion of each odd-one-out card, the clinician can emphasize the correct answer by repeating the two words that end in the same sound and then restating the word that does not have the same ending sound.
- The clinician can model segmentation of the final sound at the close of each turn. "*Brush, fish, van. Bru-SH, fi-SH, va-N. Van* is the one that does not belong. *Brush* and *fish* end with */ʃ/.*"
- For final sound matching, provide the level of scaffolding necessary for the teams to be successful. Students who have been successful with final sound judgment may not need further cues to match words containing the same final sound. Students struggling to identify final sounds may need to use the visual cues provided by the puzzle pieces in addition to the scaffolding strategies discussed previously.

WEEK 8

OVERVIEW

Session 22 Focus: Final Sound Matching

Session 23 Focus: Final Sound Matching and Final Sound Sorting

Session 24 Focus: Final Sound Matching and Final Sound Sorting and Introduction to Final Sound Segmentation

Materials Needed

- Index cards with uppercase letters printed on cards
- Alphabet cards (lowercase and uppercase)
- Small paper bag
- Dry erase marker and dry erase board
- Bags with letters *T*, *D*, *F* written on the bag
- Tape
- Final Sound Puzzle Cards
- Final Sound Cards
- Final Sound Sorting Cards
- Rhyme Generation Cards—subset (unique rimes only)

bat	cow	phone
bed	drum	pie
bee	fish	ring
bell	frog	shoe
bug	grape	skate
cake	lamp	stop
cap	light	ten
car	mop	van
chair	nose	

Intervention Notes

Session Focus: Final Sound Matching

ACTIVITY

Letter Activity (5 minutes)

Materials: Index cards with letters printed on one side (skip X).

Directions: For each letter card, the clinician takes turns asking a child to identify the name of the letter, the sound the letter makes, and a word beginning with that sound. The clinician writes the word on the back of the card. Complete half of the alphabet cards.

→ **Teaching strategies:** ***We are going to try to think of a word that begins with the sound that each letter of the alphabet makes. I'll write the words we think of on the back of these cards so that we can keep thinking of new words.***

ACTIVITY

Final Sound Matching

(25 minutes)

Materials: Final Sound Puzzle Cards, small paper bag

Directions: Place one piece of each puzzle pair in the bag and lay the remaining piece of each pair on the table. One child will pull half of a puzzle card out of the bag, show the card, and tell the group that he or she is looking for the word that ends in the same sound as the word on the card. The child can choose another child to give the answer. The child with the original half of the card determines whether or not the answer is correct and whether the two pieces match.

→ **Teaching strategies:** ***Today we are going to play the puzzle game for the rest of the time. We need to match the puzzles that end with the same sounds. It might get a little tricky because you might find two pictures that have the same sound at the end, but the puzzles don't match. That means there must be another puzzle piece with the same sound at the end, and you'll have to do more searching. Remember you can't just tell me an answer. You have to show me how you figured out the answer. You'll need to show me how you can stretch or bounce the sounds at the end of the words so that we can figure out if the words end with the same sound.***

Because children can see the puzzle pieces, they can use the shape of the puzzle as a hint. For each answer suggested, have the children repeat pairs of words aloud to determine whether they think the two pieces match. Then have the child with the puzzle piece match the pieces to self-correct. At the beginning start with just a few pairs on the table. Then practice with more pairs on the table and some pairs with the same sounds (e.g., *cake–book, sink–tack*).

Leave completed puzzles on the table. Stop the game a few times to review the completed puzzles. Model segmentation of final sounds after the children say the pair of words. ***Yes, cab and tub matched. Cab and tub end with /b/. ca-b, tu-b.***

If children are doing well on this task, play the game such that children cannot see the first half of the puzzle to use as support.

ACTIVITY

Review Initial Sounds During Final Sound Matching

Materials: None

Directions: Have children segment initial sounds for some of the puzzle words.

→ **Teaching strategies:** ***Great! You found that moose and face have the same sound at the end. They end with /s/. Now, I want you to switch and think about the beginning sounds in moose and face. What is the first sound in face? What is the last sound in face? What is the first sound in moose? What is the last sound in moose? You are right! Moose starts with /m/ and ends with /s/. And face starts with /f/ and ends with /s/.***

Session Focus: Final Sound Matching

SESSION STIMULI

Final Sound Puzzle Cards

cheese	hose
face	moose
bus	dice
clown	fan
plane	spoon
drum	comb
gum	jam
fish	brush
keys	rose
leaf	knife
chief	wolf
moon	hen
ring	king
stove	five
bed	slide
cab	tub
cake	book
sink	tack
mop	soap
cap	lamp
egg	flag
foot	goat
hat	kite
nest	coat
witch	match

IMPLEMENTATION SUGGESTIONS

Choosing Stimuli

- Continuant pairs may be easier. These pairs are listed first in the above list.
- The word pairs in which one word has a pairs blend (cap-lamp; nest-coat) will be more difficult than pairs in which each word ends in a singleton consonant.

FINAL SOUND GUIDING QUESTIONS

Say the word. Stretch or bounce the final sound.

Do [word 1] and [word 2] end with the same sound??

Does your mouth do the same thing at the end of [word 1] and [word 2]?

More on Teaching Strategies

- Continue to individualize the level of scaffolding necessary for each child to be successful. Children who have been successful with final sound judgment may not need further cues to match words with the same final sounds. Children struggling to identify final sounds may need to use the visual cues provided by the puzzle pieces in addition to the scaffolding strategies discussed previously.

WEEK 8 → SESSION 23

Session Focus: Final Sound Matching and Final Sound Sorting

ACTIVITY

Letter Activity (5 minutes)

Materials: Index cards with letters printed on one side

Directions: The clinician calls on each child to identify the name of the letter she holds up, the sound the letter makes, and a word beginning with that sound. The clinician writes the word that the child generates on the back of the card. Complete the remaining half of the alphabet cards.

→ **Teaching strategies:** ***Remember, the last time we thought of words that began with each of the letter sounds, and then we wrote the words on the backs of the cards. We didn't finish all the letters though. Today we are going to finish the rest of the cards.*** Use strategies from the previous session.

ACTIVITY

Final Sound Matching (10 minutes)

Materials: Final Sound Cards, dry erase board, dry erase marker

Directions: Select pairs of words with the same final sounds. Set up pictures on the dry erase board with half of each pair on either side of the board. Children draw a line to connect the pictures with the same ending sounds. Begin with about six pictures on each side of the board. In the second round, use more than six sets of pictures if children were generally successful in the first round.

→ **Teaching strategies:** ***Today we'll draw lines to connect the pictures that end with the same sound. Everyone will take a turn. Johanna, you can go first. What picture on this side do you want to start with? Eight. Okay, let's find the picture on the other side that has the same sound at the end as eight, eight-t-t-t. You say that.***

If a child provides an incorrect response, engage the group in a problem-solving task. ***Let's see. I'm not sure those end with the same sound. Let's say the words aloud.*** (Emphasize the final sounds.) ***I don't think those have the same sounds at the end. Now let's have*** [child] ***try again.*** Engage children in the checking of correct responses in the same way. ***Let's see. Does everyone think those words end in the same sound?***

ACTIVITY

Final Sound Sorting (10 minutes)

Materials: Final Sound Sorting Cards, three bags with letters *T, D,* and *F* and pictures taped on each bag (*boat, red, leaf*)

Directions: Children sort the picture cards by the final sound. Occasionally stop and review all cards in each bag. Ask the children to produce the final sound for each word, using the letter on the bag as a cue.

→ **Teaching strategies:** ***We are going to try to sort all these pictures today. We have to decide where to put each picture. Each picture has the same ending sound as boat, red, or leaf. Boat, boat-t-t-t. Red, red-d-d. Leaf, leafffff. Why are these letters on the bag? Yep, those are the letters for the ending sound in each of the words. Boat ends with a /t/ sound, letter T. Red ends with a /d/ sound, letter D. Leaf ends with a /f/ sound, letter F. I'll do the first one, and then it's your turn. Roof, roofffff, roof ends like leaf. I am going to put roof in the leaf bag. What is the last sound in leaf? /f/! Look, I can tell by looking at the letter on this bag.***

ACTIVITY

Review Rhyme (5 minutes)

Materials: Rhyme Generation Cards

Directions: Divide children into two teams. Alternate team turns. The clinician names the picture card and each child on the team shouts out a word that rhymes. The clinician repeats all words that the children produce. The other team can judge whether all the words rhyme or point out those that do not rhyme.

→ **Teaching strategies:** ***We'll play a quick rhyming game today. We'll have two teams. I will show a picture to your team. Everyone on the team has to try to think of a rhyming word as quickly as they can. As soon as you think of your rhyming word, you can shout it out. Here's the first card: grape.*** Children shout out answers. ***Great, I heard these words: cape, tape, and gate. Other team, do all those words rhyme with grape?***

The children should be proficient at rhyming and should be able to play the game with little assistance. The clinician should provide assistance only when children are wrong (i.e., the team accepts a non-rhyming word as a correct answer).

Session Focus: Final Sound Matching and Final Sound Sorting

SESSION STIMULI

Final Sound Cards

Note: To assist in selecting pairs, cards are sorted by final sound with continuants first.

bone	nose	stop	witch
brush	drum	boat	hook
tub	red	leaf	wreath
cup	bench	face	king
lamp	clock	eight	tack
calf	tooth	hat	egg
dice	ring	bread	dog
cat	fan	rose	frog
foot	fish	lamb	
light	cab	beach	

Final Sound Sorting Cards /t/ /d/ /f/

basket	bed	calf
bracelet	bread	chef
chocolate	bunkbed	chief
bat	cloud	cliff
boat	food	giraffe
coat	hand	half
eight	lemonade	knife
foot	mermaid	leaf
gate	mud	sheriff
meat	parade	thief
parrot	railroad	wolf
tent	road	
	salad	
	sled	
	toad	
	wood	

Rhyme Generation Cards—Subset

Subset that only includes unique rimes

bat	bed	bee	bell
bug	cake	cap	car
chair	cow	drum	fish
frog	grape	lamp	light
mop	nose	phone	pie
ring	shoe	skate	stop
ten	van		

IMPLEMENTATION SUGGESTIONS

FINAL SOUND GUIDING QUESTIONS

Say the word. Stretch or bounce the final sound.

Do [word 1] and [word 2] end with the same sound?

Does your mouth do the same thing at the end of [word 1] and [word 2]?

Session Focus: Final Sound Matching and Final Sound Sorting and Introduction to Final Sound Segmentation

ACTIVITY

Letter Activity (3–5 minutes)

Materials: Alphabet magnets, small paper bag

Directions: Each child picks a letter out of the bag, names it, and provides the sound that the letter makes.

→ **Teaching strategies:** Prompt the children to provide answers as quickly as possible. Challenge them to get through the whole alphabet in less than 3 minutes.

ACTIVITY

Final Sound Matching

(10 minutes)

Materials: Final Sound Puzzle Cards

Directions: Place one half of each puzzle in a pile, and tape the other half of each puzzle to the wall. The clinician chooses the top puzzle card and names the picture without letting the children see the puzzle piece. One child finds a picture with the same final sound and then takes the card to match the pieces.

→ **Teaching strategies:** To increase the challenge of the activity, begin with 12 puzzles and as each one is completed, add a new puzzle. Because children cannot see half of the puzzle, they will be unable to use the puzzle shape as a cue. Some of the pairs have the same final sound. If children choose a picture with the same final sound but the pieces do not match, help them to realize that the words do end with the same sound but that perhaps there is another puzzle piece that also ends with the same sound and fits.

ACTIVITY

Final Sound Sorting (10 minutes)

Materials: Final Sound Sorting Cards, bags with letters/pictures from previous session

Directions: Have teams sort cards by final sound, giving 30 seconds to each team, and then repeat. Review sorts and check accuracy at the end of each 30 seconds. The clinician prompts the children to produce the final sound of the word, using the letter as a cue. Repeat the game as time allows.

→ **Teaching strategies:** ***Let's do this sorting game one more time. We'll make two teams. Each team gets 30 seconds to sort as many pictures as you can. Don't put them in the bags yet. Just put each picture in front of the bag where you think it goes. Do as many as you can in 30 seconds. Here's the pile of cards. On your mark, get set, go!*** Team sorts cards. ***Now let's check your sorting. We'll say the name of each card and the picture on the bag and make sure that picture should go in that bag. Everyone say the words together.*** Label each sorting picture and the bag picture; elongate or iterate sounds. Have the children repeat them or say them in unison. Ask the children to produce the final sound for each word, reminding them to use the letter to help them remember the final sound.

ACTIVITY

Introduction to Final Sound Segmentation

(5 minutes)

Materials: Subset of Final Sound Cards

Directions: Segment the final sound of the words. The clinician models and the children repeat. Repeat each word as much as necessary to provide orientation to activity.

→ **Teaching strategies:** Because this is the initial introduction to this task, the clinician should provide maximal support. ***Next time we are going to work on saying the last sound in words. Let's do a little practice. What is the last sound in bone? I'll say the word and you say it after me. Say bone. Now say bonnnnne. Now say bo*** [pause] ***ne. What is the last sound in bone? That's right, /n/, bonnnne."***

Present each card to the children. Have all children in unison say the word, say the word with elongated or iterated final sound, and say the word with a pause before the final sound. Ask one child to tell the final sound. Provide additional modeling if the child does not provide the correct answer.. ***I don't think that is the last sound in foot. Listen again. foot-t-t, foo*** [pause] ***t. What is the last sound my mouth made? You say it with me: foo*** [pause] ***t. What is the last sound? What is the last sound you said?***

Session Focus: Final Sound Matching and Final Sound Sorting and Introduction to Final Sound Segmentation

SESSION STIMULI

Final Sound Puzzle Cards

cheese
face
bus
clown
plane
drum
gum
fish
keys
hose
moose
dice
fan
spoon
comb
jam
brush
rose
leaf
chief
moon
ring
stove
bed
cab
cake
sink
knife
wolf
hen
king
five
slide
tub
book
tack
mop
cap
egg
foot
hat
nest
witch
soap
lamp
flag
goat
kite
coat
match

Final Sound Sorting Cards /t/ /d/ /f/

basket
bat
eight
meat
bed
cloud
lemonade
parade
salad
wood
chief
half
sheriff
bracelet
boat
foot
parrot
bread
food
mermaid
railroad
sled
calf
cliff
knife
thief
chocolate
coat
gate
tent
bunkbed
hand
mud
road
toad
chef
giraffe
leaf
wolf

Final Sound Cards—Subset

bone
face
cup
tub
brush
lamp
foot

IMPLEMENTATION SUGGESTIONS

More on Teaching Strategies

- Remember that the goal of the final sound segmentation activity is for children to experience success as you introduce this activity. Repeat picture cards for children to experience success. Continuant final sounds may be easier than stop final sounds. For each word, use this sequence to set up the production of the answer: Say the word, say the word with the final sound elongated or iterated, and say the word with the ending sound segmented. Respond to the question: What is the last sound?
- When introducing final sound segmentation, use scaffolding strategies that allow for maximal success. In subsequent sessions, fade cues as children demonstrate signs of success. Scaffolding strategies include the following:
  - Segmentation: "What sound do you hear at the end of *moon?* Hmm, *moo...n.*" What sound do you hear at the end?
  - Facial expression: "What sound do you hear at the end of *moon?* You think you hear an */m/* sound?" (concerned facial expression) "Hmm, *moonnnn.* I hear */n/.* What do you think? You hear a */n/* sound?" (nod head) "I think I hear that too!"
  - Provide choices: "What sound do you hear at the end of *moon, moonnnn?* Do you hear */n/* at the end of *moon?* Or do you hear */f/* at the end of *moon? moonnnnn or moonffff?* Right, I think it is */n/. moo [pause] n.*"

WEEK 9

OVERVIEW

Session 25 Focus: Final Sound Segmentation

Session 26 Focus: Final Sound Segmentation and Final Sound Generation

Session 27 Focus: Final Sound Generation and Introduction to Segmentation

Materials Needed

- Index cards with letters (from Sessions 22 and 23)
- ABC magnets (uppercase and lowercase, depending on children's need for practice)
- Alphabet cards (uppercase and lowercase consonant cards only. Omit *A, E, I, O, U, Y, Q, X,* and *H* from each deck)
- Timer or stopwatch
- "Busy" picture books, such as "Where's Waldo" books or "All About Town"
- Final Sound Cards
- Final Sound Sticks, box with slots
- Two-square panels

Intervention Notes

Session Focus: Final Sound Segmentation

ACTIVITY

Letter Activity (5 minutes)

Materials: Index cards (letters printed on one side, words on opposite side)

Directions: The clinician asks children to think of one or more words for each letter card. Move quickly and do as many letters as possible.

→ **Teaching strategies:** ***Remember we used these cards before*** (Sessions 22 and 23). ***We were thinking of words that begin with each letter sound. Today we are going to see if we can think of some more words.*** If a child provides a word already written on the card, acknowledge the response as correct and ask for another word. The clinician may choose to read responses already on the card after a child chooses the card.

ACTIVITY

Final Sound Segmentation

(10 minutes)

Materials: Final Sound Cards

Directions: A child chooses a card from the pile and segments the final sound. The other children check the response by repeating the words and segmenting the final sound.

→ **Teaching strategies:** ***We need to figure out the last sound in each of these words. We'll take turns going first, but everyone needs to listen because you'll be checking the answer. Sarah, you go first. You picked light. Remember, say the word, bounce the final sound, and then say it again and break the final sound off. And then tell me the ending sound. Great, light, light-t-t, li*** [pause] ***t. Sarah says /t/ is the last sound in light. Now everyone say the word to check her answer. Do it just the way Sarah did.***

For error responses: ***Sarah says up is the last sound in cup. Let's see if she is correct. Let's all say the word together. cup, cup-p-p, cu*** [pause] ***p. Sarah said the last sound, but she also said some other sounds. Let's say the last sound all by itself. Everyone say it together: cup-p-p. What is the last sound? /p/. That's right. Sarah, say cup and bounce the last sound. Good. Now tell me the last sound in cup.***

ACTIVITY

Final Sound Segmentation

(15 minutes)

Materials: Final Sound Sticks, box with slots

Directions: The clinician presents the box with all sticks inserted. A child chooses and points to a picture, names the picture, and says the final sound. After the child tells the corresponding letter for the final sound, he or she pulls the stick out of the box to see if he or she is right.

→ **Teaching strategies:** ***We played this stick game with beginning sounds. Now let's play the stick game with final sounds. You'll pick a picture and say the name of the picture and then break the ending sound off the word. Once you figure out the ending sound, then you can tell us what letter you think makes that sound. I'll do the first one. Truck, truck-k-k, tru*** [pause] ***k. Truck ends with /k/. I think that the letter K goes with the /k/ sound. Wow, I am right!***

Place the picture stick back in the box so that there is another opportunity to respond to that picture. Allow less proficient children initially to choose a picture that has already been practiced. In subsequent turns, encourage the child to pick a new picture.

If a child's response proves to be incorrect, model the segmentation, asking the child to repeat, or ask the child to try again. If a child assigns the wrong letter, ask the group to provide an answer. When the wrong letter is still the same sound (e.g., *K*, *C*), explain that some sounds go with more than one letter.

ACTIVITY

Review Initial Sounds Embedded in Letter Activity

→ See Letter Activity above.

Session Focus: Final Sound Segmentation

SESSION STIMULI

Final Sound Cards

bone	drum	cat	clock
fan	lamb	eight	hook
brush	tooth	foot	tack
fish	wreath	hat	dog
calf	tub	light	egg
leaf	cab	bread	frog
dice	cup	red	ring
face	stop	beach	king
nose	lamp	bench	
rose	boat	witch	

Final Sound Sticks

bed	cliff	drum	fan
fish	flag	globe	glove
goat	hand	house	kite
lamp	leg	match	moon
sheep	stamp	teeth	truck

IMPLEMENTATION SUGGESTIONS

More on Teaching Strategies

- Mastery of segmentation is achieved through repeated practice on a small set of words to catch on to the notion of segmenting final sounds and then applying what is learned to a new set of words. Therefore, be less concerned with completing all the stimulus pictures and more concerned with repeated practice and successful performance. For example, begin with a word and have each child individually segment the sound, using the guiding questions. Then do the same with another word, and then a third word. Then randomly give one of the three words to each child to segment and observe whether individual children can be successful on these three words without additional scaffolding. Then introduce new words to segment and see if children can generalize their learning. If not, provide the scaffolding necessary to make children successful.
- With Final Sound Sticks, let more proficient children take turns first to provide models for less proficient children.

FINAL SOUND GUIDING QUESTIONS

Say the word. Stretch or bounce the ending sound. Say the word and break the final sound off (i.e., produce a pause between the rest of the word and the final sound). Produce the final sound in isolation.

What sound does [word] end with?

Session Focus: Final Sound Segmentation and Final Sound Generation

ACTIVITY

Letter Activity (5 minutes)

Materials: Alphabet cards

Directions: The clinician shows the group the picture side of the cards and the group determines the ending sound of the word and the letters for that sound. If the picture ends in a sound not marked by a single letter (e.g., /ch/ in *witch*) use the opportunity to briefly discuss spelling conventions.

➔ **Teaching strategies:** ***We've looked at these pictures many times, and we've paid attention to the beginning sounds in the words. But today we are going to say the names of the pictures and figure out the ending sound in each word. And then we'll see if we can figure out the letter or letters that go with the last sound in each word. So we'll only be looking at the picture side of these cards.*** If a child provides an incorrect response, have him or her try again. Correct any errors by modeling the answer and having the child imitate. ***I don't hear a /t/ sound at the end of witch. I hear /ʤ/ sound. When you spell /ʤ/ sound, you use two letters, C and H. So witch ends with a ch sound that is written by the letters CH.***

ACTIVITY

Final Sound Segmentation (20 minutes)

Materials: Final Sound Cards, game board and game pieces

Directions: Each child picks a card and identifies the final sound. A child moves forward on the game board once a correct answer is given. Put the completed cards face down on the table.

➔ **Teaching strategies:** Assist each child in iterating or elongating the final sound as a means to achieve segmentation. ***What sound do you hear at the end of brush? brushshsh. Remember to say the word, stretch it, and then break the last sound off the word.*** Have other children indicate whether they agree with the child's response, both for correct responses and incorrect responses. ***Aidan says brush ends with a /ʃ/ sound. What does everyone think?***

After completing a few cards, go back and review those cards. In unison or one after each other, have children say the words, elongate or iterate the last sound, and then produce the final sound in isolation. Then answer the question: ***What is the last sound in [target word]?***

A few times during the game, stop to review the cards that have been completed. Have children who struggle practice pictures with continuant final sounds. Or have them repeat one of the completed cards and then try a new card. Or have a peer model the segmentation process and then have the target child repeat the process with the same picture card.

ACTIVITY

Final Sound Generation (5 minutes)

Materials: Final Sound Cards, pieces of paper with a letter at the top of each, timer, picture books, as needed

Directions: Place all Final Sound Cards on the table face up. The clinician introduces each round of the activity by focusing the children on one of the picture cards. The clinician names the picture and the final sound, writing the letter(s) on a piece of paper. Ask the children to think of other words that end with the same sound. Write down words children generate.

➔ **Teaching strategies:** ***We're going to think of words that have the same ending sound as one of the pictures I choose. Let's start with hook. Hook ends with a /k/ sound. You need to think of other words that end with a /k/ sound. I'll write a K on this page and then I'll write down the words we can think of that end with /k/. Look at the pictures on the table to see if you can find any that end with /k/. Okay, clock and hook and tack. Now let's think of some other words that end with /k/. Let's set the timer for one minute.*** If children generate a word that does not end with /k/, guide them to discover that it is a wrong answer. ***Jeremy says box ends with a /k/ sound. Let's say that word and stretch that ending sound. Box, box-sssssss, /bak/*** [pause] ***/s/. Box does not end with a /k/ sound? What sound does it end with?***

The clinician can provide semantic cues. "Busy" pictures can also be used to stimulate children's thinking (e.g., *Where's Waldo?* or *All About Town* Richard Scarry books).

At first have children take turns. Later have children call out words as they think of them and then check all answers when the time is up.

Session Focus: Final Sound Segmentation and Final Sound Generation

SESSION STIMULI

Final Sound Cards

bone	fan
brush	fish
calf	leaf
dice	face
nose	rose
drum	lamb
tooth	wreath
ring	king
tub	cab
cup	stop
lamp	boat
cat	eight
foot	hat
light	bread
red	beach
bench	witch
clock	hook
tack	dog
egg	frog

IMPLEMENTATION SUGGESTIONS

FINAL SOUND GUIDING QUESTIONS

Say the word. Stretch or bounce the ending sound. Say the word and break the final sound off (i.e., produce a pause between the rest of the word and the final sound). Produce the final sound in isolation.

What sound does [word] end with?

Session Focus: Final Sound Generation and Introduction to Segmentation

ACTIVITY

Letter Activity (5 minutes)

Materials: ABC magnets, stopwatch

Directions: Have children respond as a group, providing the letter name and sound.

→ **Teaching strategies:** ***We are going to say the letter names and sounds as fast as we can. I'll show each letter and everyone say the name and the letter sound as fast as you can. Let's see how long it takes us to do this.*** Set the stopwatch. If time allows, repeat the activity and see if the group can beat their score. The clinician should identify any children who are not quickly responding to indicate who needs more assistance on letter sound knowledge.

ACTIVITY

Final Sound Generation (15 minutes)

Materials: Game board and game pieces, uppercase and lowercase alphabet cards (exclude H), busy picture books

Directions: Each child chooses four letters and places them face up in front of them. Mix lower and uppercase subsets. The children take turns generating a word that ends in the letter sound in front of them in order to move one square ahead on the game board. When the child says a word for a letter, the child can give the letter card back to the clinician. When children use all four of their cards, the remaning cards can be used to play additional rounds. Start over with all cards if time permits.

→ **Teaching strategies:** ***We're going to play a game where we have to think of words that end with certain letter sounds. Everyone pick four cards*** (place letter side up)***. We'll go around the table and everyone has to pick one card for each turn. You tell us a word that ends with the sound for the letter you picked.*** If a child cannot think of a word, provide a semantic cue or have the child look at a page in the picture books to help. If a child provides an incorrect response, repeat the word aloud a few times, emphasizing the final sound. ***Does ___ end with ___? I think it ends with ___.*** Or ***Does ___ end with___? No, that doesn't end with___. Say that word again and stretch the final sound.*** Or: ***Have [another child] say that word for you. Watch and see what sound her mouth makes at the end of the word.***

Provide summary feedback at the end of each child's turn. ***Sabrina had the letter L. She said that pail ends with the /l/ sound. She is right!***

ACTIVITY

Introduction to Segment Two–Phoneme Words with Continuant Phoneme Word Segmentation (10 minutes)

Materials: Two-square panels, CV, VC continuant word lists

Directions: Each child has a panel with two squares. The clinician says a CV or VC word and demonstrates segmenting the word into component sounds. The children imitate segmentation.

→ **Teaching strategies:** The clinician demonstrates segmentation of CV or VC words, and the children imitate segmentation by placing a hand on each square as each sound is produced. Expect children to have difficulty. Even imitation of correct segmentation may be difficult. Keep demonstrating until each child can imitate. Teach children to elongate production of words in order to segment sounds. After demonstration of each word, have the children then individually segment the word(s) just completed. In today's lesson, children should be expected only to imitate the clinician's model. Provide ample models. Repeated opportunities to imitate segmentation will help children catch on. Although many words are listed, the clinician will probably only practice a few of the words.

Today we are going to say each of the sounds in some words. We'll work with words that have two sounds. See how your cards have two squares, one for each sound. I'll show you. Let's start with zoo, zzzzzoooo. Zoo has two sounds. We need to figure out those two sounds and say each one. I'll put my hand on each square when I say each sound. Watch me. zoo, zzzzzooooo, zzzzz [pause] ***ooooo, zoo, /z/*** [put hand on one card] /^/ [put hand on second card]. ***Now we'll go around the table and everyone will take a turn breaking zoo into two sounds.*** If a child makes an error, model again and have the child imitate.

Session Focus: Final Sound Generation and Introduction to Segmentation

SESSION STIMULI

No pictures are needed for final sound generation activity.

CV and VC Continuant Sounds Word Lists

CV Words	VC Words
Fay	ace
fee	am
foe	an/Ann
knee	I'm
may	ice
moo	if
my	in
neigh	is
new	off
no	on
now	own
say	um
see	us
she	
shoe	
zoo	

The audio segments on the accompanying CD illustrate how to segment these words into sounds.

IMPLEMENTATION SUGGESTIONS

More on Teaching Strategies

WORD SEGMENTATION GUIDING QUESTIONS

Say the word, stretch the word, and break the word into sounds.

What are the two sounds in [word]?

- When introducing whole word segmentation in today's session, the clinician should have children imitate correct segmentation of CV and VC words. Begin with one word and practice it together and individually, with all children taking group and individual turns to segment the words into sounds. Some children will have difficulty even at this level of imitation. If a child does not segment correctly, the clinician can provide the model again or another child can provide the model again, and then that child can try again. Sometimes it will be necessary to break imitation down to a very simple level. For example: "Sammy, this is hard for you to do. Everyone can move their hands while Sammy and I are saying the sounds. Sammy, say *zoo*. Now say *zzzooo*. Now say */z/* [pause] */u/* and put your hand on the square when you say each sound. Say the sounds with me, *zzz* (touch first square), *ooo* (touch second square). Now you try with your squares." Use hand-over-hand assistance if necessary to place the child's hands on each square as the clinician says the sounds. Then have the child say the sounds while the clinician moves the child's hand. Then let the child try by himself. Keep reminding the children that they are segmenting words with two sounds. Note that there is nothing meaningful about the color of the squares. We used different colors so that we could prompt children with the colors. "When you say */z/* put your hand on the orange square, and when you say */u/* put your hand on the green square."
- After practicing one CV word, try a VC word. The research literature suggests that VC words may be easier to segment than CV words. However, the VC words are a bit more obscure than most of the CV words. Determine whether CV or VC are easier for your group of children. Likely only a few words may be practiced today. Remember, the goal is for children to be successful, not to get through a long list of words.
- After segmenting a word, model blending of the sounds so that children see segmentation and blending as reciprocal activities. "We broke *zoo* into two sounds: */z/* [pause] */u/*. Now let's put those sounds together: */z/* [pause] */u/*, *zzzzzzzooooooo*, *zoo*. Two sounds in *zoo*."
- When introducing the VC or CV word to be segmented, provide a context for the word. "We are going to figure out the two sounds in the word *am*. *Am*, like, I *am* a girl."
- We begin segmentation with continuant sounds because continuants are easier to segment than stops.

WEEK 10

OVERVIEW

Session 28 Focus: Segmentation of Continuant CV and VC Words; Introduction to Segmentation of Continuant CVC Words

Session 29 Focus: Segmentation and Blending of Continuant CV, VC, and CVC Words

Session 30 Focus: Segmentation and Blending of CV, VC, and CVC Words with Continuant and Stop Consonants

Materials Needed

- ➜ Alphabet cards (uppercase and lowercase depending on children's need for practice)
- ➜ Index cards with letters (from previous sessions)
- ➜ Two-square panels
- ➜ Three-square panels
- ➜ Game board and game pieces

The audio segments on the accompanying CD illustrate how to segment words into sounds.

Intervention Notes

Session Focus: Segmentation of Continuant CV and VC Words; Introduction to Segmentation of Continuant CVC Words

ACTIVITY

Letter Activity (5 minutes)

Materials: Alphabet cards

Directions: Take turns. Set the timer for 30 seconds for each child and have the child name as many sounds as he or she can. Shuffle the deck so letters are not in alphabetic order.

→ **Teaching strategies:** ***We are going to play a game today to see how fast you can tell us the sounds for letters. Each person gets a turn. Sue, you can go first. We'll set the timer for 30 seconds. I'll show you the letter and you tell me the sound. You'll do as many as you can in 30 seconds. If you say the right sound you get the card; I get the card if you say the wrong sound. Then we'll count how many you got. Remember that you are only saying the letter sounds.*** Review error cards at the end of each turn.

ACTIVITY

Segment Two–Phoneme Words with Continuant Phonemes

(20 minutes)

Materials: Two-square panels, CV and VC continuant word lists

Directions: Each child has a panel with two squares. The clinician demonstrates several VC and CV words. The clinician segments two phoneme words into individual sounds by placing one hand on each square as each sound is produced. Children imitate segmentation. Once children catch on, the clinician provides individual turns to children with a different word given to each child.

→ **Teaching strategies:** First have the children imitate segmentation in unison. Then have the children imitate segmentation of the same word one after the other, with more proficient children going first. If a child has difficulty, provide hand-over-hand assistance for a child to point to each square as each sound is produced. The clinician can produce the sounds and move the child's hand on the squares. The child can then imitate or segment in unison with the clinician. Repeat the modeled production of the words from elongating the word with no pause between sounds, to elongating with a pause between sounds, to barely elongating sounds but segmenting with a distinct pause between sounds.

Establish success on a small set of words with all children sequentially practicing these words. Then have individual children segment one of the words in the small set to see if individual children are retaining what they are practicing. Then when children are catching on, give them new words to segment. For less proficient children, have them repeat a word that another child has segmented. Have the more proficient child model and the less proficient child repeat. With each new word, have the individual child segment and then have the whole group repeat the segmentation in unison and/or individually.

There are no pictures for these words. It may be helpful to provide a context for each word. ***Let's segment in, like the toy is in the box. Our word is in.***

ACTIVITY

Introduction to Segment Three–Phoneme CVC Words with Continuant Phonemes

(5 minutes)

Materials: Three-square panels, words: *fish, moon, Sam*

Directions: The clinician demonstrates segmentation of three-phoneme words. The clinician and children do the words in unison. The children imitate segmentation by touching each square as each sound is produced.

Repeat the process for each of these words.

→ **Teaching strategies:** ***We've been breaking words into two sounds. Now let's do some words that have three sounds. Your new card has three squares, one for each sound. I'll say the word and then we need to figure out which sound goes with each square. I'll show you how it works.*** The clinician demonstrates and the children imitate. Touch each square as each sound is said. Teach children to elongate sounds in a word to figure out individual sounds. Produce segmentation with a pause between sounds. Children should be expected to imitate only and not perform task independently. Some children may be quite challenged by this task and should be provided with needed assistance until they catch on. Again, lots of repeated practice on a small set of words will establish children's segmentation skill.

Session Focus: Segmentation of Continuant CV and VC Words; Introduction to Segmentation of Continuant CVC Words

SESSION STIMULI

No pictures are needed for continuant sounds activity.

Continuant Sounds Word Lists

CV Words		CV words	CVC Words
Fay	new	am	fish
fee	no	an/Ann	moon
foe	now	ash	Sam
knee	ray	ace	
lay	row	I'm	
Lee	say	ice	
lie	see	if	
low	she	in	
may	shoe	is	
moo	so/sew	off	
my	zoo	on	
neigh		own	
		Oz	
		um	
		us	

IMPLEMENTATION SUGGESTIONS

More on Teaching Strategies

WORD SEGMENTATION GUIDING QUESTIONS

Say the word, stretch the word, and break the word into sounds.

What are the [number] sounds in [word]? What sounds do you hear in [word]?

- At this point in teaching word segmentation, the clinician should focus on the *sounds* in the words being segmented, rather than on the spelling or letters in the word. If children say the letter name (e.g., if they know how to spell one of these words), redirect their attention to sounds. "Oops, we are just thinking about sounds today. Tell me the sounds in *[target word]*."
- Make sure that each time children segment a word they follow the sequence of saying the word, stretching the word, and stretching the word with pauses, and then producing the individual sounds. All of the words in today's session include continuants; stretch the word to make the sounds more salient for children.
- Scaffolding strategies for segmenting words into sounds:
  - Model and have the child imitate. Provide whatever help is necessary for the child to imitate correctly.
  - Repeat segmentation of a single word until the child can segment the word easily and accurately. The clinician or another child models, and the target child repeats.
  - Prolong sounds (and ask guiding questions). "What are the sounds in *moo?* Listen carefully. I'll say one sound and touch the square, and then I'll say the other sound and touch the other square. *mmmm* [touch square and pause] *ooooo* [touch other square]. What are the sounds in *moo?* You show me."
- Common errors on CV segmentation include the following segmented productions: m-moo; moo-oo; moo-moo. When a child produces these errors, help him or her see what he or she has done correctly. "*m-moo.* Great, you got the first sound, */m/*. Now we need to find out what sound goes here (point to other square). Listen and watch while I do the sounds. */m/* [point to one square] */u/* [point to other square]. */m/* goes here, like you said. And */u/* goes here. Now you try."
- Children are familiar with identifying initial and final sounds in words. So pointing out that CV and VC words are just made up of an initial and final sound may help children find success with this task.
- For the CVC words, tell children what they are good at and what is new. "We are going to find the three sounds in *fish.* We have talked about the first sound and the last sound in *fish* before. But there are three sounds in *fish.* So we need to figure out the middle sound. Okay, I'll show you, and you do it after me." If a child segments only two sounds, /f/ and /sh/, and assigns those sounds to the first two squares, provide scaffolding to direct his or her attention to these sounds as the beginning and ending sounds. "You said *fish* has these sounds: */f/* and */ʃ/*. You are right. But we need to find one more sound. */f/* is the first sound in *fish, fffffish.* It goes on this square. Put your hand on this square. */ʃ/* is the last sound in *fishshshsh.* That sounds goes on this square. Put your other hand on this square. Now we need to find the sound for this square. Listen: *ffiiiiiiiiiiiiiiish.* What is that middle sound? */f/* [pause] *iiiiiiiiiii* [pause] */ʃ/.* Now let's try that word again."

Session Focus: Segmentation and Blending of Continuant CV, VC, and CVC Words

ACTIVITY

Letter Activity (5 minutes)

Materials: Index cards with letters

Directions: The child chooses card, names the letter, names its sound, and gives a word that begins with that sound. Have another child give a word that ends with that sound. The clinician writes the words on the cards. Do eight letter cards.

➜ **Teaching strategies:** Some letter cards will not have words that begin or end with that sound (e.g., the letter *h* for ending sound, the letter *x* for initial sounds). The clinician should skip that question for those letters.

ACTIVITY

Blend Two–Phoneme Words with Continuant Phonemes (5–10 minutes)

Materials: CV and VC continuant word list, game board and game pieces

Directions: The clinician produces slightly elongated sounds with a brief pause between the sounds, and the children blend the sounds together to form words. Children move one space on the board for each correct answer. Provide children with individual turns to respond, and then re-ask the question and have all children respond.

➜ **Teaching strategies:** Begin practice with words that were segmented in previous sessions and then move to including all words in the list.

We've been practicing taking words apart. I've said the word and then we've figured out what the sounds are in the word. Now we're going to put sounds together to make a word. I'll give you the sounds and you put the sounds together to make the word. Try this. /s/ [pause] ***/o/. sssss*** [pause] ***ooooo, ssssooooo, so.*** For some words, to provide context, ask: ***Who can use so in a sentence?*** (It makes no difference whether the child's sentence includes *so* or *sew*). If a child is unsuccessful, another child or the clinician models the blended word and the child imitates.

Make sure the children follow the steps outlined in the Blending Guide on the opposite page. Even if a child can blend without following these steps, saying each step aloud facilitates the learning of the other children in the group.

ACTIVITY

Segment Three–Phoneme CVC Words with Continuant Phonemes (15-20 minutes)

Materials: Three-square panels, CVC continuant word list

Directions: The clinician says a word. The clinician demonstrates segmentation of the word by pointing to one square on the card as each sound is produced. The clinician and children segment in unison. Each child is asked to imitate segmenting of each word. After practicing several words in imitation, children are asked to independently segment words previously segmented.

➜ **Teaching strategies:** ***We're going to figure out the sounds in words that have three sounds. First let's segment the word together, and then we'll take turns practicing.*** If a child is unsuccessful, give another demonstration by the clinician/another child. Move from elongation of the sounds in the word, to elongating with a slight pause between sounds, to only slight elongation of the word but longer pauses between sounds, to no elongation but distinct pauses between each sound.

Practice a small set of words until children are proficient. As individual children catch on, give them a new word to segment. For children who are not catching on, have them repeat a word already practiced or have them imitate a word segmented by another child. For all words, follow individual child segmentation with group segmentation in unison.

At the close of practice on each word, the clinician can model sound segments and demonstrate blending to re-form the word.

ACTIVITY

Review Initial Sounds and Final Sounds Embedded in Letter Activity

➜ See Letter Activity above.

Session Focus: Segmentation and Blending of Continuant CV, VC, and CVC Words

SESSION STIMULI

No pictures are needed for continuant sounds activites.

Continuant Sounds Word Lists

CV Continuants

Fay	new
fee	no
foe	now
knee	ray
lay	row
Lee	say
lie	see
low	she
may	shoe
moo	so/sew
my	zoo
neigh	

VC Continuants

ash	is
ace	oath
am	off
an/Ann	on
I'm	own
ice	Oz
if	um
in	us

CVC Continuants

face	nose
fan	nun/none
fang	race
fell	ring
fin	rose
fish	run
fun	Sam
ham	save
lace	share
leaf	shine
leash	sing
mice	soon
mom	sun
moon	van
moose	vase
mouse	vine

IMPLEMENTATION SUGGESTIONS

More on Teaching Strategies

- For most children, blending seems to be easier than segmenting. Thus, in this program, activities provide more practice on segmentation than blending. But both are important skills, and it seems important that children recognize the reciprocal nature of blending and segmenting. So activities focus on blending and segmenting the same words so that children have opportunities to put sounds together to form words and to break words apart into sounds.
- On CVC segmentation, some common errors include the following:
  - Segmenting the first and last sound, but not the middle sound. So for *moon,* the child says /m/ [pause] /n/, pointing to the first two squares in the three-panel square. For this error, the clinician needs to draw the child's attention to the fact that he or she has segmented the first and last sound but still needs to figure out the middle sound. "The */m/* sound is the first sound. It goes with this square (point to first square). */n/* is the last sound; it goes with this square (point to third square). We need to figure out this sound (point to middle square). You hold your hands on these two squares, the first and the last one. I'll say the word again, and I'll point to the middle square when I say the sound in the middle. You tell me what sound you hear me saying." The clinician then says the word and stretches the vowel sound to make it very salient. While producing the vowel sound, the clinician can point to the middle square, stop producing the vowel sound, and ask the child, "What sound am I making?" and then continue to make the sound until the child repeats it.
  - Segmenting only the first sound and then repeating the word (e.g., */m/, moon*). "Great, you got the first sound. It goes here (point to the first square). We have to figure out the other two sounds. Let's stretch the word and see if we can figure out the last sound." Have the child say and stretch the word, alone and in unison. "What is the last sound?" Then proceed with the scaffolding explained in the bulleted point above.
  - Segmenting a word into onset-rime (e.g., *m* [pause] *oon*). "Great, you said the first sound. Now we need to break the rest of the word into two sounds. Remember, *moon* has three sounds all together." Provide guidance to segment the rime into two sounds.
  - Stretching the word and sliding fingers across the squares without producing discrete sound segments. "You did a good job stretching that word. Now let's see if you can say each sound in that word. You have to break the word into sounds. Listen to the way I do it. Say each sound alone. *mmmoooonnnn. mmm -oooo -nnnn.* /m/ [pause] */u/* [pause] /n/. Now you do it."

BLENDING GUIDE

Say the sounds. Stretch the sounds with a pause between sounds.

Stretch the sounds with no pause. Say the word.

Session Focus: Segmentation and Blending of Continuant CV, VC, and CVC Words; Introduction to Segmentation of Stop CV and VC Words

ACTIVITY

Letter Activity (5 minutes)

Materials: Index cards with letters

Directions: Complete previous session's activity with eight more letters.

→ **Teaching strategies:** For teaching strategies, see Session 29.

ACTIVITY

Word Segmentation
(15–20 minutes)

Materials: CV, VC, CVC continuant word lists, two- and three-square panels

Directions: The clinician says a word in typical fashion, and a child repeats the word. The clinician then presents the word by stretching out the sounds and the child imitates. The child is asked to choose the two-square or three-square panel depending on how many sounds he or she thinks is in the word. Using the panel, the child segments the word into sounds, touching one square as each sound is produced.

→ **Teaching strategies:** ***We're going to use these squares to segment the words today. You have to decide how many sounds are in the word I give you. I'll do some first. My word is now. I think now has two sounds. So I need this panel with two squares.*** Demonstrate a couple of words with the panels.

Does your word have two sounds or three sounds? If a child chooses the wrong panel, initially correct the child. Later help the child to discover through trial and error that he or she has chosen the wrong panel.

Have an individual child segment a word and then have the group segment the same word. Make sure each time that children say the word, stretch the word, and then segment the word, as has been demonstrated previously.

Ask other children to blend the word the child has segmented. ***She said: /n/*** [pause] ***/au/. Put those sounds together and tell me the word.***

ACTIVITY

Segment Two–Phoneme Words with Stop Phonemes (5–10 minutes)

Materials: Two-square panels, CV and VC stop word lists

Directions: The clinician demonstrates and children imitate each stimulus in unison, and then each child has an individual turn to imitate. After practicing several words, children can be asked to segment each word independently, randomly choosing one of the words already practiced.

→ **Teaching strategies:** The teaching sequence is similar to that used when stimuli included continuant phonemes. Because words include stop consonants, only the vowel can be elongated. Stop consonant sounds need to be iterated (i.e., repeat sound segment: /k/ /k/ /k/ *key*). Be sure to minimize release of /k/; don't say *"kuh" "kuh" "kuh" "key"*, but instead use a short schwa vowel. Teach children to iterate sounds. Demonstrate a word and then have children practice the word in unison and in sequence. With stops, VC words may be easier than CV words. Try a few of each to see which children find easier. Provide repeated practice on a small set of words to establish the skill of segmenting stop sounds. Present words in sentence context as done previously.

We've been segmenting words that we could stretch. Now we are going to segment some words that have sounds that can't be stretched. We'll have to bounce some of the sounds. Let's do ate. aaat-t-t. aaaaa [pause] ***t-t-t. I'll show you how to segment it. We'll do it together, and then everyone gets a turn. Then we'll try another word.***

Given the practice children have had with continuant words, skill should generalize to stop sound words with minimal scaffolding. Continue to provide sufficient scaffolding so that children are successful in segmenting words.

Session Focus: Segmentation and Blending of Continuant CV, VC, and CVC Words; Introduction to Segmentation of Stop CV and VC Words

SESSION STIMULI

No pictures are needed for continuant sounds and stop sounds activities.

Continuant Sounds Word Lists

CV Continuants

Fay, fee, foe, knee, lay, Lee, lie, low, may, moo, my, neigh, new, no, now, ray, row, say, see, she, shoe, so/sew, zoo

VC Continuants

ash, ace, am, an/Ann, I'm, ice, if, in, is, oath, off, on, own, Oz, um, us

CVC Continuants

face, fan, fang, fell, fin, fish, fun, ham, lace, leaf, leash, mice, mom, moon, moose, mouse, nose, nun/none, race, ring, rose, run, Sam, save, share, shine, sing, soon, sun, van, vase, vine

Stop Sounds Word Lists

CV Stops

boy, cow, day, go, key, paw, pay, pie, tie, two

VC Stops

add, ape, at, ate, eat, egg, odd, out

IMPLEMENTATION SUGGESTIONS

More on Teaching Strategies

- Guide children each time they are segmenting a word to say the word, say the word stretching or bouncing the sounds, and say the sounds in the word. After the child segments the word, the clinician can provide summative feedback by reproducing sounds and repeating the whole word again.
- There is nothing special about the word panels. Other programs use blocks and have the children move the blocks when saying each sound. We opted to use panels and have children move their hand or their finger to mark each sound to minimize the amount of materials in front of each child. Clinicians can use blocks if this works better.
- In these early segmentation and blending activities, we do not use pictures. There are few CV and VC words that can be pictured. We also eliminated pictures to simplify the learning context. We have not found children to have difficulty remembering the words in these activities, probably because there is so much repetition of the words.
- Remember that child success is more important than getting through all words in a list. Choose words at random; the words are listed in alphabetical order for ease of presentation.

WEEK 11

OVERVIEW

Session 31 Focus: Segmentation (Stops) and Blending (Continuants): CVC

Session 32 Focus: Segmentation of CV, VC, and CVC Words (Stops and Continuants)

Session 33 Focus: Segmentation and Blending (Stops and Continuants)

Materials Needed

- ➜ Index cards with letters
- ➜ Game board and game pieces
- ➜ Barrier
- ➜ Three-square panels
- ➜ Individual Sound Boxes
- ➜ Sound Segmenting Cards in individual envelopes

Intervention Notes

Session Focus: Segmentation (Stops) and Blending (Continuants): CVC

ACTIVITY

Letter Activity (5 minutes)

Materials: Index cards with letters

Directions: Complete previous session's activity with eight more sounds to complete the alphabet.

➔ **Teaching strategies:** For teaching strategies, see Session 30.

ACTIVITY

Word Blending: CVC Words with Continuants
(10 minutes)

Materials: CVC continuant word list, game board and game pieces

Directions: Using the word list, the clinician provides isolated phonemes with pauses in between phonemes and asks a child to blend sounds to form words. The child provides a response and moves forward one space on the board.

➔ **Teaching strategies:** ***I'm going to say three sounds and I want you to put the sounds together and figure out the word. I'll do the first one. /m/*** [pause] ***/u/*** [pause] ***/n/. What is the word?*** If children have difficulty, the clinician should model by saying the sounds without elongation but pause between each sound, then with elongation with a pause between sounds, then with elongation with a slight pause between sounds, then elongation with no pause between sounds, and then produce the word.

Make sure, when producing the word, that children blend and say the word with typical prosody. If the child produces the word without typical prosody, the clinician should model the appropriate prosody. Perform the task by speaking in unison with the child. Repeat until the child is able to produce the word with elongated phonemes and then with typical prosody/duration.

ACTIVITY

Word Segmentation: CVC Words with Stops (15 minutes)

Materials: CVC stop word list, three-square panels

Directions: The clinician demonstrates segmentation and the children imitate in unison. Point to individual squares in sequence when producing individual sounds.

➔ **Teaching strategies:** ***We're going to figure out the sounds in words that have three sounds. First let's do the word together and then we'll take turns practicing.*** As done before, begin repeating a small set of words and then include other words as children demonstrate success.

Demonstrate iteration of the stop sounds with the vowel sound elongated. The clinician demonstrates and children imitate. Point to each square while producing each phoneme. Each child imitates each word. If a child has difficulty, return to the clinician model and then ask the child to imitate. Children who have the greatest difficulty can go last after having the opportunity to observe the word segmented by several other children. The clinician can orally segment the word while a child points to each box as each sound is produced. Provide hand-over-hand assistance to the child in pointing to boxes, if needed, having the child repeat each sound as the clinician moves the child's finger to point to each square.

ACTIVITY

Review Initial Sounds and Final Sounds Embedded in Letter Activity

➔ See Letter Activity above.

Session Focus: Segmentation (Stops) and Blending (Continuants): CVC

SESSION STIMULI

No pictures are needed for segmentation and blending activities.

Continuant Sounds Word Lists

CVC Words

face	mice	Sam
fan	mom	save
fang	moon	share
fell	moose	shine
fin	mouse	sing
fish	nose	soon
fun	nun/none	sun
ham	race	van
lace	ring	vase
leaf	rose	vine
leash	run	

Stop Sounds Word Lists

CVC Words

bed	gate
boat	goat
book	jug
cake	kite
cat	pig
coat	tack
dog	top
duck	

IMPLEMENTATION SUGGESTIONS

More on Teaching Strategies

- Blending strategies:
    - Demonstrate blending: Produce sounds with pauses, produce elongated sounds with pauses, produce elongated sounds with no pauses, and produce the word.
    - Vary presentation format based on child's proficiency. Use short pauses with children who are having difficulty blending and longer pauses for children who are successful at blending.
    - Provide the sounds and then give choices of which word is being presented. For children having great difficulty, make the foil very different from the target: "What word? Is it *sun* or *cat?*" For children having some difficulty, make the foil similar to the target: "What word? Is it *sun* or *some?*"
- Segmenting words with stop sounds may be more difficult for some children than continuant sound words were. Provide the support necessary for children to be successful. Again, lots of repetition should be provided.
- Always have children proceed through the steps of saying the word, stretching/iterating the word, and then segmenting the word into sounds. Doing each step with each word supports the learning of all the children in the group.

WEEK 11 ➔ SESSION 32

Session Focus: Segmentation of CV, VC, and CVC Words (Stops and Continuants)

ACTIVITY

Letter Activity (5 minutes)

Materials: Alphabet cards

Directions: Take turns. Set the timer for 30 seconds for each child and have the child name as many sounds as he or she can. Shuffle the deck so letters are not in alphabetic order.

➔ **Teaching strategies:** For teaching strategies, see Session 28

ACTIVITY

Word Segmentation: CV, VC, CVC Words with Stops or Continuants

(25 minutes)

Materials: Individual Sound Boxes

Directions: Initially all children should have a set of Individual Sound Boxes. The clinician demonstrates segmentation of a word and children imitate in unison. Point to individual squares in sequence when producing individual sounds. After practicing the sound boxes, place one set in the center of the table. Have the children take turns choosing one and completing segmentation.

➔ **Teaching strategies:** The clinician demonstrates and the children imitate. Point to each square while producing each sound. First, children segment words in unison. Then children can also take turns in sequence, segmenting the same word. If a child has difficulty, the clinician demonstrates and the child imitates again. Or perhaps have two children segment in unison. Children who have the greatest difficulty can go last after having the opportunity to observe the word segmented by several other children. Clinician can orally segment a word while a child points to each box as a sound is produced; then the child tries to do it alone. Provide hand-over-hand assistance as needed. CV and VC may be easier than CVC. Words with continuants may be easier than stops.

For the last 10 minutes, place one set of Individual Sound Boxes in the center of the table and have children take turns picking pictures and segmenting words. When one set is placed in the center of the table, assist children having difficulty initially to choose words with continuants. Have children having difficulty imitate segmentation of a word that another child has just segmented. Or have the child segment a word that another child practiced in a previous turn.

It is not necessary to get through all of the pictures but rather the focus should be on child learning and success.

Each word should be said, stretched/iterated, and then segmented. Include all steps for all children and all words.

ACTIVITY

Review Initial Sounds and Final Sounds Embedded in Letter Activity

➔ See Letter Activity above.

Session Focus: Segmentation of CV, VC, and CVC Words (Stops and Continuants)

SESSION STIMULI

Individual Sound Boxes

CV and VC Words

Stops	Continuants
ape	knee
bee	mow
bow	see
boy	sew
cow	shoe
egg	show
pie	
tie	
toe	
two	

CVC Words

Stops	Continuants
bed	face
bike	fan
boat	fin
book	fish
cake	mail
cat	moon
coat	moose
dog	mouse
duck	nose
gate	rose
kite	run
pig	shell
tack	sun
top	van
	vine

IMPLEMENTATION SUGGESTIONS

More on Teaching Strategies

- Taking note of the errors children make will provide a good basis on which to plan for subsequent sessions. The same types of errors are observed across children.

Session Focus: Segmentation and Blending (Stops and Continuants)

ACTIVITY

Letter Activity (5 minutes)

Materials: Alphabet cards

Directions: Take turns. Set the timer for 30 seconds for each child and have the child name as many sounds as he or she can. Shuffle the deck so letters are not in alphabetic order.

➔ **Teaching strategies:** For teaching strategies, see Session 28.

ACTIVITY

Word Blending (10 minutes)

Materials: Sound Segmenting Cards

Directions: Spread the picture pieces on the table (picture side down). The clinician says individual phonemes of word. One child blends the sounds together to identify the word and then flips the picture pieces over and puts them together as a means to check the accuracy of his or her response.

➔ **Teaching strategies:** Have children raise their hands; allow more proficient children to respond first and thus provide models for less proficient children. If children discover after putting together the picture pieces that the response is incorrect, provide the individual sounds again, and engage children in blending the sounds together. If a child provides an incorrect response, ask other children for agreement. Have the target child turn over one picture piece to use as a cue and re-present the sound segments in the word.

ACTIVITY

Word Segmentation (20 minutes)

Materials: Sound Segmenting Cards, barrier for child to work behind, envelopes

Directions: Place picture pieces in individual envelopes for children to choose. Each child chooses an envelope and takes the pieces out. The child then identifies the number of sounds in the word, based on the number of pieces, and then provides the group with the individual sounds in the word. Another child is chosen to receive the "message" to "decode" the word being sent.

➔ **Teaching strategies:** Guide children through the steps of the activity. ***Everyone is going to have a chance to be the teacher. When you're the teacher you get to sit behind this barrier.*** [child's name], ***choose one of the envelopes and put your picture together. Tell the group how many sounds are in the word you have. The number of picture pieces is the same as the number of sounds in the word. Now say the word to yourself. Don't say it out loud. We want to guess. Say the word to yourself and then tell us the sounds in the word. Can you call on someone to guess the word?***

If a child has difficulty segmenting, the clinician can first guide the child to identify the initial and final sound and then the remaining sound.

Children can be the "teacher" in pairs, pairing a less proficient child with a more proficient child.

ACTIVITY

Review Rhyme During Word Segmentation

Materials: None

Directions: The child generates a rhyming word for the word segmented.

➔ **Teaching strategies:** After the child has segmented a word into sounds, the clinician represents the word (game in the following example) and asks for a rhyme. ***Okay, now that we figured out the sounds in game, tell me a word that rhymes with game. You are right, tame rhymes with game. Can someone tell me the sounds in tame? The sounds in tame will be almost the same as the sounds in game.***

Session Focus: Segmentation and Blending (Stops and Continuants)

SESSION STIMULI

Sound Segmenting Cards

Two Pieces	Three Pieces
ape	cake
egg	cheese
key	fish
shoe	game
	knees
	log
	man
	mop
	thief
	toes
	witch

IMPLEMENTATION SUGGESTIONS

More on Teaching Strategies

- In the word-blending task, continue to use shorter pauses between sounds if a group is having difficulty blending a given word. If there are some students who are able to blend sounds with longer pauses, allow them to answer first, and less confident students can answer later in the activity. Blending seems to be easier with shorter pauses.
- If, during the word-blending task, a student provides an incorrect response, try counting the pieces on the table versus the number of sounds in the word the student provided or allow him or her to flip over the puzzle pieces and put the puzzle together. "Mary says */g/ /ɑ/ /m/* makes *going*. Before we turn over the pieces, let's count the sounds in *going, /g/ /o/ /I/ /ŋ/*, holding up one finger for each sound. I count four sounds, but I only see three pieces. There's something not right here. Let's try putting the first two sounds together: */g/ /ɑ/, /g/ /ɑ/*, that makes */gɑ/*. Now you add */m/, /gɑ/ /m/*. Put those sounds together. Let's say it together. *Game!* Let's turn over the pieces and see."
- During the word segmentation task, struggling students may want to work with a partner when it's their turn to be the "teacher." Have the two students consult quietly together to determine the sounds in the word before presenting them to the rest of the group. What is most important is that children are successful in segmenting. It may be necessary to violate the game rules (e.g., have child-teacher say word, then stretch/bounce sounds, then isolate sounds).

WEEK 12

OVERVIEW

Session 34 Focus: Segmentation, Including Words with Blends

Session 35 Focus: Segmentation, Including Words with Blends

Session 36 Focus: Segmentation and Blending

Materials Needed

- ➜ Index cards with letters
- ➜ Alphabet cards (lowercase or uppercase depending on children's need for practice)
- ➜ Blocks
- ➜ Barrier
- ➜ Three-square panels
- ➜ Four-square panels
- ➜ Individual Sound Boxes
- ➜ Sound Segmenting Cards

Intervention Notes

Session Focus: Segmentation, Including Words with Blends

ACTIVITY

Letter Activity (5 minutes)

Materials: Index cards with letters

Directions: Each child chooses a card, names the letter and sound, and asks another child "Tell me a word that begins with the ___ sound." Then the clinician gives a word that ends with the sound.

➜ **Teaching strategies:** The clinician should occasionally give a wrong answer. If children don't catch the wrong answer, clinician may need to prompt, "I don't know if my answer is correct."

ACTIVITY

Word Segmentation: Two- and Three-Sound Words (CV, VC, CVC)

(10 minutes)

Materials: Individual Sound Boxes

Directions: A child chooses a picture from the pile, says the word, and segments the word, pointing to a box for each sound in the word.

➜ **Teaching strategies:** Mix cards up so that children randomly select the different types of word stimuli. Place one set of the individual sound box pictures in the middle of the table. Individual children select a picture and then segment the word. A child then passes the picture card to another child and asks that child to segment the word again. Provide support and scaffolding when children have difficulty.

ACTIVITY

Word Segmentation: Blends–CCV, VCC, CCVC Words (15 minutes)

Materials: Three-square panels, four-square panels, Blend Words List

Words to use: See opposite page

Directions: The clinician tells the children how many sounds are in a word. The clinician says the word and elongates or iterates sounds as appropriate. The clinician models segmentation of the word and the children then imitate, one at a time. Point to each square as a sound is produced.

➜ **Teaching strategies:** ***Today we are going to do some more work on breaking words into sounds. These words may be a little more difficult than some of the other words we have done. But we'll do them together. We won't have pictures for these words. Okay, let's start with fly. Fly has three sounds. So pick the three-square panel. Let's figure out the three sounds in fly. I'll do this one first, and then you do it together after me. And then we'll take turns.***

If children have difficulty repeating the clinician's model, assist the child in identifying the initial and final sounds, showing the child which squares correspond to those sounds. Then model the word again, using iteration and elongation to bring the child's attention to the remaining sounds. If a child has difficulty, a model will again be given for the child to imitate. Have the children identify the initial and final sounds and then middle sound(s), as needed. Practice an individual word several times before moving on to the next word. Having some success with segmenting blends is more important than completing all of the words.

The words are presented in columns on the opposite page in the hypothesized order of difficulty. Words with final nasal blends are very difficult, and children may have limited success, even in imitation of segmentation.

Session Focus: Segmentation, Including Words with Blends

SESSION STIMULI

Individual Sound Boxes

CV and VC Words

Stops	Continuants
ape	knee
bee	mow
bow	see
boy	sew
cow	shoe
egg	show
pie	
tie	
toe	
two	

CVC Words

Stops		Continuants	
bed	dog	face	
bike	duck	fan	nose
boat	gate	fin	rose
book	kite	fish	run
cake	pig	mail	shell
cat	tack	moon	sun
coat	top	moose	van
		mouse	vine

Blend Words List

fly	sky	ask
block	spoon	fist
play	snow	dust
glass	stone	mask
	slide	ox

IMPLEMENTATION SUGGESTIONS

Choosing Stimuli

The words for blend segmentation are arranged in columns in the hypothesized order of difficulty. Remember that success is more important than getting through all the words. Initial blends are easier than final blends.

WORD SEGMENTATION GUIDING QUESTIONS

Say the word. Stretch or bounce the sounds. Break the word into sounds.

More on Teaching Strategies

- If children are having little difficulty on the VC, CV, and CVC words, spend more time on second activity, words with blends.
- Segmentation of words with blends proves to be much more difficult for children than segmenting words without blends. Pulling apart two consonants is more difficult than separating a V-C combination. Thus we provide explicit practice on blend words rather than assuming the segmentation of VC, CV, and CVC will generalize to words with blends. Typical errors are omission of the inner sound; for example, leaving out the /k/ in segmenting *sky* or leaving out the /s/ in segmenting *fist*. The goal for today is success, and so lots of repetition is suggested. Success is more important than practicing all the blend combinations. Final nasal blends (e.g., *jump, land*) are the most difficult blends for children to segment. Thus, here we practice with other blends and introduce and practice nasal blends in Sessions 35 and 36.
- As when segmentation was started, begin with imitation and then give children a chance for individual turns. When all sounds are not segmented, show the child where the sounds belong on the sound panel and repeat the word by elongating/bouncing sounds to help the child figure out the omitted sound(s).

WEEK 12 → SESSION 35

Session Focus: Segmentation, Including Words with Blends

ACTIVITY

Letter Activity (5 minutes)

Materials: Alphabet cards

Directions: As a group, children will name the letter shown by the clinician and provide its sound. The group will use the carrier phrase, *This is ___ and ___ says ___.*

→ **Teaching strategies:** This task should present no difficulties to children. Challenge the group to see how quickly all letters names and sounds can be provided.

ACTIVITY

Word Segmentation (15 minutes)

Materials: Blocks, Individual Sound Boxes Word List

Directions: The clinician says a word from the list of words for Initial Sound Boxes (opposite page). The child chooses a number of blocks and segments the word into sounds.

→ **Teaching strategies:** The individual sound box pictures will not be used so that children have to figure out how many sounds are in the word on their own.

We are going to segment words into sounds again today. But you have to figure out how many sounds are in the word before you can figure out the sounds. Let me show you with the first word. I need to figure out the sounds in fish. fish, ffffiiiiishshsh. How many sounds are in fish? I think there are three sounds in fish. So I am going to take three blocks. Line up three blocks in front of self. ***Now I have to figure out the three sounds: /f/, /i/, /ʃ/.*** Say each sound as one block is moved for each sound. Demonstrate again with a word with all stop sounds (e.g., *coat*).

When children choose the wrong number of blocks, let them try to segment the word and figure out that they have the wrong number of blocks. Provide guidance as needed.

ACTIVITY

Segmentation: Word Blends–CCV, VCC, CCVC Words (10 minutes)

Materials: Three-square panels, four-square panels, Blend Words List

Directions: The clinician tells children how many sounds are in a word. The clinician says the word and elongates or iterates sounds as appropriate. The clinician models segmentation of the word and the children then imitate, one at a time. Point to each square as a sound is produced.

Practice segmenting words in the order of the words presented above. Clinician tells children which panel to use.

→ **Teaching strategies:** Continue with this activity from the last session. Begin with a few words practiced in the previous session. Then focus on new words. Continue with repeated modeling and imitation. As children are successful in imitation, then provide individual turns with children segmenting words without the preceding model.

We have been practicing these words together. Now I am going to let you do them alone. We'll take turns breaking words into sounds. Joshua, you can go first. Show me the sounds in fly. Great, you did a good job. Now everyone show me the sounds in fly, just like Joshua did. Sophie, you can do the next word. Show me the sounds in snow. Great, you did it perfectly: /s/ /n/ /o/. Those are the three sounds in snow. Now everyone do it together.

For the children who are successful segmenting words with blends, provide the opportunity to segment final nasal blend words (*ant, land, jump*).

For children who are struggling with the blend words, skip the final nasal blend words.

Children may benefit from explicit cueing about blends. These words have two consonant sounds next to each other. Pay attention to your mouth and break the two consonants apart at the beginning of fly.

Session Focus: Segmentation, Including Words with Blends

SESSION STIMULI

Individual Sound Boxes Word Lists

CV and VC Words

Stops	Continuants
ape	knee
bee	mow
bow	see
boy	sew
cow	shoe
egg	show
pie	
tie	
tow	
two	

CVC Words

Stops		Continuants	
bed	dog	face	nose
bike	duck	fan	rose
boat	gate	fin	run
book	kite	fish	shell
cake	pig	mail	sun
cat	tack	moon	van
coat	top	moose	vine
		mouse	

Blend Words List

fly	sky	ask	land
block	spoon	fist	ant
play	snow	dust	jump
glass	stone	mask	
	slide	ox	

IMPLEMENTATION SUGGESTIONS

Choosing Stimuli

- Words with L-blends (e.g., fly, block) may be easier than other blends. Homorganic blends /sn/ may be more difficult than non-homorganic blends /sk/. The two sounds in homorganic blends have the same articulatory placement.

More on Teaching Strategies

- Call children's attention to the changes in articulatory position of sounds as they produce the two sounds in the blend.

WORD SEGMENTATION GUIDING QUESTIONS

Say the word, stretch the word, and break the word into sounds.

What are the [number] sounds in [word]? What sounds do you hear in [word]?

Session Focus: Segmentation and Blending

ACTIVITY

Letter Activity (5 minutes)

Materials: Alphabet cards

Directions: As a group, the children will name the letter shown by the the clinician and provide a word that begins with that sound.

➜ **Teaching strategies:** Challenge children by making each response a race between two children. ***Okay, this round it's Mary versus Tom. Are you ready, contestants? Here is your letter. Great, Mary knows it's G. Now, which of you can name a word that starts with a /g/ sound? Go!***

ACTIVITY

Word Segmentation/ Blending (10 minutes)

Materials: Sound Segmenting Cards, barrier

Directions: Each child has an envelope containing the pieces of their picture and takes turns being the teacher. The child puts the pieces together to determine the word, then provides the segmented phonemes for the group. The group will blend the sounds to form the word.

➜ **Teaching strategies:** Have children work in pairs to segment the word. Have children say the word to themselves and then provide segmented phonemes out loud. If a child has trouble, assist in identifying the initial and final sounds first.

ACTIVITY

Word Segmentation (15 minutes)

Materials: Blocks, Segmentation Word List

Directions: Children are asked today to segment words that they have not practiced segmenting before. The clinician will say a word for a child. The child will say the word, say the word with the sounds elongated/iterated, and then choose the number of blocks. Then the child will produce the isolated sounds. Individual turns will be followed by group turns.

➜ **Teaching strategies:** The list of words to be segmented in this session include verbs, adjectives, and less picturable nouns to assure that they are words the children have not practiced segmenting in previous sessions. Child performance and need for scaffolding in today's session will provide a good indication of the child's level of proficiency in segmenting words of various types (syllable structure, types of sounds).

Today we are going to break a lot of new words into sounds. We don't have pictures. So everyone will need to listen carefully to remember the words. I want everyone to watch closely as your friends figure out the sounds in words, because you will get a chance to break that word into sounds after your friend breaks the word apart.

The words today require children independently to determine the number of sounds in the word. If children ask for the wrong number of blocks, allow them to try to segment the word with the number of blocks they have chosen. This allows them to discover their own errors. Orally problem solve with the child to then arrive at the correct number of sounds. If someone thinks a word was segmented incorrectly, have him or her segment the word out loud. Allow children to make mistakes in segmenting the word as well as make mistakes in checking the accuracy of the other children's responses. Children then can be engaged in a problem-solving task to decipher the correct response.

ACTIVITY

Review Initial Sounds Embedded in Letter Activity

➜ See Letter Activity above.

SESSION STIMULI

Sound Segmenting Cards

No pictures are needed for segmentation activity.

Two Pieces	**Three Pieces**
ape	cake
egg	cheese
shoe	fish
key	game
	knees
	log
	man
	mop
	thief
	toes
	witch

Segmentation Word List

CVC Words	**Words with Blends**
huge	pink
bake	roast
dive	best
fight	fresh
talk	skip
leap	east
thin	blow
mean	climb
move	float
name	swim
noise	bent
pain	drink
sing	twist
fudge	stamp

IMPLEMENTATION SUGGESTIONS

Choosing Stimuli

The words for the second segmentation activity vary greatly in difficulty. Clinicians should select words for individual children based on their past performance. The varied list provides the clinician the opportunity to challenge children who have more skill and to observe the range of ability across the children in the group. If a child is not successful with a word given, the clinician can substitute an easier word. *"Oops, that word is really hard. Let's try a different word."*

More on Teaching Strategies

- Having the child choose the number of blocks provides the child an opportunity to problem solve. If the child chooses the wrong number of blocks, guide the child to figure out his error only after trying to segment. "You chose four blocks for bake, but you don't seem to be finding four sounds. Maybe you should have chosen three blocks."

References

Adams, M., Foorman, B., Lundberg, I., & Beeler, T. (1998). *Phonemic awareness in young children: A classroom curriculum.* Baltimore: Paul H. Brookes Publishing Co.

Al Otaiba, S., & Fuchs, D. (2002). Characteristics of children who are unresponsive to early literacy intervention: A review of the literature. *Remedial and Special Education, 23,* 300–316.

American Speech-Language-Hearing Association. (2002). *Knowledge and skills needed by speech-language pathologists with respect to reading and writing in children and adolescents [Knowledge and Skills].* Retrieved March 2014 from www. asha.org/policy

Anthony, J., & Lonigan, C. (2004). The nature of phonological awareness: Converging evidence from four studies of preschool and early grade school children. *Journal of Educational Psychology, 96,* 43–55.

Anthony, J., Lonigan, C., Burgess, S., Driscoll, K., Phillips, B., & Cantor, B. (2002). Structure of preschool phonological sensitivity: Overlapping sensitivity to rhyme, words, syllables, and phonemes. *Journal of Experimental Child Psychology, 82,* 65–92.

Anthony, J., Lonigan, C., Driscoll, K., Phillips, B., & Burgess, S. (2003). Phonological sensitivity: A quasi-parallel progression of word structure units and cognitive operation. *Reading Research Quarterly, 38*, 470–487.

Aram, D., Ekelman, B., & Nation, J. (1984). Preschoolers with language disorders: 10 years later. *Journal of Speech and Hearing Research, 27,* 232–244.

Aram, D., & Nation, J. (1980). Preschool language disorders and subsequent language and academic difficulties. *Journal of Communication Disorders, 13,* 159–179.

Ball, E., & Blachman, B. (1988). Phoneme segmentation training: Effect on reading readiness. *Annals of Dyslexia, 38,* 208–225.

Ball, E., & Blachman, B. (1991). Does phoneme awareness training in kindergarten make a difference in early word recognition and developmental spelling? *Reading Research Quarterly, 26,* 49–66.

Blachman, B., Ball, E., Black, R., & Tangel, D. (2000). *Road to the code: A phonological awareness program for young children.* Baltimore: Paul H. Brookes Publishing Co.

Boudreau, D., & Hedberg, N. (1999). A comparison of early literacy skills in children with specific language impairment and their typically developing peers. *American Journal of Speech-Language Pathology, 8,* 249–260.

Bradley, L., & Bryant, P. (1983). Categorizing sounds and learning to read: A causal connection. *Nature, 301*, 419-421.

Bus, A., & Van IJzendoorn, M. (1999). Phonological awareness and early reading: A meta-analysis of experimental training studies. *Journal of Educational Psychology, 91,* 403–414.

Catts, H. (1993). The relationship between speech-language impairments and reading disabilities. *Journal of Speech and Hearing Research, 36,* 948–958.

Catts, H., Adlof, S., Hogan, T., & Ellis Weismer, S. (2005). Are specific language impairment and dyslexia distinct disorders? *Journal of Speech, Language, and Hearing Research, 48,* 1378–1396.

Catts, H., Fey, M., Tomblin, J.B., & Zhang, X. (2002). A longitudinal investigation of reading outcomes in children with language impairments. *Journal of Speech, Language, and Hearing Research, 45,* 1142–1157.

Catts, H., Fey, M., Zhang, X., & Tomblin, J.B. (2001). Estimating the risk of future reading difficulties in kindergarten children: A research-based model and its clinical implementation. *Language, Speech, and Hearing Services in Schools, 32,* 38–50.

Catts, H., & Kamhi, A. (1986). The linguistic basis of reading disorders: Implications for the speech-language pathologist. *Language, Speech, and Hearing Services in Schools, 17,* 329–341.

Catts, H., & Vartiainen, T. (1993). *Sounds abound: Listening, rhyming, and reading.* Moline, IL: LinguiSystems.

Dayton, N., & Schuele, C.M. (1997, November). *Effects of phonological awareness training on young children with specific language impairment.* Paper presented at the annual convention of the American Speech-Language-Hearing Association, Boston.

Ehri, L., Nunes, S., Willows, D., Schuster, B., Yaghoub-Zadeh, Z., & Shanahan, T. (2001). Phonemic awareness instruction helps children learn to read: Evidence from the National Reading Panel's meta-analysis. *Reading Research Quarterly, 36,* 250–287.

Ericson, L., & Juliebo, M. (1998). *The phonological awareness handbook for kindergarten and primary teachers.* Newark, DE: International Reading Association.

Foorman, B., Francis, D., Fletcher, J., Schatschneider, C., & Mehta, P. (1998). The role of instruction in learning to read: Preventing reading failure in at-risk children. *Journal of Educational Psychology, 90,* 37–55.

Francis, D., Shaywitz, S., Stuebing, K., Shaywitz, B., & Fletcher, J. (1996). Developmental lag versus deficit models of reading disability: A longitudinal, individual growth curves analysis. *Journal of Educational Psychology, 88,* 3–17.

Fuchs, D., & Fuchs, L. (2006). Introduction to Response to Intervention: What, why, and how valid is it? *Reading Research Quarterly, 41,* 93–99. doi: 10.1598/RRQ.41.1.4

Fuchs, D., Fuchs, L., & Vaughn, S. (2008). *Response to intervention: A framework for reading educators.* Newark, DE: International Reading Association.

Gillon, G. (2004). *Phonological awareness: From research to practice.* New York: Guilford Press.

Hall, P., & Tomblin, J.B. (1978). A follow-up study of children with articulation and language disorders. *Journal of Speech and Hearing Disorders, 43,* 227–241.

Hoover, W., & Gough, P. (1990). The simple view of reading. *Reading and Writing: An Interdisciplinary Journal, 2,* 127–160.

Individuals with Disabilities Education Improvement Act (IDEA) of 2004, PL 108-446, 20 U.S.C. §§ 1400 *et seq.*

International Reading Association. (1998). *Position statement: Phonemic awareness and the teaching of reading.* Newark, DE: Author. Retrieved from www.reading.org

International Reading Association. (2000). *Teaching all children to read: The roles of the reading specialist—A position statement of the International Reading Association.* Newark, DE: Author.

Juel, C. (1996). What makes literacy tutoring effective? *Reading Research Quarterly, 31,* 268–269.

Justice, L., Schuele, C.M., Kingery, B., Knighton, K., & Lee, M. (2004, November). *Multi-tiered phonemic awareness intervention for kindergartners.* Paper presented at the annual convention of the American Speech-Language-Hearing Association, Philadelphia.

Kamhi, A., & Koenig, L. (1985). Metalinguistic awareness in normal and language-disordered children. *Language, Speech, and Hearing Services in Schools, 16,* 199–210.

Kamhi, A., Lee, R., & Nelson, L. (1985). Word, syllable, and sound awareness in language-disordered children. *Journal of Speech and Hearing Disorders, 50,* 207–212.

Larrivee, L., & Catts, H. (1999). Early reading achievement in children with expressive phonological disorders. *American Journal of Speech-Language Pathology, 8,* 118–128.

Lewis, B., & Freebairn, L. (1992). Residual effects of preschool phonology disorders in grade school, adolescence, and adulthood. *Journal of Speech and Hearing Research, 35,* 819–831.

Lewis, B., Freebairn, L., & Taylor, H.G. (2000). Follow-up of children with early expressive phonology disorders. *Journal of Learning Disabilities, 25,* 586–597.

Lewis, B., Freebairn, L., & Taylor, H.G. (2002). Correlates of spelling abilities in children with early speech sound disorders. *Reading and Writing: An Interdisciplinary Journal, 15,* 389–407.

Lonigan, C., Burgess, S., Anthony, J., & Barker, T. (1998). Development of phonological sensitivity in 2- to 5-year-old children. *Journal of Educational Psychology, 90,* 294–311.

Mattingly, I. (1972). Reading, the linguistic process, and linguistic awareness. In J. Kavanagh & I. Mattingly (Eds.), *Language by ear and by eye: The relationships between speech and reading* (pp. 133–147). Cambridge, MA: The MIT Press.

Mellard, D., & Johnson, E. (2007). *Practitioner's guide to implementing response to intervention.* Thousand Oaks, CA: Corwin Press.

Metsala, J., & Walley, A. (1998). Spoken vocabulary growth and the segmental restructuring of lexical representations: Precursors to phoneme awareness and early reading ability. In J. Metsala & L. Ehri (Eds.), *Word recognition in beginning literacy* (pp. 89–120). Mahwah, NJ: Lawrence Erlbaum Associates.

Moats, L.C. (2000). *Speech to print: Language essentials for teachers.* Baltimore: Paul H. Brookes Publishing Co.

Moats, L.C. (2010). *Speech to print: Language essentials for teachers* (2nd ed.). Baltimore: Paul H. Brookes Publishing Co.

National Institute of Child Health and Human Development. (2000a). *Report of the National Reading Panel. Teaching children to read: An evidence-based assessment of the scientific research literature on reading and its implications for reading instruction* (NIH Publication No. 00-4769). Washington, DC: U.S. Government Printing Office.

National Institute of Child Health and Human Development. (2000b). *Report of the National Reading Panel. Teaching children to read: An evidence-based assessment of the scientific research literature on reading and its implications for reading instruction: Report of the Subgroups* (NIH Publication No. 00-4754). Washington, DC: U.S. Government Printing Office.

No Child Left Behind Act of 2001, PL 107-110, 115 Stat. 1425, 20 U.S.C. §§ 6301 *et seq.*

Raitano, N., Pennington, B., Tunick, R., Boada, R., & Shriberg, L. (2004). Pre-literacy skills of subgroups of children with speech sound disorders. *Journal of Child Psychology and Psychiatry, 45,* 821–835.

Robertson, C., & Salter, W. (1995). *The phonological awareness book.* Moline, IL: LinguiSystems.

Scarborough, H., & Brady, S. (2002). Toward a common terminology for talking about speech and reading: A glossary of the "phon" words and some related terms. *Journal of Literacy Research, 34,* 299–336.

Scarborough, H., & Dobrich, W. (1990). Development of children with early language delay. *Journal of Speech and Hearing Research, 33,* 70–83.

Schatschneider, C., Francis, D., Foorman, B., Fletcher, J., & Mehta, P. (1999). The dimensionality of phonological awareness: An application of response theory. *Journal of Educational Psychology, 91,* 439–449.

Schuele, C.M., & Boudreau, D. (2008). Phonological awareness intervention: Beyond the basics. *Language, Speech, and Hearing Services in Schools, 39,* 3–20.

Schuele, C.M., Justice, L., Cabell, S., Knighton, K., Kingery, B., & Lee, M. (2008). Field-based evaluation of a two-tiered instruction for enhancing kindergarten phonological awareness. *Early Education and Development, 19,* 726–752.

Schuele, C.M., Justice, L., Knighton, K., & Kingery, B. (2002, November). *Phonological awareness instruction: A collaborative state-wide pilot project.* Paper presented at the annual convention of the American Speech-Language-Hearing Association, Atlanta, GA.

Schuele, C.M., Paul, K., & Mazzaferri, K. (1998). *Phonological awareness training: Is it worth the time?* Paper presented at the annual convention of the American Speech-Language-Hearing Association, San Antonio, TX.

Schuele, C.M., & van Kleeck, A. (1987). Precursors to literacy: Assessment and intervention. *Topics in Language Disorders, 7*(2), 32–44.

Sirin, S. (2010). Socio-economic status and academic achievement: A meta-analytic review of research. *Review of Educational Research, 75,* 417–453.

Smith, S., Simmons, D., Gleason, M., Kame'enui, E., Baker, S., Sprick, M., et al. (2001). An analysis of phonological awareness instruction in four kindergarten basal reading programs. *Reading and Writing Quarterly, 17,* 25–51.

Spencer, E., Schuele, C.M., Guillot, K., & Lee, M. (2008). Phonemic awareness skill of speech-language pathologists and other educators. *Language, Speech, and Hearing Services in Schools, 39,* 512–520.

Stahl, S., & Murray, B. (1994). Defining phonological awareness and its relationship to early reading. *Journal of Educational Psychology, 86,* 221–234.

Stark, R., Bernstein, L., Condino, R., Bender, M., Tallal, P., & Catts, H. (1984). Four-year follow-up study of language-impaired children. *Annals of Dyslexia, 34,* 49–68.

Tomblin, J.B., Zhang, A., Buckwalter, P., & Catts, H. (2000). The association of reading disability, behavior disorders, and language impairment among second-grade children. *Journal of Child Psychology and Psychiatry, 41,* 473–482.

Torgesen, J., & Mathes, P. (2000). *A basic guide to understanding, assessing, and teaching phonological awareness.* Austin, TX: PRO-ED.

Torgesen, J., Morgan, S., & Davis, C. (1992). Effects of two types of phonological awareness training on word learning in kindergarten children. *Journal of Educational Psychology, 84,* 364–370.

Troia, G. (1999). Phonological awareness intervention research: A critical review of the experimental methodology. *Reading Research Quarterly, 34,* 28–52.

van Kleeck, A. (1994). Metalinguistic development. In G. Wallach & K. Butler (Eds.), *Language learning disabilities in school-age children and adolescents: Some principles and applications* (pp. 53–98). New York: Charles E. Merrill.

van Kleeck, A., Gillam, R., & McFadden, T. (1998). A study of classroom-based phonological awareness training for preschoolers with speech and/or language disorders. *American Journal of Speech-Language Pathology, 7,* 65–76.

Wagner, R., Torgesen, J., & Rashotte, C. (1994). Development of reading-related phonological processing abilities: New evidence of bidirectional causality from a latent variable longitudinal study. *Developmental Psychology, 30,* 73–87.

Wagner, R., Torgesen, J., Rashotte, C., Hecht, S., Barker, T., Burgess, S., et al. (1997). Changing relations between phonological processing abilities and word-level reading as children develop from beginning to skilled readers: A 5-year longitudinal study. *Developmental Psychology, 33,* 468–479.

Walker, D., Greenwood, C., Hart, B., & Carta, J. (1994). Prediction of school outcomes based on early language production and socioeconomic factors. *Child Development, 65,* 606–621.

Walley, A., Metsala, J., & Garlock, V. (2003). Spoken vocabulary growth: Its role in the development of phoneme awareness and early reading ability. *Reading and Writing: An Interdisciplinary Journal, 16,* 5–20.

Warrick, N., & Rubin, H. (1992). Phonological awareness: Normally developing and language delayed children. *Journal of Speech-Language Pathology and Audiology, 16*(1), 11–20.

Warrick, N., Rubin, H., & Rowe-Walsh, S. (1993). Phoneme awareness in language-delayed children: Comparative studies and intervention. *Annals of Dyslexia, 43,* 153–173.

Yopp, H. (1988). The validity and reliability of phonemic awareness tests. *Reading Research Quarterly, 23,* 159–177.

Master Word List

Master Word List

WORDS	CARD SET NAMES																		
	Rhyme Judgment Cards	Rhyme Odd-One-Out Cards	Rhyme Puzzle Cards	Rhyme Sorting Cards	Rhyme Generation Cards	Initial Sound Judgment Cards	Initial Sound Odd-One-Out Cards	Initial Sound Puzzle Cards	Initial Sound Sorting Cards /k/ /g/ /m/	Initial Sound Cards	Initial Sound Sticks	Final Sound Judgment Cards	Final Sound Odd-One-Out Cards	Final Sound Puzzle Cards	Final Sound Sorting Cards /t/ /d/ /f/	Final Sound Sticks	Final Sound Cards	Sound Segmenting Cards	Individual Sound Boxes
ant		ant																	
ape					ape													ape	ape
bad															bad				
bag	bag					bag						bag							
ball					ball	ball		ball		ball	ball								
basket															basket				
bat				bat	bat														
beach																	beach		
bear	bear		bear					bear											bed
bed	bed	bed	bed		bed			bed			bed	bed	bed	bed	bed	bed			bee
bee			bee	bee	bee			bee											
bees																			
bell			bell		bell														bike
bench																	bench		
bike						bike						bike							boat
boat		boat	boat										boat		boat		boat		
bone		bone	bone										bone				bone		book
book	book	book	book		book	book	book	book				book	book	book					bow
bow	bow																		
box		box			box	box	box												boy
boy					boy	boy				boy									
bracelet															bracelet				
bread															bread		bread		
bridge												bridge							
brush												brush	brush	brush			brush		
bug	bug	bug		bug	bug			bug				bug							
bunkbed															bunkbed				
bus	bus					bus	bus				bus	bus	bus	bus					
cab													cab	cab			cab		cake

cage												cage							
cake	cake	cake		cake	cake	cake	cake					cake		cake				cake	
calf													calf		calf		calf		
can									can										
candy									candy										
cane	cane	cane			cane														
cap	cap	cap			cap							cap		cap					
cape	cape																		
car			car		car	car			car	car									
carrot									carrot										cat
cat	cat	cat	cat	cat	cat	cat			cat	cat	cat		cat				cat		
caterpillar									caterpillar										
chain					chain			chain											
chair	chair				chair			chair											
cheese		cheese			cheese	cheese				cheese	cheese			cheese				cheese	
chef															chef				
cherry					cherry	cherry													
chicken										chicken									
chief														chief	chief				
chime		chime																	
chin					chin														
chocolate															chocolate				
class		class																	
cliff															cliff	cliff			
clock		clock		clock					clock								clock		
cloud													cloud		cloud				
clown									clown	clown			clown	clown					coat
coat			coat		coat		coat		coat		coat	coat		coat	coat				
comb	comb	comb							comb			comb		comb					
computer									computer										
cone	cone																		
cop		cop	cop	cop															cow
corn							corn	corn	corn				corn						

(continued)

Master Word List *(continued)*

WORDS	CARD SET NAMES: Rhyme Judgment Cards	Rhyme Odd-One-Out Cards	Rhyme Puzzle Cards	Rhyme Sorting Cards	Rhyme Generation Cards	Initial Sound Judgment Cards	Initial Sound Odd-One-Out Cards	Initial Sound Puzzle Cards	Initial Sound Sorting Cards /k/ /g/ /m/	Initial Sound Cards	Initial Sound Sticks	Final Sound Judgment Cards	Final Sound Odd-One-Out Cards	Final Sound Puzzle Cards	Final Sound Sorting Cards /t/ /d/ /f/	Final Sound Sticks	Final Sound Cards	Sound Segmenting Cards	Individual Sound Boxes
cow						cow			cow										
cowboy									cowboy										
crown									crown										
cup		cup										cup					cup		
dart																			
dice	dice	dice						dice						dice			dice		
dime		dime								dime		dime	dime						
dish			dish		dish	dish													dog
dog		dog	dog		dog	dog		dog		dog	dog	dish					dog		
door			door			door		door											
dove	dove																		
drink			drink																
drum	drum		drum		drum							drum	drum	drum		drum	drum		
duck	duck	duck			duck			duck			duck	duck							duck
ear		ear																	
egg												egg	egg	egg			egg	egg	egg
eight			eight												eight		eight		
face		face			face	face	face					face		face			face		face
fan	fan	fan	fan				fan	fan		fan	fan	fan				fan	fan		fan
feet													feet						
fin																			fin
finger						finger													
fish	fish	fish	fish		fish	fish	fish					fish	fish	fish		fish	fish	fish	fish
five		five											five	five					
flag	flag													flag		flag			
flower										flower									
food															food				
foot	foot						foot					foot	foot	foot	foot		foot		
four			four			four	four			four									

fox		fox				fox	fox	fox											
frog		frog	frog		frog												frog		
game									game	game							game		
garbage									garbage										
gas		gas					gas						gas						
gate	gate		gate		gate	gate		gate	gate			gate			gate				gate
ghost									ghost										
giraffe															giraffe				
girl					girl	girl		girl	girl										
glass													glass						
globe																globe			
glove	glove															glove			
goat		goat				goat			goat	goat	goat			goat		goat			
golf									golf										
goose		goose			goose														
gorilla									gorilla										
grape					grape														
grass																			
guitar									guitar										
gum		gum	gum				gum							gum					
gumball									gumball										
half															half				
ham		ham										ham							
hand												hand			hand	hand			
hat		hat	hat	hat	hat			hat		hat		hat	hat	hat			hat		
head			head																
heart										heart									
hen												hen		hen					
hoe					hoe														
hook	hook		hook								hook						hook		
horse												horse	horse						
hose				hose										hose					
house	house		house					house				house	house			house			

(continued)

Master Word List *(continued)*

WORDS	Rhyme Judgment Cards	Rhyme Odd-One-Out Cards	Rhyme Puzzle Cards	Rhyme Sorting Cards	Rhyme Generation Cards	Initial Sound Judgment Cards	Initial Sound Odd-One-Out Cards	Initial Sound Puzzle Cards	Initial Sound Sorting Cards /k/ /g/ /m/	Initial Sound Cards	Initial Sound Sticks	Final Sound Judgment Cards	Final Sound Odd-One-Out Cards	Final Sound Puzzle Cards	Final Sound Sorting Cards /t/ /d/ /f/	Final Sound Sticks	Final Sound Cards	Sound Segmenting Cards	Individual Sound Boxes
	CARD SET NAMES																		
ice	ice																		
jack					jack														
jail																			
jam										jam				jam					
jar										jar	jar								
jug			jug	jug															
kangaroo									kangaroo										
key					key	key			key									key	
keys		keys										keys	keys	keys					
kick									kick										
kids									kids										
king	king	king			king		king	king	king	king			king	king			king		
kitchen									kitchen										
kite		kite				kite			kite		kite		kite	kite		kite			kite
knee				knee	knee	knee													knee
knees																		knees	
knife														knife	knife				
lake				lake						lake									
lamb	lamb	lamb										lamb	lamb				lamb		
lamp					lamp		lamp	lamp						lamp		lamp	lamp		
leaf		leaf			leaf		leaf				leaf	leaf	leaf	leaf	leaf		leaf		
leg								leg					leg			leg			
lemonade															lemon-ade				
light		light	light		light	light	light					light					light		
lips						lips													
lock				lock															
log										log								log	
mail						mail			mail										mail
man									man					man				man	

map		map							map	map			map						
mask									mask										
mat				mat	mat														
match	match							match	match			match		match		match			
meat									meat						meat				
menu									menu										
mermaid															mermaid				
mice		mice											mice						
milk									milk										
money									money										
monkey							mon-key		monkey										
moon	moon		moon		moon	moon	moon	moon	moon	moon		moon		moon		moon			moon
moose		moose												moose					moose
mop	mop	mop	mop	mop		mop	mop			mop	mop	mop	mop	mop				mop	
mountain									mountain										
mouse	mouse	mouse	mouse			mouse	mouse			mouse	mouse	mouse	mouse						mouse
mouth									mouth										
mow																			mow
mud															mud				
muffin									muffin										
mug				mug															
nail						nail	nail	nail											
nest							nest	nest						nest					
net						net				net									
night			night				night												
nose	nose	nose		nose	nose	nose	nose	nose		nose		nose					nose		nose
nut						nut		nut											
one	one					one		one											
owl																			
pan		pan	pan			pan													
parade															parade				
parrot															parrot				

(continued)

Master Word List *(continued)*

WORDS	CARD SET NAMES: Rhyme Judgment Cards	Rhyme Odd-One-Out Cards	Rhyme Puzzle Cards	Rhyme Sorting Cards	Rhyme Generation Cards	Initial Sound Judgment Cards	Initial Sound Odd-One-Out Cards	Initial Sound Puzzle Cards	Initial Sound Sorting Cards /k/ /g/ /m/	Initial Sound Cards	Initial Sound Sticks	Final Sound Judgment Cards	Final Sound Odd-One-Out Cards	Final Sound Puzzle Cards	Final Sound Sorting Cards /t/ /d/ /f/	Final Sound Sticks	Final Sound Cards	Sound Segmenting Cards	Individual Sound Boxes
pear			pear				pear												
pen		pen								pen									
phone	phone	phone	phone		phone		phone					phone							
pie		pie			pie	pie		pie			pie								pie
pig		pig			pig	pig	pig			pig									pig
pin					pin			pin											
plant		plant																	
plane														plane					
plate			plate																
pool								pool											
pot								pot											
race	race																		
railroad															railroad				
rain		rain	rain		rain		rain	rain					rain						
rake		rake		rake			rake	rake		rake		rake							
rat										rat									
red	red																red		
rice												rice							
ring	ring				ring							ring	ring	ring			ring		
road													road		road				
rock				rock															
roof													roof						
rope	rope											rope	rope						
rose				rose									rose	rose			rose		rose
rug		rug	rug	rug	rug					rug									
run																			run
sail								sail											
salad															salad				
sand													sand						

see																			see
seven						seven		seven											
sew																			sew
sheep						sheep	sheep			sheep			sheep			sheep			
shell											shell								shell
sheriff															sheriff				
ship						ship		ship					ship						
shoe			shoe		shoe	shoe	shoe	shoe		shoe								shoe	shoe
show																			show
sink			sink			sink	sink	sink						sink					
skate	skate		skate		skate														
sky										sky									
sled		sled										sled			sled				
slide														slide					
snail										snail									
snake		snake		snake	snake								snake						
snow	snow																		
soap	soap					soap								soap					
sock		sock		sock	sock		sock	sock		sock	sock								
soup																			
spoon	spoon		spoon											spoon					
stamp																stamp			
star			star		star														
stool		stool																	
stop			stop	stop	stop												stop		
stove		stove										stove	stove	stove					
sun	sun	sun			sun	sun	sun			sun	sun	sun							sun
table					table	table				table									
tack								tack						tack			tack		tack
tail						tail													
tape	tape					tape						tape							
teeth																teeth			

(continued)

Master Word List *(continued)*

WORDS	CARD SET NAMES: Rhyme Judgment Cards	Rhyme Odd-One-Out Cards	Rhyme Puzzle Cards	Rhyme Sorting Cards	Rhyme Generation Cards	Initial Sound Judgment Cards	Initial Sound Odd-One-Out Cards	Initial Sound Puzzle Cards	Initial Sound Sorting Cards /k/ /g/ /m/	Initial Sound Cards	Initial Sound Sticks	Final Sound Judgment Cards	Final Sound Odd-One-Out Cards	Final Sound Puzzle Cards	Final Sound Sorting Cards /t/ /d/ /f/	Final Sound Sticks	Final Sound Cards	Sound Segmenting Cards	Individual Sound Boxes
ten		ten			ten					ten		ten							
tent						tent		tent							tent				
thief															thief			thief	
three				three							three								
thumb		thumb																	
tie		tie																	tie
time					time							time	time						
tire							tire												
toad															toad				
toe																			
toes				toes			toes											toes	
tool		tool																	
tooth	tooth									tooth		tooth					tooth		
top		top	top	top		top													top
tow																			tow
toy																			
train	train		train		train														
tree		tree	tree	tree	tree														
truck	truck											truck				truck			
tub		tub											tub	tub			tub		
two			two		two	two													two
van		van			van		van	van		van			van						van
vase	vase	vase					vase	vase		vase		vase	vase						
vine																			vine
well			well																
wheel											wheel								
wig																			
wing								wing											
witch		witch										witch		witch			witch	witch	
wolf					wolf	wolf						wolf	wolf	wolf	wolf				
wood															wood				
wreath																	wreath		

B

How to Create Your IPA Program Materials Kit

Most of the activities require ancillary materials. These resources are referenced in the IPA Program Materials Kit Inventory (see the last page of this appendix for reference; a reproducible version is available on the accompanying CD-ROM), as well as on the first pages of the appropriate Week and Session on the first pages of the overview for each week. Some of the materials are included on the CD-ROM, but other materials might be found in your classroom or can be easily made from inexpensive materials. Directions for assembling your own IPA Program Materials Kit are found here.

STEP 1

Create Storage Box

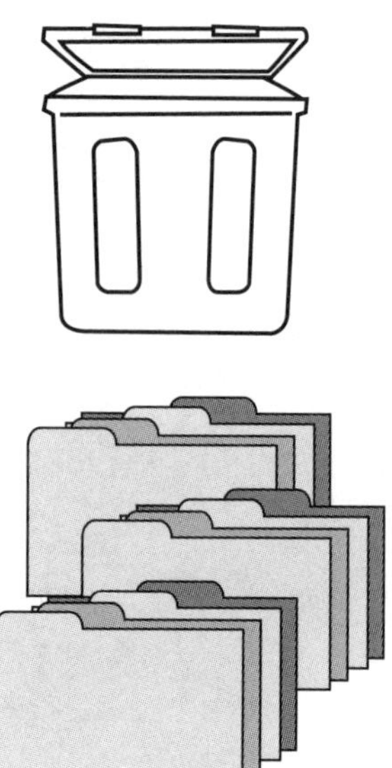

Materials: Plastic storage box with lid, thirteen hanging file portfolios, black marker for labeling

Directions: Obtain a plastic storage box with a lid to store your materials—one in which you can hang files will work best. Label twelve hanging portfolios by week (e.g. Week 1, Week 2, Week 3). You will use these to store materials for each of the weekly units. Label the thirteenth hanging portfolio "Other Materials" and use it to store materials that are used in repeated weeks.

STEP 2

Gather Commercially Available Items

- ❑ **Alphabet magnets:** Use a standard set of magnetic letters. The letter set can be uppercase or lowercase, as long as it differs in case style from the case style of the alphabet puzzle.

- ❑ **Alphabet puzzle:** Use a foam rubber or wood puzzle with letters in alphabetical order. The puzzle can be uppercase or lowercase, as long as it differs in case style from the case style of the alphabet magnets.

- ❑ **Alphabet picture cards:** Alphabet flash cards can be found at any toy store or bookstore. Cards contain an uppercase letter or lowercase letter on one side and a picture of an object beginning with the sound on the other side (e.g., letter "A" on one side and a picture of an apple on the other). Either lowercase or uppercase letters can be used in the activities.

- ❑ **Blocks** (approximately 30 small colored blocks): Use small colored blocks in segmentation activities. Alternatively, small objects such as teddy bear counters can be used.

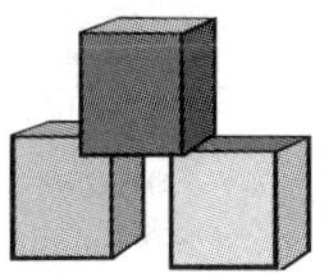

- ❑ **Dry erase marker and dry erase board or large pieces of paper**

- ❑ **Game pieces:** Any small manipulative may be used as a game piece (e.g., action figures, LEGOs®, erasers, buttons) to move along the game boards provided on the CD. Will need 6 to 8, depending on group size.

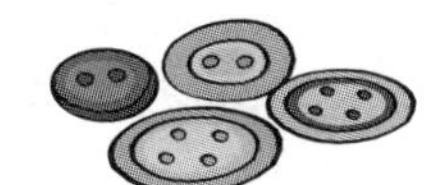

- ❑ **Magnetic board** (about 12" x 14" or 11" x 17"): A small cookie sheet works fine. Alternatively, any flat metal surface may be used (e.g., side of a filing cabinet, side of a desk).

- ❑ **Mirror** (optional): Any small, hand-held mirror.
- ❑ **"Busy" picture books:** Any small child's board book or picture book, such as "Where's Waldo" books or "All About Town".

- ❑ **Timer or stopwatch**

- ❑ **Tongue depressors:** 42 needed to use with the cards to make sound sticks.
- ❑ **Small paper lunch bags:** 10 bags for various activities. Attach a picture to the outside for several of the sorting activities.
- ❑ **Double-sided tape and regular tape**
- ❑ **Envelopes and plastic bags:** 16 small or letter size envelopes to store Sound Segmenting Cards; larger envelopes or self-closure plastic bags (e.g., quart size) to store all other picture card sets.
- ❑ **Shoe box with lid:** Used with the contact paper.
- ❑ **Contact paper:** Used to cover the shoebox and lid and then slots are cut in the lid so that the tongue depressors fit snugly into the slots. Approximately 12 slots are cut.
- ❑ **Index cards:** 3″ x 5″ cards, lined on one side.

STEP 3

Prepare Materials

Materials: Shoe box with lid, contact paper, scissors, index cards, black marker for labeling, two manila folders, tape, two small paper lunch bags

Directions:

- ❑ **Box with slots:** Cover a shoe box and lid with colored contact paper. Cut slots in the lid so that the tongue depressors fit snugly into the slots. Twelve slots are needed.

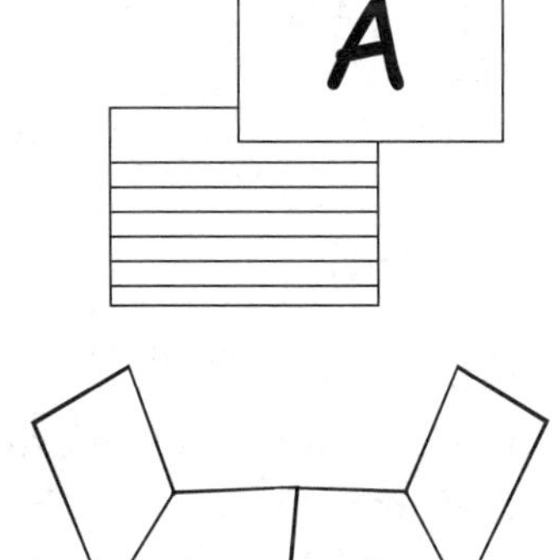

- ❑ **Index cards with uppercase letters:** Write uppercase letters on the plain sides of 3″ × 5″ index cards. Leave the lined side blank to record child responses. Create 26 cards, one for each letter of the alphabet.
- ❑ **Barrier:** Tape two folders together to create a U-shaped barrier to obstruct children's view.
- ❑ **Two small paper lunch bags:** Label one "Same Sounds" and the other "Different Sounds."

STEP 4

Print CD-ROM Materials

Note: All materials can be laminated for repeated use.

Materials: Light blue, light yellow, light green, and white card stock paper; white plain paper; scissors; tongue depressors; manila folders; small paper lunch bags; double-sided tape; envelopes and/or plastic bags; black marker for labeling

Directions: Print all files except Individual Sound Boxes on card stock paper for durability. Files can be printed in color or black and white. If you choose to print files in color, note that the Individual Sound Boxes file should be printed in black and white (see the instructions that follow).

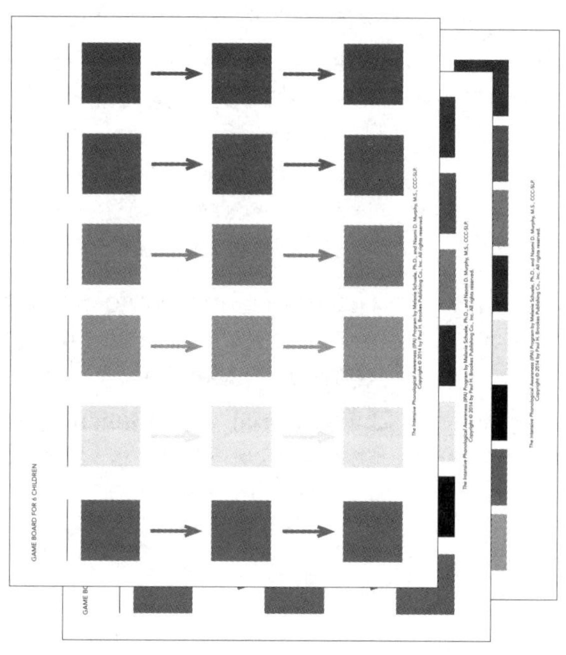

- ❑ Game boards
  - ❑ WEEKS 1, 3, 4, 6, 10, 11:
    - ❑ **Game Board for 6 Children.pdf**
    - ❑ **Game Board for 7 Children.pdf**
    - ❑ **Game Board for 8 Children.pdf**

    Thre pages of game boards (one for 6 children, one for 7 children, one for 8 children)

  Print two copies of the game board that corresponds to the number of children in your group on plain white paper. Laminate the pages, and use a dry erase marker to write each player's name on the lines at the tops of each column. Paste the pages inside one manila folder.

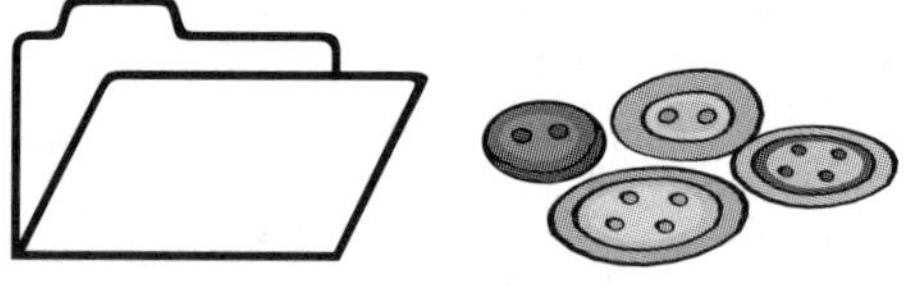

Week 1 Materials

- ❑ Alphabet picture cards
- ❑ Game board and game pieces
- ❑ Optional: Mirror
- ❑ **Rhyme Judgment Cards W1.pdf,** *3 pages (28 cards)*

  These cards contain two pictures each. Print on light blue card stock. Cut along dotted lines and laminate.
- ❑ **Rhyme Generation Cards W1.pdf, subset,** *3 pages (16 cards)*

  These are single pictures placed on individual cards. Print on light blue card stock. Cut along dotted lines and laminate.
- ❑ **Rhyme Odd-One-Out Cards W1.pdf,** *5 pages (25 cards)*

  These are strips containing three pictures, two of which rhyme. Print on light blue card stock. Cut and laminate each row of three pictures. Do not cut on the solid lines. Picture strip will include three pictures separated by solid lines.
- ❑ **Rhyme Puzzle Cards W1.pdf, subset,** *2 pages (4 pairs of cards)*

  These cards contain two pictures each separated by various zigzag lines. Print on light blue card stock, cut along all dotted lines, and laminate. The right side of each puzzle pair is designated with a black dot.

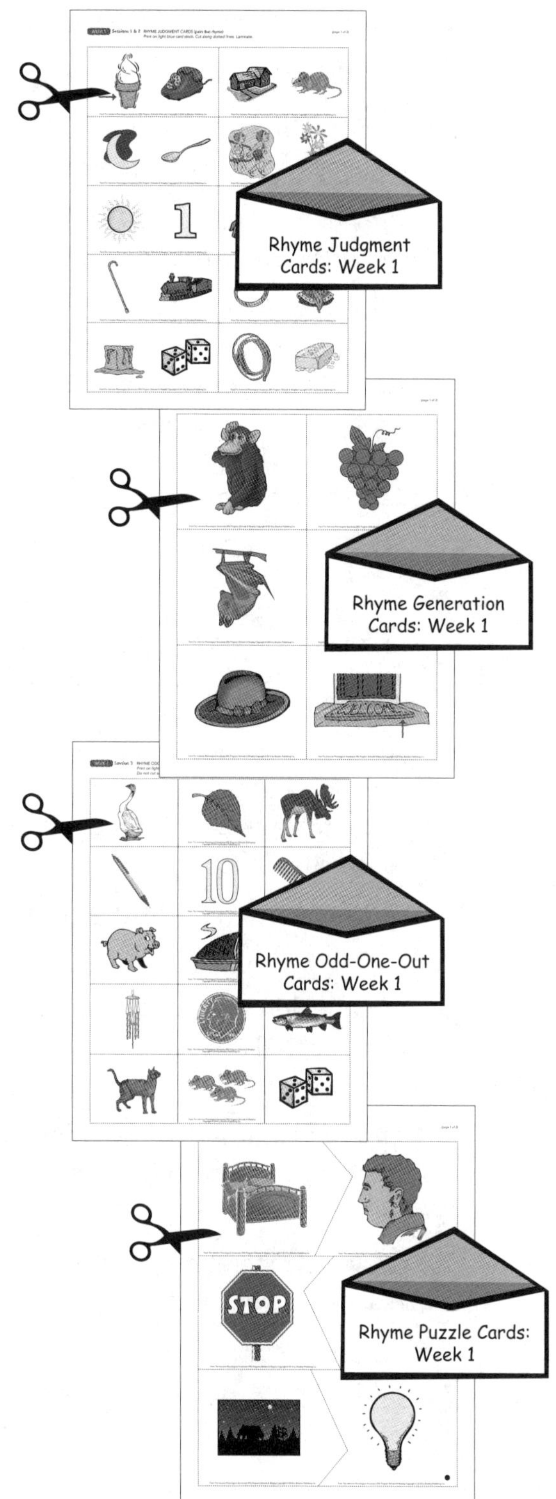

Week 2 Materials

- ❑ Alphabet picture cards (lowercase)
- ❑ Small paper lunch bag (unmarked)
- ❑ Rhyme Puzzle Cards W2a.pdf, *9 pages (25 pairs of cards)*
- ❑ Rhyme Puzzle Cards W2b.pdf, *9 pages (25 pairs of cards)*

  These cards contain two pictures each separated by various zigzag lines. Print on light blue card stock, cut along all dotted lines, and laminate. The right side of each puzzle pair is designated with a black dot.

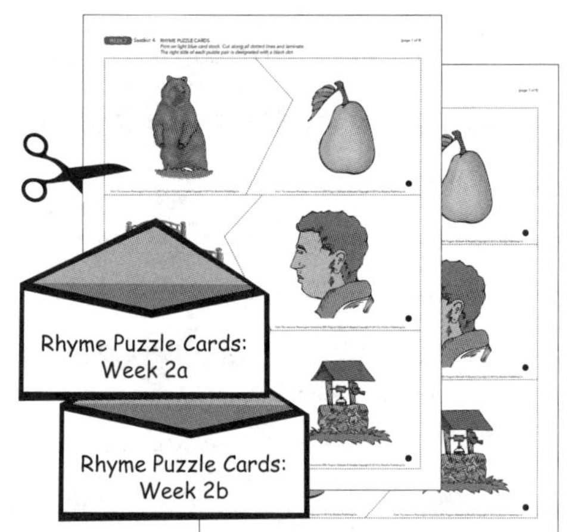

- ❑ Rhyme Odd-One-Out Cards W2.pdf, *5 pages (25 cards)*

  These are strips containing three pictures, two of which rhyme. Print on light blue card stock. Cut and laminate each row of three pictures. Do not cut on the solid lines. Picture strip will include three pictures separated by solid lines.

- ❑ Rhyme Sorting Cards W2a.pdf, *2 pages (12 cards)*
- ❑ Rhyme Sorting Cards W2b.pdf, *5 pages (28 cards)*

  These are single pictures placed on individual cards. Print on light blue card stock. Cut along dotted lines and laminate.

- ❑ Rhyme Generation Cards W2.pdf, subset, *1 page (6 cards)*

  These are single pictures placed on individual cards. Print on light blue card stock. Cut along dotted lines and laminate.

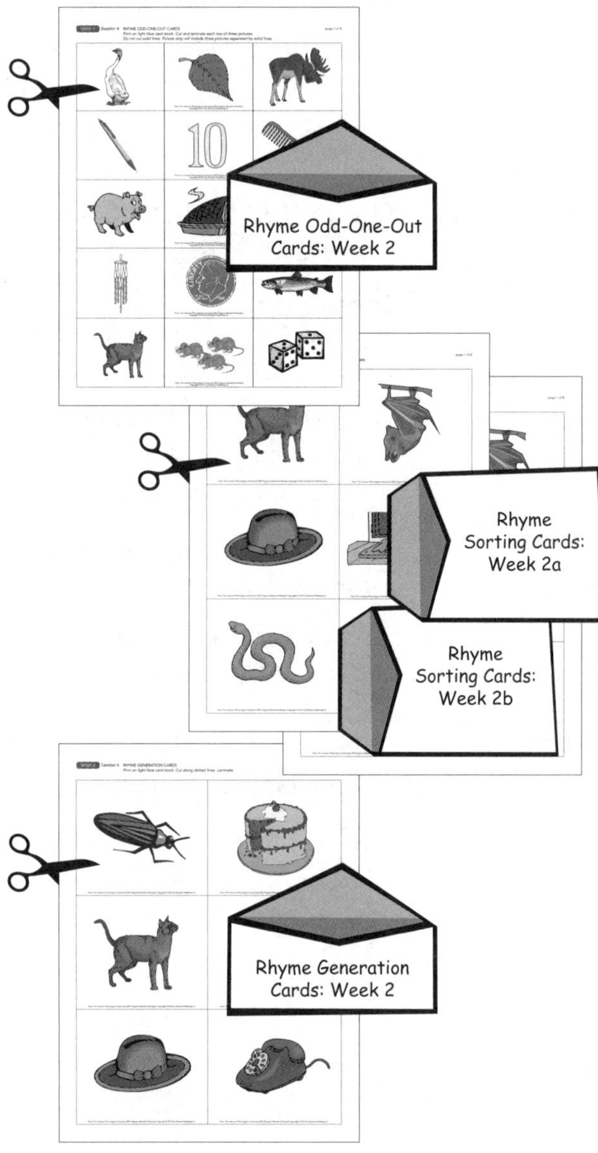

Week 3 Materials

- ❑ Alphabet puzzle (uppercase)
- ❑ Alphabet picture cards (uppercase)
- ❑ Game board and game pieces
- ❑ Small paper lunch bag (unmarked)
- ❑ Paper
- ❑ Marker
- ❑ Rhyme Generation Cards W3a.pdf, *8 pages (48 cards)*
- ❑ Rhyme Generation Cards W3b.pdf, *7 pages (40 cards)*

  These are single pictures placed on individual cards. Print on light blue card stock. Cut along dotted lines and laminate.

- ❑ Initial Sound Judgment Cards W3.pdf, subset, *1 page (8 cards)*

  These cards contain two pictures each. Print on light yellow card stock. Cut along dotted lines and laminate.

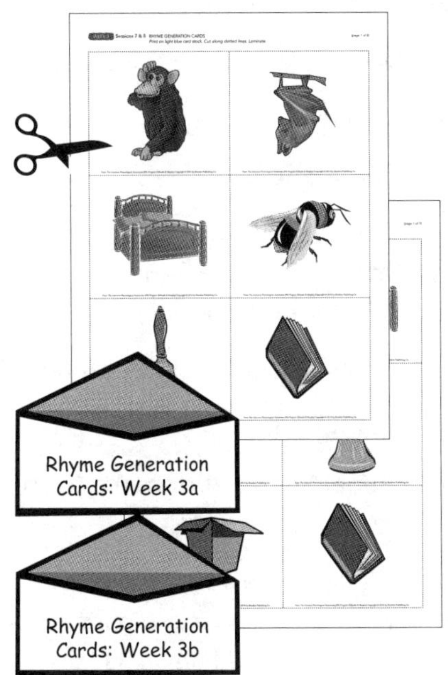

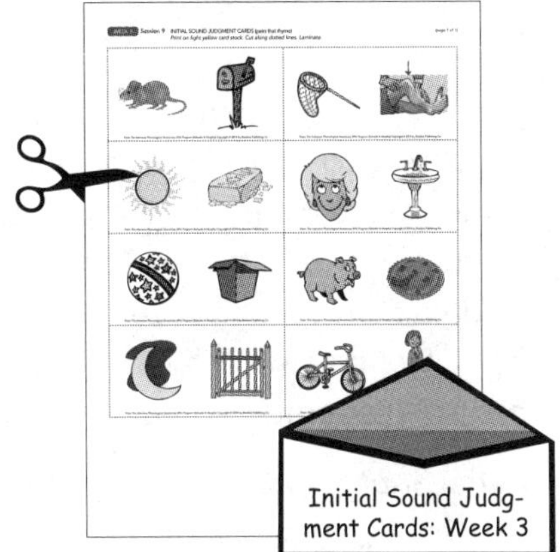

Week 4 Materials

- ❑ Alphabet magnets (lowercase)
- ❑ Alphabet puzzle (lowercase)
- ❑ Alphabet picture cards (lowercase)
- ❑ Magnetic board
- ❑ Two small paper lunch bags (one marked "Same Sounds," other marked "Different Sounds")
- ❑ Small paper lunch bag (unmarked)
- ❑ Game board and game pieces
- ❑ Initial Sound Judgment Cards W4.pdf, *3 pages (29 cards)*

  These cards contain two pictures each. Print on light yellow card stock. Cut along dotted lines and laminate.

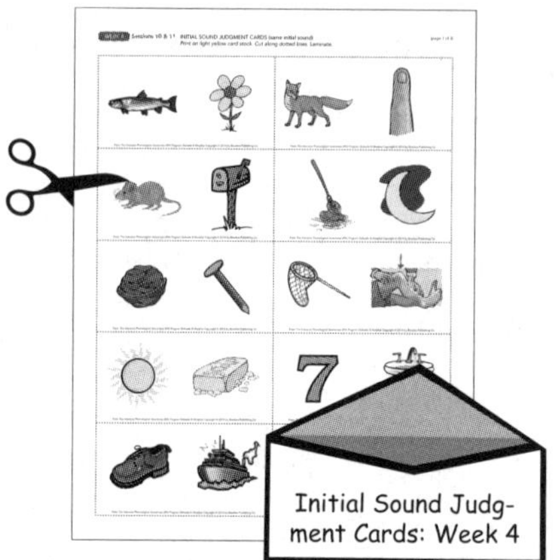

- ❑ Initial Sound Odd-One-Out Cards W4.pdf, *5 pages (25 cards)*

  These are strips containing three pictures, two of which begin with the same sound. Print on light yellow card stock. Cut and laminate each row of three pictures. Do not cut on the solid lines. Picture strip will include three pictures separated by solid lines.

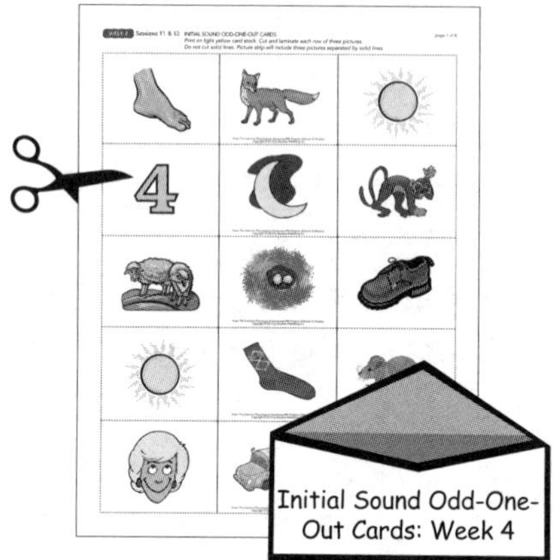

- ❑ Initial Sound Puzzle Cards W4.pdf, subset, *3 pages (7 pairs of cards)*

  These cards contain two pictures each separated by various zigzag lines. Print on light yellow stock, cut along all dotted lines, and laminate. The right side of each puzzle pair is designated with a black dot.

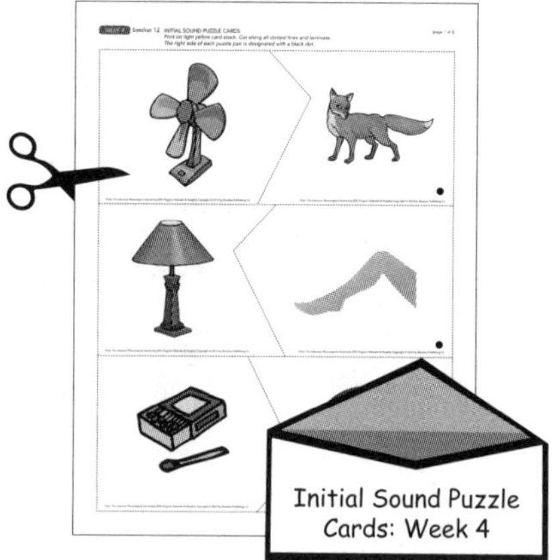

Week 5 Materials

- ❑ Alphabet magnets (uppercase)
- ❑ Alphabet puzzle (uppercase)
- ❑ Alphabet picture cards (lowercase)
- ❑ Magnetic board
- ❑ Dry erase marker and dry erase board
- ❑ Tape
- ❑ Three small paper lunch bags with letters on front of each: M; G; C and K
- ❑ Small paper lunch bag (unmarked)
- ❑ Initial Sound Puzzle Cards W5.pdf, *8 pages (23 pairs of cards)*

  These cards contain two pictures each separated by various zigzag lines. Print on light yellow stock, cut along all dotted lines, and laminate. The right side of each puzzle pair is designated with a black dot.
- ❑ Initial Sound Cards W5.pdf, *8 pages (43 cards)*

  These are single pictures placed on individual cards. Print on light yellow card stock. Cut along dotted lines and laminate.
- ❑ Initial Sound Sorting Cards W5.pdf, *4 pages (46 cards)*

  These are single pictures placed on individual cards. Print on yellow card stock. Cut along dotted lines and laminate. Label 3 small paper lunch bags with the capital letters M; G; C and K.
- ❑ Initial Sound Segmentation Cards W5.pdf, subset, *2 pages (8 cards)*

  These are single pictures placed on individual cards. Print on yellow card stock. Cut along dotted lines and laminate.

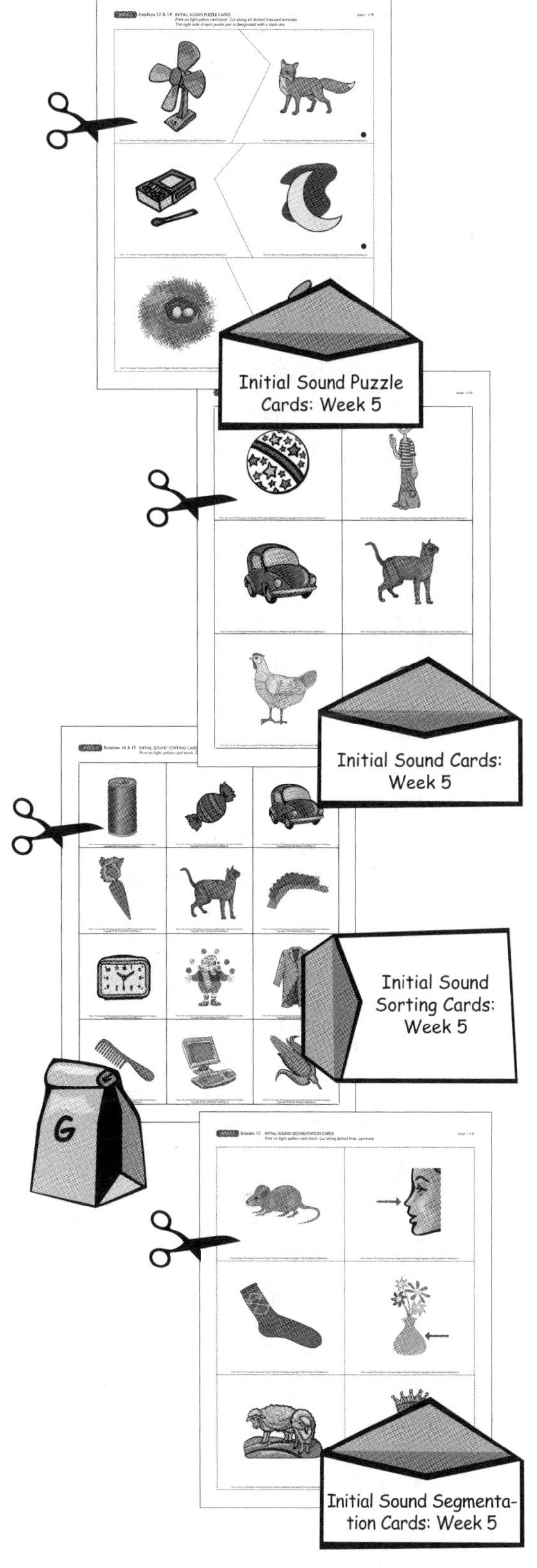

Week 6 Materials

- ❑ Alphabet magnets (lowercase)
- ❑ Magnetic board
- ❑ Two large pieces of paper
- ❑ Marker
- ❑ Box with slots
- ❑ Game board and game pieces
- ❑ "Busy" picture books, such as "Where's Waldo" books or "All About Town"
- ❑ Initial Sound Cards W6.pdf, *8 pages (43 cards)*

  These are single pictures placed on individual cards. Print on light yellow card stock. Cut along dotted lines and laminate.

- ❑ Initial Sound Sticks W6.pdf, *1 page (22 sticks)*

  Print on white card stock and cut along the dotted lines. Attach one picture to the top of each tongue depressor using double-sided tape. Write the letter for the initial sound on the bottom of each stick.

- ❑ Rhyme Generation Cards W6.pdf, *6 pages (36 cards)*

  These are single pictures placed on individual cards. Print on light blue card stock. Cut along dotted lines and laminate.

- ❑ Final Sound Judgment Cards W6.pdf, subset, *2 pages (8 cards)*

  These cards contain two pictures each. Print on light green card stock. Cut along dotted lines and laminate.

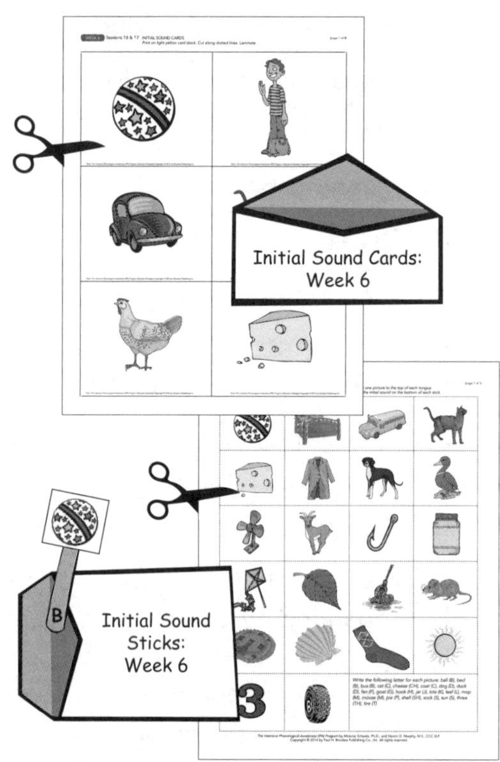

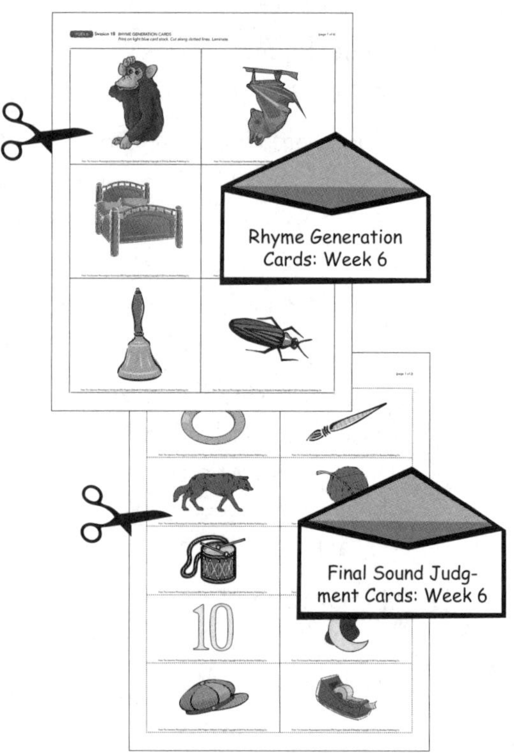

Week 7 Materials

- ❑ Alphabet picture cards (uppercase)
- ❑ Alphabet magnets (uppercase)
- ❑ Two small paper lunch bags (one marked "Same Sounds," other marked "Different Sounds")
- ❑ Final Sound Judgment Cards W7.pdf, *7 pages (30 cards)*

  These cards contain two pictures each. Print on light green card stock. Cut along dotted lines and laminate.

- ❑ Final Sound Odd-One-Out Cards W7.pdf, *5 pages (25 cards)*

  These are strips containing three pictures, two of which end with the same sound. Print on light green card stock. Cut and laminate each row of three pictures. Do not cut on the solid lines. Picture strip will include three pictures separated by solid lines.

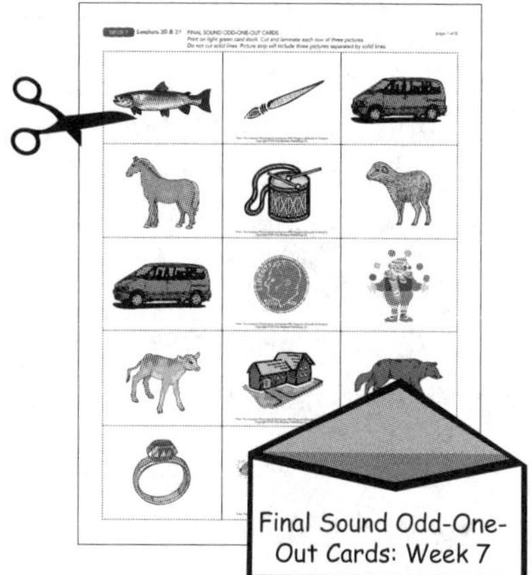

- ❑ Final Sound Puzzle Cards W7.pdf, subset, *2 pages (4 pairs of cards)*

  These cards contain two pictures each separated by various zigzag lines. Print on light green stock, cut along all dotted lines, and laminate. The right side of each puzzle pair is designated with a black dot.

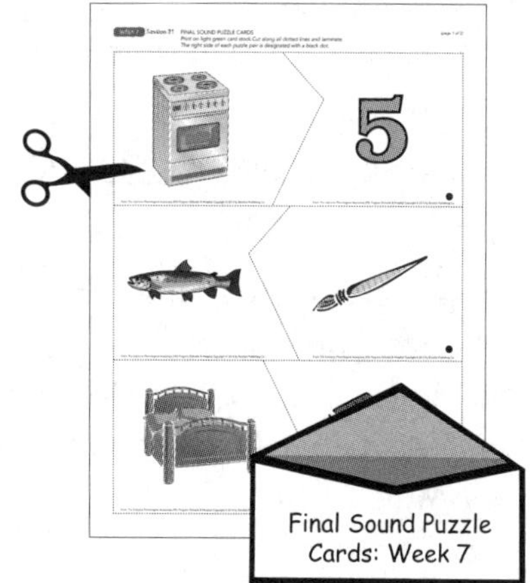

Week 8 Materials

- ❑ Index cards with uppercase letters
- ❑ Alphabet picture cards (uppercase and lowercase)
- ❑ Small paper lunch bag
- ❑ Dry erase marker and dry erase board
- ❑ Three small paper lunch bags with letters on front of each: T, D, F
- ❑ Tape
- ❑ Final Sound Puzzle Cards W8.pdf, *9 pages (25 pairs of cards)*

  These cards contain two pictures each separated by various zigzag lines. Print on light green stock, cut along all dotted lines, and laminate. The right side of each puzzle pair is designated with a black dot.

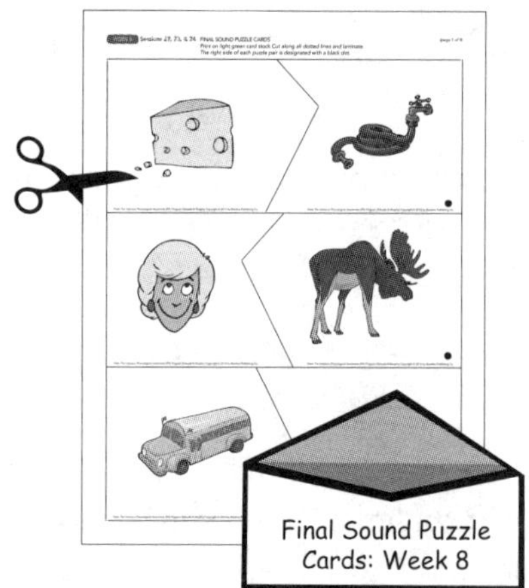

- ❑ Final Sound Cards W8a.pdf, *7 pages (38 cards)*
- ❑ Final Sound Cards W8b.pdf, *2 pages (7 cards)*

  These are single pictures placed on individual cards. Print on light green card stock. Cut along dotted lines and laminate.

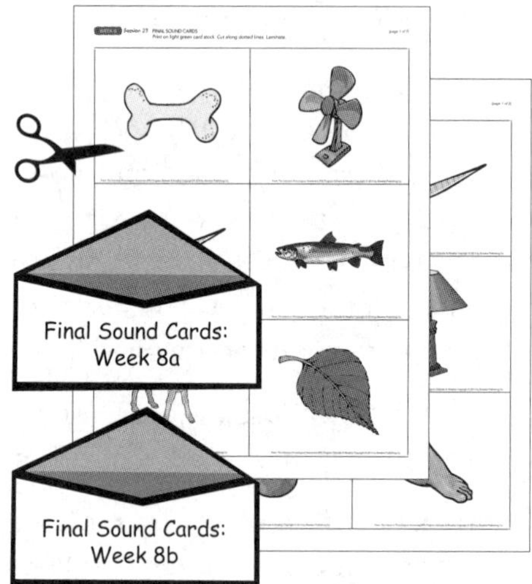

- ❑ Final Sound Sorting Cards W8.pdf, *4 pages (39 cards)*

  These are single pictures placed on individual cards. Print on light green card stock. Cut along dotted lines and laminate. Label 3 small paper lunch bags with the capital letters T, D, and F.

- ❑ **Rhyme Generation Cards W8.pdf, subset,** *5 pages (26 cards)*

  These are single pictures placed on individual cards. Print on light blue card stock. Cut along dotted lines and laminate.

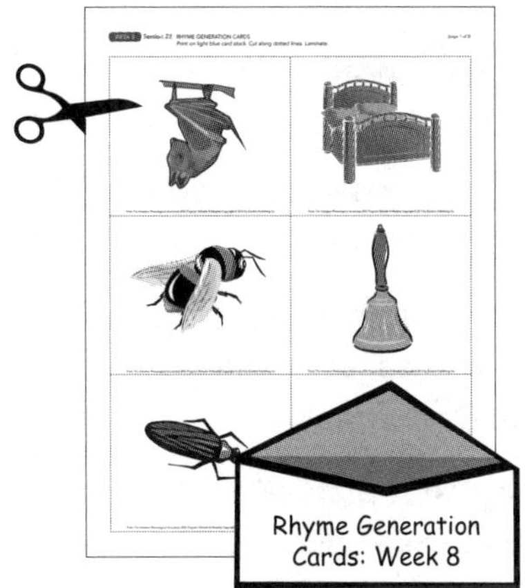

Week 9 Materials

- ❑ Index cards with uppercase letters (from Week 8, Sessions 22 and 23)
- ❑ Alphabet magnets (uppercase or lowercase, depending on children's need for practice)
- ❑ Alphabet picture cards (uppercase and lowercase consonant cards only. Omit A, E, I, O, U, Y, Q, X, and H from each deck)
- ❑ Timer or stopwatch
- ❑ "Busy" picture books, such as "Where's Waldo" books or "All About Town"
- ❑ Box with slots
- ❑ Final Sound Cards W9.pdf,
  7 pages (38 cards)

  These are single pictures placed on individual cards. Print on light green card stock. Cut along dotted lines and laminate.

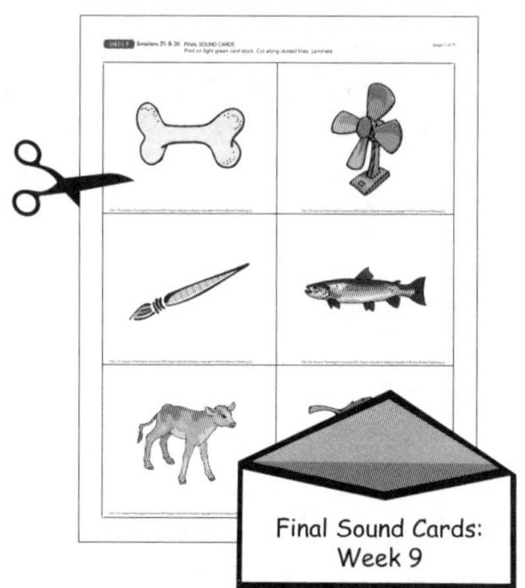

- ❑ Final Sound Sticks W9.pdf,
  1 page (20 sticks)

  Print on white card stock and cut along the dotted lines. Attach one picture to the top of each tongue depressor using double-sided tape. Write the letter for the final sound on the bottom of each stick.

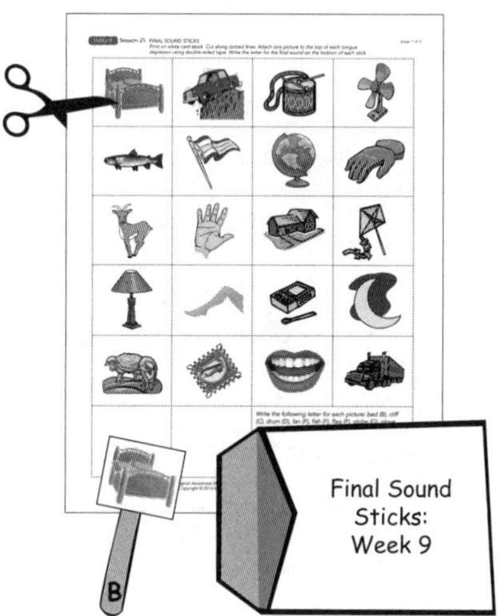

- ❑ Two-Square Sound Segmenting Panels W9.pdf, *4 pages (8 panels)*

  Print on white card stock. Cut along dotted lines and laminate.

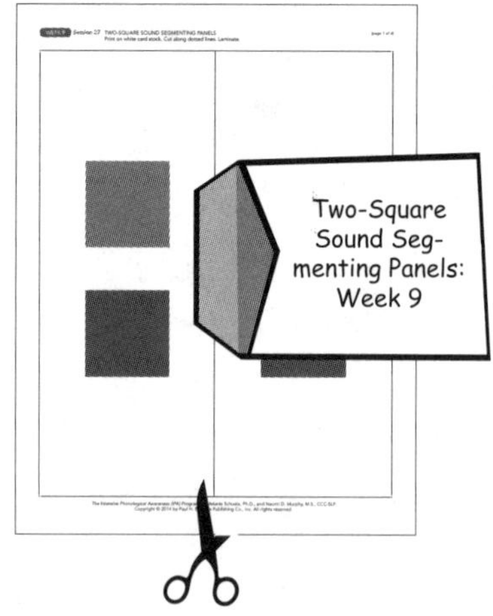

Week 10 Materials

- ❑ Alphabet picture cards (uppercase or lowercase depending on children's need for practice)
- ❑ Index cards with uppercase letters (from previous sessions)
- ❑ Game board and game pieces
- ❑ Two-Square Sound Segmenting Panels W10a.pdf, *4 pages (8 panels)*

  Print on white card stock. Cut along dotted lines and laminate.
- ❑ Three-Square Sound Segmenting Panels W10b.pdf, *4 pages (8 panels)*

  Print on white card stock. Cut along dotted lines and laminate.

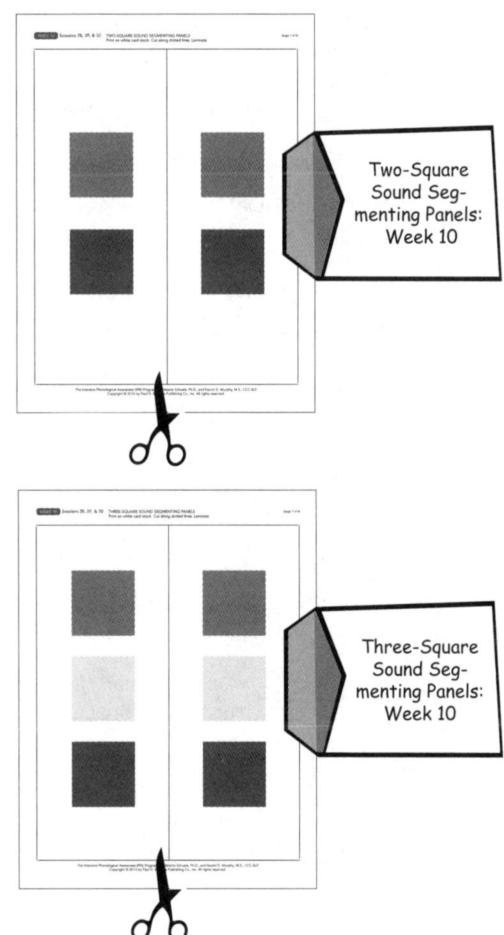

Week 11 Materials

- ❑ Index cards with uppercase letters (from previous sessions)
- ❑ Game board and game pieces
- ❑ Tape two folders together to create a U-shaped barrier to obstruct children's view.
- ❑ Three-Square Sound Segmenting Panels W11.pdf, *4 pages (8 panels)*

  Print on white card stock. Cut along dotted lines and laminate.

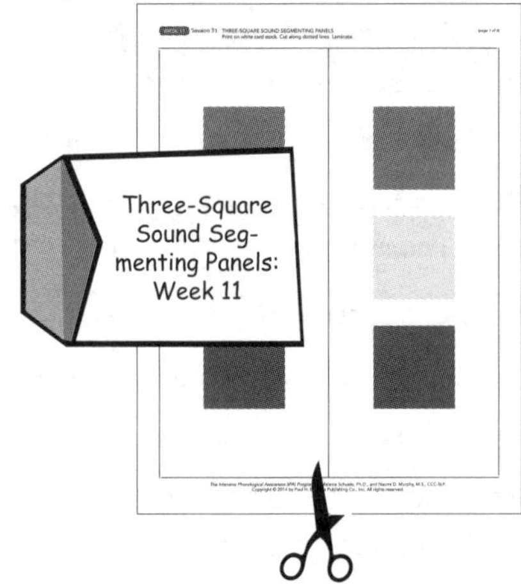

- ❑ Individual Sound Boxes W11.pdf, *23 pages (45 cards)*

  Print in black and white on plain white paper. Cut along dotted lines. Sort pictures into sets of 6 like pictures, and divide into CV and VC stops, CV and VC continuants, CVC stops, and CVC continuants. Generate enough copies so each child and teacher has a set (number of sets will depend on number of children in group).

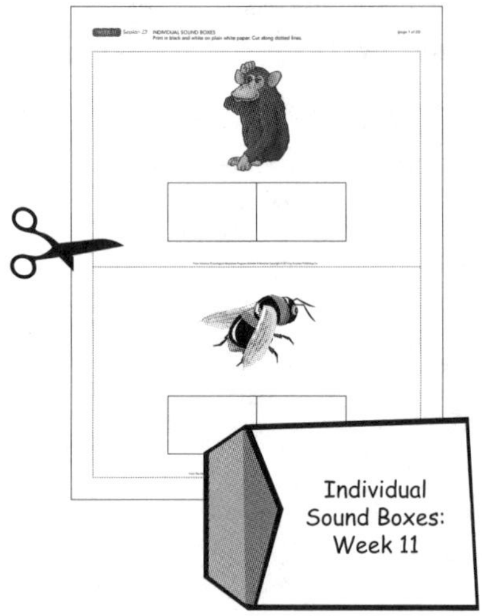

- ❑ Sound Segmenting Cards W11.pdf, *8 pages (16 cards)*

  Print on plain white paper. Cut along dotted lines, laminate, and place the pieces for each picture in individual envelopes.

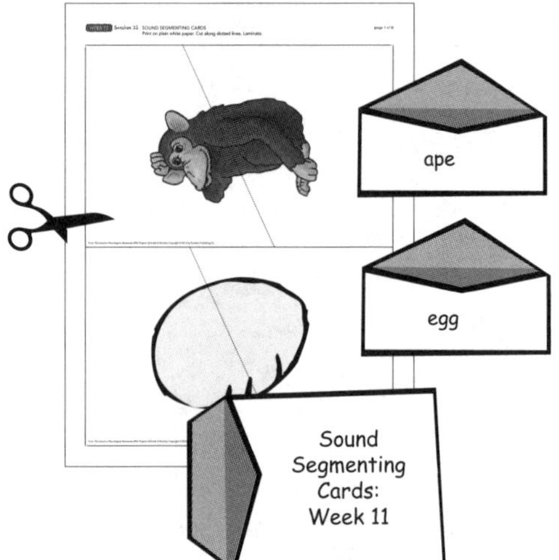

Week 12 Materials

- ❑ Index cards with uppercase letters (from previous sessions)
- ❑ Alphabet picture cards (lowercase or uppercase depending on children's need for practice)
- ❑ Blocks
- ❑ Tape two folders together to create a U-shaped barrier to obstruct children's view.
- ❑ Three-Square Sound Segmenting Panels W12a.pdf, *4 pages (8 panels)*
- ❑ Four-Square Sound Segmenting Panels W12b.pdf, *4 pages (8 panels)*

  Print on white card stock. Cut along dotted lines and laminate.

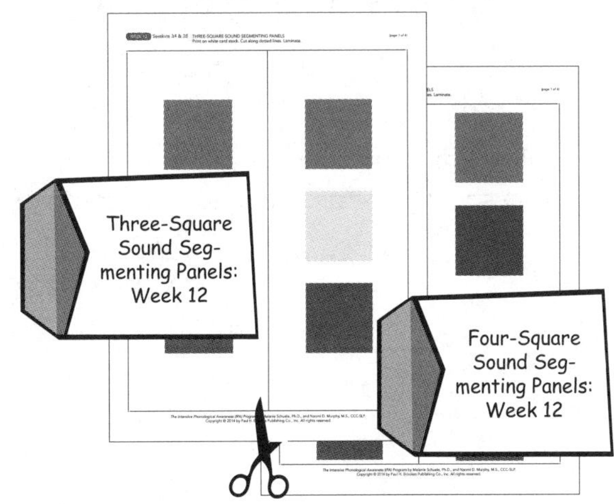

- ❑ Individual Sound Boxes W12.pdf, *23 pages (45 cards)*

  Print in black and white on plain white paper. Cut along dotted lines. Sort pictures into sets of 6 like pictures, and divide into CV and VC stops, CV and VC continuants, CVC stops, and CVC continuants. Generate enough copies so each child and teacher has a set (number of sets will depend on number of children in group).

- ❑ Sound Segmenting Cards W12.pdf, *8 pages (16 cards)*

  Print on plain white paper. Cut along dotted lines, laminate, and place the pieces for each picture in individual envelopes.

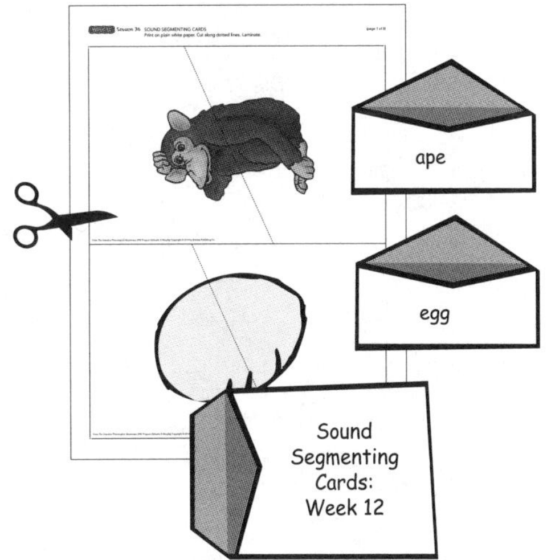

STEP 5

Organize and Store Kit

Materials: None

Directions: Print out checklist from CD. Use checklist to assure your kit is complete.

IPA Program Materials Kit Inventory Sheet by Week

Week 1
- ☐ Rhyme Judgment Cards W1.pdf, *3 pages (28 cards)*
- ☐ Rhyme Generation Cards W1.pdf, subset, *3 pages (16 cards)*
- ☐ Rhyme Odd-One-Out Cards W1.pdf, *5 pages (25 cards)*
- ☐ Rhyme Puzzle Cards W1.pdf, subset, *2 pages (4 pairs of cards)*

Week 2
- ☐ Rhyme Puzzle Cards W2a.pdf, *9 pages (25 pairs of cards)*
- ☐ Rhyme Puzzle Cards W2b.pdf, *9 pages (25 pairs of cards)*
- ☐ Rhyme Odd-One-Out Cards W2.pdf, *5 pages (25 cards)*
- ☐ Rhyme Sorting Cards W2a.pdf, *2 pages (12 cards)*
- ☐ Rhyme Sorting Cards W2b.pdf, *5 pages (28 cards)*
- ☐ Rhyme Generation Cards W2.pdf, subset, *1 page (6 cards)*

Week 3
- ☐ Rhyme Generation Cards W3a.pdf, *8 pages (48 cards)*
- ☐ Rhyme Generation Cards W3b.pdf, *7 pages (40 cards)*
- ☐ Initial Sound Judgment Cards W3.pdf, subset, *1 page (8 cards)*

Week 4
- ☐ Initial Sound Judgment Cards W4.pdf, *3 pages (29 cards)*
- ☐ Initial Sound Odd-One-Out Cards W4.pdf, *5 pages (25 cards)*
- ☐ Initial Sound Puzzle Cards W4.pdf, subset, *3 pages (7 pairs of cards)*

Week 5
- ☐ Initial Sound Puzzle Cards W5.pdf, *8 pages (23 pairs of cards)*
- ☐ Initial Sound Cards W5.pdf, *8 pages (43 cards)*
- ☐ Initial Sound Sorting Cards W5.pdf, *4 pages (46 cards)*
- ☐ Initial Sound Segmentation Cards W5.pdf, *2 pages (8 cards)*

Week 6
- ☐ Initial Sound Cards W6.pdf, *8 pages (43 cards)*
- ☐ Initial Sound Sticks W6.pdf, *1 page (22 sticks)*
- ☐ Rhyme Generation Cards W6.pdf, *6 pages (36 cards)*
- ☐ Final Sound Judgment Cards W6.pdf, subset, *2 pages (8 cards)*

Week 7
- ☐ Final Sound Judgment Cards W7.pdf, *7 pages (30 cards)*
- ☐ Final Sound Odd-One-Out Cards W7.pdf, *5 pages (25 cards)*
- ☐ Final Sound Puzzle Cards W7.pdf, subset, *2 pages (4 pairs of cards)*

Week 8
- ☐ Final Sound Puzzle Cards W8.pdf, *9 pages (25 pairs of cards)*
- ☐ Final Sound Cards W8a.pdf, *7 pages (38 cards)*
- ☐ Final Sound Cards W8b.pdf, *2 pages (7 cards)*
- ☐ Final Sound Sorting Cards W8.pdf, *4 pages (39 cards)*
- ☐ Rhyme Generation Cards W8.pdf, subset, *5 pages (26 cards)*

Week 9
- ☐ Final Sound Cards W9.pdf, *7 pages (38 cards)*
- ☐ Final Sound Sticks W9.pdf, *1 page (20 sticks)*
- ☐ Two-Square Sound Segmenting Panels W9.pdf, *4 pages (8 panels)*

Week 10
- ☐ Two-Square Sound Segmenting Panels W10a.pdf, *4 pages (8 panels)*
- ☐ Three-Square Sound Segmenting Panels W10b.pdf, *4 pages (8 panels)*

Week 11
- ☐ Three-Square Sound Segmenting Panels W11.pdf, *4 pages (8 panels)*
- ☐ Individual Sound Boxes W11.pdf, *23 pages (45 cards)*
- ☐ Sound Segmenting Cards W11.pdf, *8 pages (16 cards)*

Week 12
- ☐ Three-Square Sound Segmenting Panels W12a.pdf, *4 pages (8 panels)*
- ☐ Four-Square Sound Segmenting Panels W12b.pdf, *4 pages (8 panels)*
- ☐ Individual Sound Boxes W12.pdf, *23 pages (45 cards)*
- ☐ Sound Segmenting Cards W12.pdf, *8 pages (16 cards)*

Other Materials

☐ Alphabet magnets	☐ Index cards with uppercase letters
☐ Alphabet picture cards (two sets)	☐ IPA Program Implementation Record
☐ Alphabet puzzle	☐ Magnetic board
☐ Barrier	☐ Markers
☐ Blocks	☐ Mirror
☐ Box with slots	☐ Paper
☐ Child Attendance Record	☐ Scope & Sequence
☐ Daily Implementation Record	☐ Small paper lunch bags
☐ Dry erase marker and dry erase board	☐ Tape
☐ Game Boards and game pieces	☐ Timer or stopwatch

IPA Program Materials Kit Inventory Sheet by Week

Week 1

- ❑ Rhyme Judgment Cards W1.pdf, *3 pages (28 cards)*
- ❑ Rhyme Generation Cards W1.pdf, subset, *3 pages (16 cards)*
- ❑ Rhyme Odd-One-Out Cards W1.pdf, *5 pages (25 cards)*
- ❑ Rhyme Puzzle Cards W1.pdf, subset, *2 pages (4 pairs of cards)*

Week 2

- ❑ Rhyme Puzzle Cards W2a.pdf, *9 pages (25 pairs of cards)*
- ❑ Rhyme Puzzle Cards W2b.pdf, *9 pages (25 pairs of cards)*
- ❑ Rhyme Odd-One-Out Cards W2.pdf, *5 pages (25 cards)*
- ❑ Rhyme Sorting Cards W2a.pdf, *2 pages (12 cards)*
- ❑ Rhyme Sorting Cards W2b.pdf, *5 pages (28 cards)*
- ❑ Rhyme Generation Cards W2.pdf, subset, *1 page (6 cards)*

Week 3

- ❑ Rhyme Generation Cards W3a.pdf, *8 pages (48 cards)*
- ❑ Rhyme Generation Cards W3b.pdf, *7 pages (40 cards)*
- ❑ Initial Sound Judgment Cards W3.pdf, subset, *1 page (8 cards)*

Week 4

- ❑ Initial Sound Judgment Cards W4.pdf, *3 pages (29 cards)*
- ❑ Initial Sound Odd-One-Out Cards W4.pdf, *5 pages (25 cards)*
- ❑ Initial Sound Puzzle Cards W4.pdf, subset, *3 pages (7 pairs of cards)*

Week 5

- ❑ Initial Sound Puzzle Cards W5.pdf, *8 pages (23 pairs of cards)*
- ❑ Initial Sound Cards W5.pdf, *8 pages (43 cards)*
- ❑ Initial Sound Sorting Cards W5.pdf, *4 pages (46 cards)*
- ❑ Initial Sound Segmentation Cards W5.pdf, *2 pages (8 cards)*

Week 6

- ❑ Initial Sound Cards W6.pdf, *8 pages (43 cards)*
- ❑ Initial Sound Sticks W6.pdf, *1 page (22 sticks)*
- ❑ Rhyme Generation Cards W6.pdf, *6 pages (36 cards)*
- ❑ Final Sound Judgment Cards W6.pdf, subset, *2 pages (8 cards)*

Week 7

- ❑ Final Sound Judgment Cards W7.pdf, *7 pages (30 cards)*
- ❑ Final Sound Odd-One-Out Cards W7.pdf, *5 pages (25 cards)*
- ❑ Final Sound Puzzle Cards W7.pdf, subset, *2 pages (4 pairs of cards)*

Week 8

- ❑ Final Sound Puzzle Cards W8.pdf, *9 pages (25 pairs of cards)*
- ❑ Final Sound Cards W8a.pdf, *7 pages (38 cards)*
- ❑ Final Sound Cards W8b.pdf, *2 pages (7 cards)*
- ❑ Final Sound Sorting Cards W8.pdf, *4 pages (39 cards)*
- ❑ Rhyme Generation Cards W8.pdf, subset, *5 pages (26 cards)*

Week 9

- ❑ Final Sound Cards W9.pdf, *7 pages (38 cards)*
- ❑ Final Sound Sticks W9.pdf, *1 page (20 sticks)*
- ❑ Two-Square Sound Segmenting Panels W9.pdf, *4 pages (8 panels)*

Week 10

- ❑ Two-Square Sound Segmenting Panels W10a.pdf, *4 pages (8 panels)*
- ❑ Three-Square Sound Segmenting Panels W10b.pdf, *4 pages (8 panels)*

Week 11

- ❑ Three-Square Sound Segmenting Panels W11.pdf, *4 pages (8 panels)*
- ❑ Individual Sound Boxes W11.pdf, *23 pages (45 cards)*
- ❑ Sound Segmenting Cards W11.pdf, *8 pages (16 cards)*

Week 12

- ❑ Three-Square Sound Segmenting Panels W12a.pdf, *4 pages (8 panels)*
- ❑ Four-Square Sound Segmenting Panels W12b.pdf, *4 pages (8 panels)*
- ❑ Individual Sound Boxes W12.pdf, *23 pages (45 cards)*
- ❑ Sound Segmenting Cards W12.pdf, *8 pages (16 cards)*

Other Materials

❑ Alphabet magnets	❑ Index cards with uppercase letters
❑ Alphabet picture cards (two sets)	❑ IPA Program Implementation Record
❑ Alphabet puzzle	❑ Magnetic board
❑ Barrier	❑ Markers
❑ Blocks	❑ Mirror
❑ Box with slots	❑ Paper
❑ Child Attendance Record	❑ Scope & Sequence
❑ Daily Implementation Record	❑ Small paper lunch bags
❑ Dry erase marker and dry erase board	❑ Tape
❑ Game Boards and game pieces	❑ Timer or stopwatch

This kit is for use with *The Intensive Phonological Awareness (IPA) Program.* Please refer to the book's lessons for specific instructions on how to use the materials included in this kit. ISBN-13: 978-1-59857-118-9 ISBN-10: 1-59857-118-4 Paul H. Brookes Publishing Co., Inc. www.brookespublishing.com

Index

Note. *f* indicates figures, *t* indicates tables.